Microsoft®
Office 365
FOR
DUMMIES®

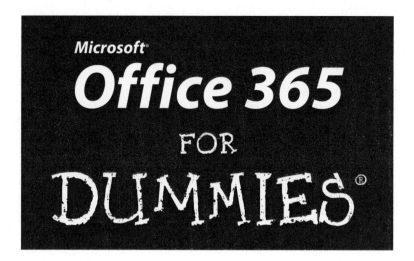

Microsoft®

Office 365

FOR

DUMMIES®

by Ken Withee and Jennifer Reed

WILEY

John Wiley & Sons, Inc.

Microsoft® Office 365 For Dummies®

Published by
John Wiley & Sons, Inc.
111 River Street
Hoboken, NJ 07030-5774
www.wiley.com

Copyright © 2012 by John Wiley & Sons, Inc., Hoboken, New Jersey

Published by John Wiley & Sons, Inc., Hoboken, New Jersey

Published simultaneously in Canada

For general information on our other products and services, please contact our Customer Care Department within the U.S. at 877-762-2974, outside the U.S. at 317-572-3993, or fax 317-572-4002.

For technical support, please visit www.wiley.com/techsupport.

Wiley publishes in a variety of print and electronic formats and by print-on-demand. Some material included with standard print versions of this book may not be included in e-books or in print-on-demand. If this book refers to media such as a CD or DVD that is not included in the version you purchased, you may download this material at http://booksupport.wiley.com. For more information about Wiley products, visit www.wiley.com.

Library of Congress Control Number: 2011945670

ISBN 978-1-118-10450-7 (pbk); ISBN 978-1-118-22395-6 (ebk); ISBN 978-1-118-23241-5 (ebk); ISBN 978-1-118-25833-0 (ebk)

Manufactured in the United States of America

10 9 8 7 6 5 4 3 2 1

WILEY

About the Authors

Ken Withee is President of Portal Integrators LLC (www.portalint.com), a software development company focused on developing world class business applications for the SharePoint platform. He lives with his wife Rosemarie in Seattle, Washington and is the author or coauthor of several books including *Microsoft Office 365 For Dummies* (Wiley, 2011), *SharePoint 2010 Development For Dummies* (Wiley, 2011), *Professional Microsoft Project Server 2010* (WROX, 2012), *Microsoft Business Intelligence For Dummies* (Wiley, 2010), *Professional Microsoft SQL Server 2011 Reporting Services* (WROX, 2011), and *Professional Microsoft SQL Server 2008 Reporting Services* (WROX, 2008). Ken has also written a number of other published works in a number of journals and magazines.

Ken earned a Master of Science degree in Computer Science studying under Dr. Edward Lank at San Francisco State University. Their work has been published in the LNCS journals and was the focus of a presentation at the IASTED conference in Phoenix. Their work has also been presented at various other Human Computer Interaction conferences throughout the world.

Ken has more than 12 years of professional computer and management experience working with a vast range of technologies. He is a Microsoft Certified Technology Specialist and is certified in SharePoint, SQL Server, and .NET.

Jennifer Reed is the founder and president of Cloud611 (www.cloud611.com), a Seattle-based company offering web design and development services, strategic social media consulting, and small business cloud solutions using Microsoft technologies.

Jenn holds a bachelor's degree in Economics and has for many years provided consulting services to small businesses and nonprofit organizations on technology solutions, creative communications, database design, web design and development, SharePoint implementation, and project management. Known affectionately as "the half-geek" because she is equally comfortable in the tech and non-technical "worlds," Jenn is a PMI-certified project management professional and Certified Scrum Master who excels at translating ambiguous requirements into actionable strategies and measurable projects.

Jenn lives with her husband Rick and son Siddha in the farming community of Snohomish 45 miles northeast of Seattle. When not working on a book, Jenn spends her spare time growing an organic garden on the family's five-acre farm overlooking the Snohomish Valley and Mt. Rainier to the south. She blogs at www.askthehalfgeek.com about technology, project management, social media, and life. She also serves as a Trustee for the Crisis Clinic (www.crisisclinic.org) and is an active member of the Project Management Institute (www.pmi.org).

Dedication

I dedicate this book to my wife and best friend, Rosemarie Withee, who encouraged me daily throughout this time intensive process. I owe her another year's worth of late nights and weekends and hope to make it up to her during our long future together. I love you!

— Ken Withee

My work on this book would not have been possible without the love and support of my husband and best friend Rick Reed and my wonderful son Siddha. I dedicate this book to both of you for understanding my late nights and busy weekends, forgiving my absence at sports practices and basketball games, stepping up and learning to cook and bake when I became too busy, and encouraging, supporting, and loving me. I love you both and you complete me.

— Jennifer Reed

Authors' Acknowledgments

Ken Withee: I would like to acknowledge my grandma Tiny Withee who turns 99 this year and is still going strong. I would also like to acknowledge my wife Rosemarie Withee, mother Maggie Blair, father Ken Withee, sister Kate Henneinke, and parents-in-law Alfonso and Lourdes Supetran and family.

An extraordinary amount of special thanks to Katie Mohr, Blair Pottenger, Beth Taylor, Amy Bates, and the rest of the *For Dummies* team for providing more support than I ever thought possible. It is truly amazing how much work goes into a single book.

Jennifer Reed: I owe my deepest gratitude to my husband Rick Reed for providing valuable feedback as my non-technical, test "dummy" reader and for helping me find my "voice."

I am indebted to my clients, employers, co-workers, and friends for the opportunities to learn and enrich my life, and grateful that I can share those positive, relevant experiences in this book.

It's been an honor and a pleasure to have the support and guidance of Katie Mohr, Blair Pottenger, Beth Taylor, and Amy Bates, and the rest of the *For Dummies* team. They are truly a dream team to work with.

I also warmly acknowledge my co-author, Ken Withee, who introduced me to the exciting world of book writing. Without his inspiration, this book would not have been possible.

Publisher's Acknowledgments

We're proud of this book; please send us your comments at http://dummies.custhelp.com. For other comments, please contact our Customer Care Department within the U.S. at 877-762-2974, outside the U.S. at 317-572-3993, or fax 317-572-4002.

Some of the people who helped bring this book to market include the following:

Acquisitions, Editorial, and Vertical Websites

Project Editor: Beth Taylor

Acquisitions Editor: Katie Mohr

Copy Editor: Beth Taylor

Technical Editor: Amy Bates

Editorial Manager: Jodi Jensen

Editorial Assistant: Amanda Graham

Sr. Editorial Assistant: Cherie Case

Cover Photo: © iStockphoto.com / Iakov Kalinin

Cartoons: Rich Tennant (www.the5th wave.com)

Composition Services

Project Coordinator: Katie Crocker

Layout and Graphics: Lavonne Roberts

Proofreaders: Lauren Mandelbaum, Bonnie Mikkelson

Indexer: Valerie Haynes Perry

Publishing and Editorial for Technology Dummies

> **Richard Swadley,** Vice President and Executive Group Publisher
>
> **Andy Cummings,** Vice President and Publisher
>
> **Mary Bednarek,** Executive Acquisitions Director
>
> **Mary C. Corder,** Editorial Director

Publishing for Consumer Dummies

> **Kathleen Nebenhaus,** Vice President and Executive Publisher

Composition Services

> **Debbie Stailey,** Director of Composition Services

Contents at a Glance

Introduction *1*

Part 1: Recognizing the Cloud Momentum *7*
Chapter 1: Getting to Know the Cloud 9
Chapter 2: Moving to the Office 365 Cloud.......................................23

Part 11: Getting Connected with E-mail,
Calendar, and Contacts *37*
Chapter 3: Unleashing the Power of Exchange Online.......................39
Chapter 4: Giving Productivity a Boost 51

Part 111: Exploring SharePoint Online........................... *63*
Chapter 5: Collaborating Has Never Been This Easy!........................65
Chapter 6: Going Beyond Websites: SharePoint Scenarios 87
Chapter 7: Microsoft Office Integration 103
Chapter 8: Demystifying SharePoint Online Administration............121
Chapter 9: Understanding SharePoint Online Development............139

Part 1V: Diving into the Office Web Apps *161*
Chapter 10: Introducing the Office Web Apps 163
Chapter 11: Getting into the Word Web App 169
Chapter 12: Plunging into the Excel Web App 179
Chapter 13: Powering Up the PowerPoint Web App 187
Chapter 14: Figuring Out the OneNote Web App.............................195

Part V: Instant Messaging and Online Meetings *207*
Chapter 15: Getting Empowered by Lync Online 209
Chapter 16: Your Presence Unlimited...219

Part V1: Preparing to Move *227*
Chapter 17: Meeting Office 365 Requirements................................229
Chapter 18: Planning for Your Office 365 Implementation..............239
Chapter 19: Implementing Office 365 251
Chapter 20: Managing Office 365 261

Part VII: The Part of Tens 275

Chapter 21: Ten Signs It's Time for You to Move to the Cloud 277
Chapter 22: Ten Office 365 Value Propositions 285
Chapter 23: Ten Tips for Increasing Productivity and Efficiency
with Office 365 293

Glossary 299

Index 305

Table of Contents

Introduction *1*

    About This Book 1
    How To Use This Book 2
    How This Book Is Organized 2
        Part I: Recognizing the Cloud Momentum 2
        Part II: Getting Connected with E-mail, Calendar, and Contacts 2
        Part III: Exploring SharePoint Online 3
        Part IV: Diving into the Office Web Apps 3
        Part V: Instant Messaging and Online Meetings 3
        Part VI: Preparing to Move 3
        Part VII: The Part of Tens 4
    Icons Used In This Book 4
    Let's Get Started! 5

Part 1: Recognizing the Cloud Momentum *7*

    Chapter 1: Getting to Know the Cloud. 9

        Defining Cloud Computing 10
        Understanding the History of Cloud Computing 12
            Knowing where we are now 12
            Looking forward: Where we go from here 14
            Recognizing why you should care 14
        Introducing the Microsoft Cloud Products 16
            Smart computing with Windows Azure 16
            Opting for the private cloud — Services dedicated to
                your organization 17
            Achieving cloud productivity with Office 365 17
        Knowing the Different Microsoft Office 365 Plans 18
            Analyzing the Office 365 for professionals and small
                businesses plan (P Plan) 18
            Breaking down the Office 365 for mid-size businesses and
                enterprises plan (E Plans) 19
            Answering the needs of the kiosk workers (K Plans) 20
            Examining the Office 365 for education plan (A Plans) ... 21

Chapter 2: Moving to the Office 365 Cloud.......................**23**

Discovering Office 365 Features and Benefits...........................24
  Generating greater productivity..................................24
  Accessing from anywhere...24
  Working with what you know......................................26
  Robust security and reliability..................................26
  IT control and efficiency..27
Getting Familiar with Office 365 Products.............................27
  Pay-as-you-go flexibility..28
  Native apps experience integrated into web apps..................29
  Latest versions of the office apps — always......................29
Severing Ties to Your Desk..29
  Using OWA..30
  Grouping conversations in your inbox.............................30
  Archiving just got personal.....................................31
  Collaborating made easy...31
  Creating communities for the corporate world....................32
  Sharing information with customers and partners with
    extranet sites...32
Going Virtual with Intuitive Communications.........................33
  Text, voice, and video in a single app and service...............33
  From conversations to ad hoc meetings – Yes, it's possible........34
  Online meetings unleashed.......................................34
  Interacting with photos and activity feeds.......................35

**Part II: Getting Connected with E-mail,
Calendar, and Contacts................................. 37**

Chapter 3: Unleashing the Power of Exchange Online............**39**

Gaining Flexibility and Reliability..................................40
  Deployment flexibility..40
  Deployment predictability.......................................41
  Flexible provisioning...42
  Continuous availability...42
  Simplified administration.......................................42
Accessing from Anywhere...43
  From your Outlook e-mail client.................................44
  From the web..44
  From your phone...44
  From your Mac...45
  From any e-mail client..45
  Manage inbox overload..46
  Efficient collaboration...46
  Enhanced voicemail...47

Protecting Information...47
    Archiving and retention 48
    Information protection and control 48

Chapter 4: Giving Productivity a Boost. 51

Understanding the Office 365 Productivity Advantage 52
    Productivity on the go...52
    Enhanced collaboration...52
    Instant Messaging with presence..54
Managing Your Mailbox..54
    Meaningful conversations with the conversation view 54
    Getting deleted items back 56
    Accessing other e-mail accounts through Office 365.................56
Optimizing Your Calendar and Contacts......................................57
    Setting up your OOF when you're OFF...................................57
    Setting up a conference room 58
    Using the Scheduling Assistant...59
    Creating a public group...60
Integrating Social Networking Platforms 61

Part III: Exploring SharePoint Online 63

Chapter 5: Collaborating Has Never Been This Easy! 65

Using SharePoint Online At Work...65
Working with My Site 66
    Viewing and editing your profile...67
    Tagging and noting 68
    Adding tags and notes to web pages.....................................69
    Managing content in your personal site 70
    Adding files to your document libraries 70
Creating a Personal Blog..71
Using Team Sites for External Sharing..73
    Setting up the Team Site 73
    Restoring a previous version of a document or item...................74
    Staying in sync with team calendars and tasks 76
    Sharing Team Sites with external users................................77
Setting up the Intranet with the Publishing Template.................78
    Configuring the permissions for your site.............................79
    Changing the logo 80
    Creating additional pages 80
    Publishing pages 83
    Updating the home page...84
    Displaying site pages in the navigation.................................85
Managing the Press Release Subsite..85

Chapter 6: Going Beyond Websites: SharePoint Scenarios. 87

Managing Digital Content 87
  Document libraries 88
  Slide library 91
  Adding tags and notes..93
  Document Sets 95
Using Search Functionality..97
Using SharePoint Online Services 100
  Excel Services..100
  Access Services...100
  Visio Services 101
  InfoPath Forms Services 101

Chapter 7: Microsoft Office Integration 103

Integrating Office 2010 with SharePoint Online...................................104
  Getting a Backstage view 104
  Using the PowerPoint Broadcast feature....................................106
  Coauthoring documents 108
  Enabling versioning control 109
  Outlook and Outlook alerts 110
Offline Access with SharePoint Workspace 112
  Setting up SharePoint Workspace 112
  Synchronizing documents libraries and lists..............................114
Integrating SharePoint Online with Access 2010.................................115
  Understanding Access databases...115
  Translating Access lingo into SharePoint terms.........................116
  Exporting an Access table to a SharePoint List 116
  Using the Publish to Access Services feature in Access 2010......118

Chapter 8: Demystifying SharePoint Online Administration 121

Appreciating the Concept of a SharePoint Farm 122
  Administering the SharePoint Farm and why you
    don't want to do it..123
  Multitenancy explained...124
  Delegating administration tasks 125
Understanding SharePoint Online Administrator Responsibilities 126
  Turning on external sharing..126
  Creating a new site collection 128
  Assigning a new site collection owner to the
    new site collection 129
  Managing the user profiles 129
  Importing a new custom taxonomy into the Term Store.............130
Exercising the Powers Vested on the Site Collection Administrator....132
  Sharing your site externally..132
  Creating a new team subsite and/or new document libraries 132
  About content and content types 133

Managing the look and feel...135
Managing the galleries 135
Managing permissions and groups...................................137

Chapter 9: Understanding SharePoint Online Development 139

Going Over SharePoint Development 140
Using a Web Browser As a Development Tool 140
    Developing SharePoint sites...................................141
    Adding lists, libraries, and pages..........................145
Cracking Open SharePoint Designer 149
    Peering into the looking glass with SharePoint Designer 149
    Taking a spin around SharePoint Designer 152
    Finding site-creation tools 152
    Unwrapping the Ribbon 153
    Steering the navigation features 154
    Configuring with settings windows 156
    Viewing gallery windows 156
    Developing in editor windows.................................157

Part IV: Diving into the Office Web Apps 161

Chapter 10: Introducing the Office Web Apps....................163

Exploring Office Web Apps Environments and Benefits.........164
    Supporting Office Web Apps with the right
        browser and devices......................................165
    Comparing Office Web Apps and Office Professional Plus..........166
Experiencing Office Web Apps Front and Back 166
    Supported file types and oddities...........................167
    Understanding the engine behind the user experience...............167

Chapter 11: Getting into the Word Web App.....................169

Comparing Word Web App and Word 169
Getting the Basics..170
    Using the Word Web App interface........................170
    Working with documents..173
    Editing and Reading Modes 174
Working with Advanced Functions 175
    Styles 175
    Tables 176

Chapter 12: Plunging into the Excel Web App 179

Comparing Excel Web App and Excel.................................180
Covering the Basics..180
    Using the Excel Web App interface 181
    Working with workbooks..182
    Editing and Reading Modes 183

Using Advanced Features 184
   Adding functions...184
   Manipulating data...185
   Coauthoring workbooks in the cloud.....................................186

Chapter 13: Powering Up the PowerPoint Web App 187
Going Over the Basics...188
   Comparing the PowerPoint Web App and PowerPoint 2010.......188
   Using the PowerPoint Web App user interface.............................189
   Working with presentations 191
Using Advanced Functions..193
   Broadcasting a slide show..193
   Adjusting alignments, bullets, and numbered lists 194
   Adding pictures and Smart Art graphics 194

Chapter 14: Figuring Out the OneNote Web App 195
Exploring Basic Functions 196
   Introduction to Microsoft OneNote..196
   Comparing OneNote Web App and OneNote 2010 198
   Using the OneNote Web App interface 200
   Working with notebooks...200
   The Editing and Reading Views..202
Using Advanced Features 202
   Tagging and proofing your notes...202
   Managing pages and sections...203
   Viewing and restoring page versions 204
   Inserting pictures, tables, and hyperlinks................................205

Part V: Instant Messaging and Online Meetings 207

Chapter 15: Getting Empowered by Lync Online 209
Benefitting from Lync Online 210
   Connecting you, your team, and your work................................210
   Letting people know your presence status 211
   Starting a conversation 212
   Managing contacts and conversations 213
   Lync Integration with Outlook and SharePoint Online................214
Conferencing and Collaborating with Lync....................................214
   Using voice and video features 216
   Using best practices for a successful Lync meeting 216
Understanding the Lync Web App Join Experience...........................217

Chapter 16: Your Presence Unlimited............................219
    Understanding Why Presence Drives Productivity.............................220
        Exploring the Lync user interface...220
        Location, location, location..221
        Is my contact present? Looking for contacts in Lync.................221
        Working with ambient Activity Feed....................................222
        Using the Soft Phone feature..223
        Having your devices at your fingertips.................................224
    Presence Indicator in Office Applications.....................................224
        Click-to-Communicate through Lync from Outlook...................224
        Viewing presence status with Exchange Online and
            Outlook Web App...225
        Locating presence in Word, Excel, and PowerPoint..................226
    Presence Indicator in SharePoint Lists and Libraries......................226

Part VI: Preparing to Move... **227**

Chapter 17: Meeting Office 365 Requirements..................229
    Cloud Attraction..229
    Looking at the Pros and Cons of the Cloud...................................231
    Overall Office 365 Requirements...232
        Geographic requirements..232
        Software requirements..233
        Internet access requirements...234
    Figuring Out Browser Requirements..235
    Lync Requirements...236

Chapter 18: Planning for Your Office 365 Implementation........239
    Choosing an Office 365 Plan...239
    Laying the Groundwork..241
        Planning phase...242
        Preparing phase..246
    Office 365 Online Documentation..248
    Choosing a Partner..248

Chapter 19: Implementing Office 365.............................251
    Getting Users Ready for Office 365..252
        Training...252
        Support..253
    Migrating to Office 365...254
        Activating licensing...255
        Migrating mailbox data (Exchange)......................................256
        Migrating portal content and functionality (SharePoint)...........258
        Throwing the switch..259
        Configuring mobile phones..259

Chapter 20: Managing Office 365 . . . .**261**

Going Over Office 365 Management 261
Managing Exchange Online 266
    Managing your organization.. 267
    Managing yourself or someone else...................................... 268
Managing Lync Online.. 269
    Domain federation 269
    Public instant messaging 270
    User information 270
Managing SharePoint 271
    Managing site collections 271
    InfoPath Form Services 271
    User Profiles 272
    SharePoint Term Store.. 273

Part VII: The Part of Tens **275**

Chapter 21: Ten Signs It's Time for You to Move to the Cloud **277**

You've Experienced a Document-Versioning Nightmare 278
Your Job Includes Maintaining Your IT Infrastructure.......................... 278
A Malfunctioning In-House Server Nearly Obliterated Your Data 279
You Think That "On Demand" Can Apply To Your Business................. 279
Popping Packaging Bubbles No Longer Excites You 280
You've Made Your Workplace Green but Feel You Can Do More 281
Opportunity Knocked While You're on Vacation.................................... 281
You Covet Enterprise-Class Web Conferencing 282
Your IT Department Needs a Morale Boost 283
You Are Ready to Take On Gartner Research 2012 Predictions 283

Chapter 22: Ten Office 365 Value Propositions **285**

Offloaded Responsibility 286
Reduced Infrastructure.. 286
Predictable Costs... 287
Reduced Complexity 287
Anywhere Access 288
Synchronized Data 288
Integrated Software 289
Mobile Access to Enterprise Data 289
Increased IT Efficiency.. 290
Self-Service Enterprise Software... 291

**Chapter 23: Ten Tips for Increasing Productivity and
Efficiency with Office 365** 293

Leveraging the Service Health Dashboard to Save Time......................294
Don't Lose Sleep over Confidential Data in Your Lost Phone.................294
Sharing the Workload to Manage SharePoint
    Online External Users...295
Chatting in Outlook Web App 295
Publishing Your Calendar...296
Doing Something With Content in the Backstage View 297
Leveraging Microsoft's Three-Screen Strategy
    to Drive Productivity..297
Taking Your Files Offline and Resyncing Them 298
Administering Data Security Is No Longer an Onerous
    Technical Task..298

Glossary *299*

Index *305*

Introduction

· ·

Any fool can make things bigger and more complex. It takes a touch of genius — and a lot of courage — to move in the opposite direction.

— Albert Einstein

*I*n the last few years, the cloud has taken the information technology community by storm. As companies have struggled with the learning curve and cost of adopting Enterprise class software on their own the cloud has created a simplified and streamlined alternative. The complexity of keeping software running has been taken out of the equation. The result is that organizations can focus on using software to drive business and competitive advantage instead of using critical resources to keep the lights blinking green.

Office 365 is the newest cloud offering by Microsoft and bundles the popular SharePoint, Exchange, Lync, and Office into a single product that is accessed over the Internet. Because Microsoft runs these server products in their data centers with their engineers, you can be assured that they know what they are doing. After all, who better to manage these products than the same people who actually built them in the first place? To ease the mind of the risk averse, Microsoft puts their company name and piles of cash behind Office 365 in a very attractive service level agreement.

For those who are still not convinced, Microsoft has taken the unique step of designing Office 365 in a way that lets you use the Enterprise software in a hybrid environment. Should you want to keep some of your data and management in house you can still use Office 365. If you feel more comfortable moving to Office 365 in waves, then it is designed to accommodate you. You can start with a pilot group in order to prove out the benefits that the cloud provides before turning your trust over to Microsoft engineers. Microsoft is convinced that after you try Office 365, it will change your perspective on Enterprise software forever, and you will never look back.

About This Book

This book is about understanding Microsoft Office 365. This book looks at the cloud in general to give you the fundamentalsand then dives into the specifics of the Microsoft cloud. The Office 365 product consists of a number of sub-products and applications, and the book walks you through all of them. If you are considering moving to Office 365 or have already moved, then this book is the first book you should read in order to get up to speed on the concepts and terms as quickly as possible.

How To Use This Book

This book is designed to be read as you want to find out about the specific components of Office 365. You do not need to read the parts of the book in any order. It is recommended that you read the first part first to gain foundational knowledge of the cloud and, in particular Office 365, but then feel free to jump around as you see fit.

How This Book Is Organized

This book is organized into seven parts.

Part 1: Recognizing the Cloud Momentum

This part provides the fundamental knowledge you need to understand in order to get a handle on the momentum the cloud has experienced in recent years. This part walks you through the definition of the cloud and some of the various products that fall under the cloud category. In addition, it provides a very high-level overview of the Office 365 environment and walks you through some of the key benefits and features of the product as a whole, as well as the components that make up the product, including SharePoint Online, Exchange Online, Lync Online, and Office Professional Plus.

Part II: Getting Connected with E-mail, Calendar, and Contacts

I bet that you probably use e-mail more than any other communication mechanism other that talking with someone face to face. Actually, many of the people we know use e-mail more than even talking with someone in person! The component of Office 365 that is responsible for e-mail is called Exchange Online, and this part walks you through that product, including the calendar and contacts functionality.

Part III: Exploring SharePoint Online

Part III of the book discusses one of the most important aspects of Office 365 — SharePoint Online. The part walks you through some of the basics of SharePoint, including communication and collaboration, as well as content management and Microsoft Office integration. Finally, this part discusses some of the different roles and responsibilities that come along with using SharePoint and then walks you through some of the technical aspects of the platform, including SharePoint development.

Part IV: Diving into the Office Web Apps

This part dives into the Office Web Apps by starting with an overview and definition of Web Apps, followed by a dive into each particular app. In particular, it talks about the Word Web App, Excel Web App, PowerPoint Web App, and finally the OneNote Web App. The Web Apps are exciting because you can work with these popular Office products from any computer with an Internet connection, using nothing more than a web browser. Find yourself on an awesome cruise and in need of revising a critical proposal but without a decent computer? No problem, you can use the ship's loaner computer and its web browser to sign in and make the changes you need. Remember, Office 365 is in the cloud, so all you need is an Internet connection to get to most of your Enterprise data.

Part V: Instant Messaging and Online Meetings

One of the components of Office 365 is called Lync Online and that is the subject of this part of the book. The part starts off with an overview of Lync and describes some of the key benefits you achieve such as connecting with colleagues and conducting ad-hoc online meetings. Finally, this part discusses how Lync integrates with the other components of Office 365 to form a wholly connected environment where you are always only a click away from a co-worker, colleague, or partner, regardless of what you are doing in Office 365.

Part VI: Preparing to Move

A big piece of Office 365 is moving your people and processes into the new environment. This part walks you through the requirements to Office 365 and then moves into more detailed topics such as preparing, planning, and implementing. Finally, this part discusses some of the specifics around managing Office 365 after you have made the switch.

Part VII: The Part of Tens

The Part of Tens provides a quick reference to three topics to keep in mind when thinking about Office 365. Chapter 21 provides a list of ten signs that you should move to the cloud right away. Chapter 22 lists out ten value propositions that you should consider when moving to Office 365. And finally, Chapter 23 walks you through some of the best ways to increase efficiency when using Office 365.

Icons Used In This Book

The familiar *For Dummies* icons offer visual clues about the material contained within this book. Look for the following icons throughout the chapters:

Whenever you see a Tip icon take note. We use the tip icon whenever we want you to pay particular attention. Throughout the process of writing the book, we worked closely with Microsoft on any bugs or issues that have come up. When we found something worth a special note, we use this icon for emphasis.

Whenever you see a Remember icon get out your notebook. The Remember icon is used to point out key concepts that you should remember as you walk through the Office 365 product. Of course, you can always use the online cheatsheet, too.

Throughout our careers we've come across many roadblocks. It often takes hours to figure something out the first time and then only minutes the next time you encounter it. Often the root cause of your problems is a bug or some quirky behavior. We have tried to call out whenever you should take note of something and beware of how it will affect your Office 365 environment.

Office 365 is designed to be simple and intuitive; however, nothing is ever as easy as it appears. When we talk about something that is fairly technical in depth, we use the Technical Stuff icon. You definitely don't need to understand every technical detail, but it is there if you decide you want to dig further.

Let's Get Started!

Office 365 is was one of the most highly anticipated products in Microsoft's history. Even before the launch, major customers were moving their infrastructure over to the Microsoft cloud in order to reap the cost savings, predictability, and peace of mind that comes with the cloud. Because Microsoft has included many of their most popular Enterprise products in the Office 365 offering, it becomes a game changer from the very beginning. As with any technology, however, there is a learning curve. Microsoft has done everything they could to make Office 365 as user friendly and intuitive as possible but you will still require guidance. This book is the first step in your Office 365 journey and is designed to get you up to speed as quickly as possible. If you are ready to take your first step, then you can get started!

Part I
Recognizing the Cloud Momentum

The 5th Wave · By Rich Tennant

"We're still working out the kinks in our cloud computing environment."

In this part . . .

In this part, you get an overview of this new buzzword known as the cloud. You also get a brief history on how we got this puffy new creature and what it means to move into it. We help get your feet wet with a broad understanding of the Microsoft cloud and how Office 365 fits into the mix. Finally, you look into Office 365 in particular and take a gander at all of the products stuffed into the offering. This includes Exchange Online for e-mail, SharePoint Online for your portal needs, Lync Online for instant and ad-hoc meetings and communication, and Office Professional Plus.

Chapter 1

Getting to Know the Cloud

In This Chapter

▶ Understanding cloud computing

▶ Discovering the various Microsoft cloud products

▶ Determining the right Office 365 plan for your business

"The cloud services companies of all size. The cloud is for everyone. The cloud is a democracy."

— Marc Benioff, CEO, Salesforce.com

*E*veryone is talking about the cloud. It's everywhere. It's on TV, it's on YouTube, it's in the papers, and it's on billboards. The term as it relates to technology has as many definitions as there are keys on your computer. When *Cloud Computing Journal* gathered 21 experts to define cloud computing in early 2009, they came up with definitions ranging from overly simplified to downright too technical for the average person affected by this paradigm shift sweeping across the globe.

If you are confused about cloud computing, despair not. Even Larry Ellison (Chief Executive Officer of Oracle Corporation, a major enterprise software company) once said: ". . . Maybe I'm an idiot, but I have no idea what anyone is talking about."

This chapter is for those of you who have a keen interest in understanding the basic principles of cloud computing with the intent of leveraging that knowledge to help your business, your organization, or your professional career. If you are a business owner who is contemplating a move to the cloud, this chapter's overview of key cloud computing players (specifically Microsoft cloud product offerings) will hopefully provide the push to help you make your decision.

Defining Cloud Computing

The cloud is a metaphor for the Internet. In very simplistic terms, cloud computing means that your applications or software, data, and computing needs are accessed, stored, and occur over the Internet or the cloud.

Perhaps one of the best ways to illustrate the concept of cloud computing is through the story of how Saleforce.com grew from a start-up in a rented apartment to the world's fastest growing software company in less than a decade.

In his book *Behind the Cloud,* Marc Benioff describes how he saw an opportunity to deliver business software applications in a new way. He wanted to make software easier to purchase and simpler to use without the complexities of installation, maintenance, and constant upgrades. His vision was to sell software as a service. Companies would pay a monthly fee, per user, only for those services they used delivered via the Internet. The idea was to host the software on a website and for it to be available to companies anytime, anywhere.

By using the Internet as the delivery platform, an on-demand service in an infrastructure gave Saleforce.com customers the ability to use software fully managed not by their own IT department but by their cloud service provider, Saleforce.com.

For most small businesses, this type of deployment model is referred to as the *public cloud* where the cloud computing service is owned by a provider offering the highest level of efficiency. For organizations where a "one-size-fits-all" approach doesn't work, two other deployment models for cloud computing are available: private clouds and hybrid clouds (see Figure 1-1).

A *private cloud* is typically dedicated to one organization on its own highly secure, private network. A *hybrid cloud* is simply a combination of the public and private clouds. As an example, applications in a hybrid cloud may be run in a public cloud but customer information is stored in a database in a private cloud.

Regardless of the deployment model used, cloud computing means that your business applications are outsourced somewhere on the Internet where you don't have to worry about paying for capacity you don't need. It also means that the version of the software you're using is always the latest version; it is accessible anytime, anywhere.

Cloud Computing Deployment Models

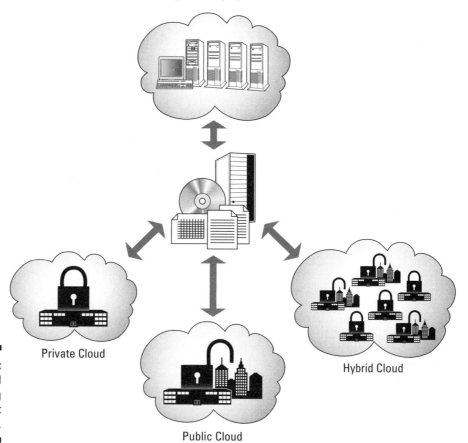

Private Cloud

Public Cloud

Hybrid Cloud

Figure 1-1:
Cloud
Computing
Deployment
Models.

As a consumer or end user, cloud computing means that you can create documents and media files by using software hosted online, store your files in a location somewhere on the Internet (not on your hard drive), and easily share your files with others. This is your personal cloud in a public deployment model. If you want to, you can synchronize your files in the cloud to your computer's local hard drive.

In this sense, the advantages of cloud computing is not limited to just big or small companies. It is also beneficial to individual end users or consumers. As such, Benioff is right: The cloud truly is a democracy.

Understanding the History of Cloud Computing

Contrary to general belief, cloud computing is not a new concept. The arrival of Salesforce.com in the late 1990s was indeed a milestone, but the idea of an "intergalactic computer network" was first introduced in the 1960s by J. C. R. Licklider, one of the most influential men in the history of computer science. Licklider headed a group at the Advance Research Projects Agency (ARPA) in 1962 to improve the military's use of computers and brought time-sharing and networking capabilities to the forefront of computer technology and research.

Other people attribute the emergence of cloud computing to John McCarthy, another computer scientist who in the 1960s proposed that computing be delivered as a public utility similar to service bureaus that provided services to businesses for a fee.

The popular "Did You Know/Shift Happens" series from xplane.com claims that the computer inside a cellphone is a million times cheaper, a thousand times more powerful, and about a hundred thousand times smaller than the computers in the 1960s. We don't dispute that claim especially since back then, massive computing was conducted with supercomputers and mainframes occupying whole buildings. Thousands of central processing units (CPUs) were connected to divide the computing tasks of supercomputers in order to get results faster. The very high cost for creating and maintaining these supercomputers precipitated the discovery of more economical computing means.

Knowing where we are now

Today, computing has developed along numerous paths. Not only are businesses able to use the services of specialized providers for massive computing, they also benefit from the lower cost of these services stemming from the efficiencies of shared infrastructure.

After Salesforce.com pioneered the delivery of enterprise applications over the Internet in 1999, Amazon.com followed suit in 2002 by offering a suite of cloud-based storage, computation, and even human intelligence through the Amazon Mechanical Turk. In 2006, Amazon.com launched the Elastic Compute Cloud (EC2) as a commercial web service that offers small businesses and individuals computer capacity in the cloud.

The surge of new technologies, social media innovations, and Web 2.0 altered the media landscape in 2009. Google and others soon focused their attention on browser-based enterprise class Software-as-a-Service (SaaS) product offerings, such as Google Apps and Microsoft Office 365.

In addition to SaaS, cloud computing offers two other service models: Platform-as-a-Service (PaaS) and Infrastructure-as-a-Service (IaaS). Figure 1-2 illustrates the three kinds of cloud computing service models.

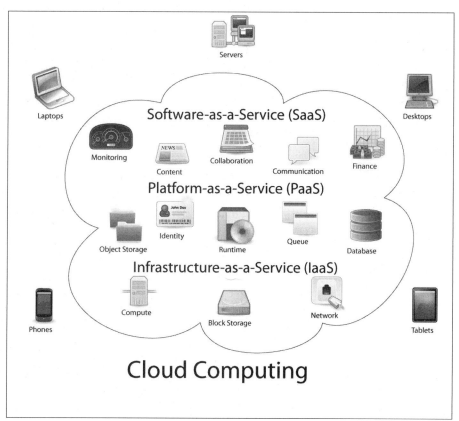

Figure 1-2:
Cloud
Computing
Service
Models.

In PaaS, users (mostly developers) are able to create new online applications in platforms provided by the PaaS provider. Google App Engine and Windows Azure are examples of a PaaS service model.

In an IaaS service model, organizations have access to computing power and storage capacity, using a cloud provider's hardware. This enables them to have control over the infrastructure and run applications in the cloud at a reduced cost. Amazon Web Services offer several IaaS cloud hosting products that can be purchased by the hour. Rackspace is another player in the IaaS market offering managed and cloud hosting services. The Microsoft offering in the IaaS service model is the use of remote desktops and virtual machines with Windows Azure.

Looking forward: Where we go from here

Pew Research Center's most recent survey indicates that an overwhelming majority of highly engaged technology stakeholders and critics agree that by 2020 most people won't do their work with software running on a general-purpose PC. Instead, they will work in Internet-based as well as smartphone applications.

Undoubtedly, the cloud will continue to expand across industries to dominate informational transactions and ultimately provide access to sophisticated yet affordable networks from the comfort of our own homes.

As the number of social network users and cloud-based workers grow, leading technology giants including Microsoft, Google, Apple, and Facebook will provide important contributions to cloud computing in terms of "killer apps" and reliable online services.

Recognizing why you should care

In the early 20th century, people were skeptical about cars and viewed the new invention as horseless carriages, based on a centuries-old dominant paradigm: the horse and carriage.

Gottlieb Daimler, the inventor of the automobile, estimated long-term auto popularity to be no more than a million cars. A Michigan Savings Bank president once advised Henry Ford's lawyer not to invest in Ford Motor Company in 1903 because "the horse is here to stay but the automobile is only a novelty, a fad."

Today, over 600 million cars are on the road . . . and not many horses. The important role cars play in our daily lives has proven both Daimler and the Michigan Savings Bank president wrong. Prior constraints to the production of cars have been overcome to bring the cars to the masses.

The "horseless carriage" syndrome

When the first cars came out, they looked very similar to the horse and carriage but without the horse (see the figure below). The problem with the design was that the engineers back then didn't understand the opportunities of the new paradigm (faster and safer cars). The engineers insisted on putting a whip holder into the early car models before realizing that without a horse, there was no need for a whip holder! We may not fully grasp the true potential of cloud computing, but it's a good idea not to fall prey to the horseless carriage syndrome.

Businesses of all sizes face a similar change. Just as in the early days of the automobile industry, much is unknown about where this paradigm shift is going to take us. What we do know is that cloud computing promises not just cheaper but also faster, easier, flexible, and more-effective IT solutions for any type of organization.

As more and more work is done on the cloud, the economies of scale will kick in and barriers to cloud adoption (such as security and privacy) will begin to fall. Strength in cloud adoption will change perceptions and focus on the further developments of the technology will accelerate, unlocking more economic benefits for the businesses. The whole cloud ecosystem will change and adapt just as the horseless carriage evolved into an essential and irreplaceable commodity of modern life.

Introducing the Microsoft Cloud Products

Microsoft has made and continues to make significant investments to grow its cloud-based businesses. The software giant last year launched its largest-ever ad campaign touting "Cloud Power" and its benefits over traditional server-based computing. To Microsoft, *Cloud Power* means three scenarios: public cloud, private cloud, and cloud productivity. The goal of this effort, according to Chief Creative Officer, Central Marketing Group Gayle Troberman, is to ". . . make sense of all the options and help customers harness the power of the cloud in the manner that best suits their business needs."

Microsoft's cloud solutions consist of a productivity offering, a cloud platform, and a private cloud.

Smart computing with Windows Azure

Windows Azure is a set of technologies and services that empowers businesses to take advantage of the scalability and agility of cloud computing. The technology not only allows businesses to store data in the cloud but also allows them to build and connect applications in the cloud similar to how businesses currently do it on premises. The flexibility of this platform makes it easy to scale up or down to meet business needs under a pay-for-use business model. If you are a developer, Windows Azure is a great platform to develop and run applications in .NET, PHP, and Java, hosted in Microsoft data centers. The platform essentially eliminates the need to buy servers and allocate resources to manage the infrastructure, allowing organizations to focus more on responding to customer needs and growing their business.

The database component to the Windows Azure platform is *SQL Azure.* This relational database is hosted in the cloud, is built on Microsoft's SQL technology, and runs in the same datacenters as Microsoft's Windows Azure.

The growing list of Windows Azure platform users includes companies and organizations, such as 3M, NASA, General Mills, Volvo, Xerox, T-Mobile, and Pixar.

In a white paper published by Microsoft entitled "The Economics of the Cloud," you find that Pixar Animation Studios runs its computer-animation rendering process on Windows Azure because every frame of its movies would take eight hours to render if it were running on a single processor. This means that on a single processor, an entire movie would take 272 years to render! With the Windows Azure platform however, Pixar is able to get the job done as fast as they need to because the cloud business model allows a user to pay the same for 1 machine running for 1,000 hours as he would for accelerating the process by running 1,000 machines for 1 hour.

Hyper-V makes you go on a Target shopping spree — A Microsoft case study

Imagine over 1,750 stores with no IT personnel whatsoever in any of those stores. How do you manage the business application that runs the processes to ensure that shelves are stocked and checkouts are quick, while at the same time saving millions of dollars in hardware, electrical, and maintenance cost?

To deliver on its "Expect More, Pay Less" brand promise, Target uses Hyper-V virtualization technology to support 15,000 virtual machines running mission-critical applications on 30,000 endpoints across its retail network. With this cost-effective technology, Target plans to retire 8,650 servers and implement a two-server-per-store policy by 2012.

So the next time you find yourself in an engaging shopping spree, know that your experience has something to do with Hyper-V and cloud computing.

Opting for the private cloud — Services dedicated to your organization

In a private cloud implementation, you still enjoy the benefits of public cloud computing, namely: self-service, scalability, and elasticity. In addition, your dedicated resources allow more control and customization regardless of whether your implementation exists on-premises or off-premises.

The core component for Microsoft's private cloud is the server virtualization technology called *Windows Server Hyper-V (Hyper-V)*. With Hyper-V, you are able to consolidate multiple server roles as separate virtual machines (VMs) running on a single, physical machine. To illustrate how this works, take a cue from retail giant Target who relies on a virtual solution to optimize its customer's shopping experience (see the "Hyper-V makes you go on a Target shopping spree — A Microsoft case study" sidebar).

There are a number of Microsoft Private Cloud Service Partners listed at `http://pinpoint.microsoft.com` who offer cloud services implementation and configuration to meet the needs of any business type or size.

Achieving cloud productivity with Office 365

Microsoft Office 365 combines the familiar and trusted communication (Exchange Online) and collaboration (SharePoint Online and Lync Online) software into the cloud. In addition, the same Microsoft Outlook and

Microsoft Office applications you know now work seamlessly with this cloud service.

Microsoft's three-screen strategy extends the cloud to the PC, browser, and the phone. This means that the software, devices, phones, and browsers already in your arsenal all work in harmony to give your workers access to information anytime, anywhere. With presence on all three screens — and all portals pointing to the cloud — businesses and consumers become more productive and efficient as the cloud becomes a part of their daily lives.

Knowing the Different Microsoft Office 365 Plans

As a cloud productivity solution in one place, Microsoft Office 365 offers service plans for professionals and small businesses, mid-size businesses and enterprises, and the education community. All plans are designed to help an organization's business needs for security, reliability, and productivity.

Analyzing the Office 365 for professionals and small businesses plan (P Plan)

This pay-as-you-go set of web-enabled tools allows users to access e-mail, documents, calendar, contacts, and online meetings on any device, any time, from anywhere for $6 per user, per month, for businesses not needing more than 50 users or accounts. Subscription to Plan P includes the following key features:

- Exchange Online for e-mail, calendar, and contacts. Mailbox storage is allocated at 25GB with e-mail attachments up to 25 MB
- Office Web Apps for online viewing and basic editing of Word, Excel, PowerPoint, and OneNote
- SharePoint Online for collaboration and creating a professional-looking public-facing website
- Lync Online for instant messaging, online meetings, PC-to-PC audio and video calls, and presence
- Microsoft Forefront Online Protection for Exchange provides premium antivirus and anti-spam protection
- Online community support only, no phone support

Breaking down the Office 365 for mid-size businesses and enterprises plan (E Plans)

The enterprise family of plans for Office 365 comes in four versions (E1 through E4) with prices ranging from $10–$27 per month, per user. The enterprise version comes with Exchange Online, SharePoint Online, Lync Online, and Office Professional Plus. Table 1-1 lists the cost (per user, per month) for the subscription and the key features associated with each of these plans.

Table 1-1	Enterprise Plans Pricing Model			
Office 365 Plan E Family (per user, per month)	**E1 ($10)**	**E2 ($16)**	**E3 ($24)**	**E4 ($27)**
Advanced administration capabilities, active directory integration, and 24/7 IT Administrator support	✓	✓	✓	✓
E-mail, calendar, contacts, personal archive, and 25GB mailbox storage	✓	✓	✓	✓
Sites to share documents and information	✓	✓	✓	✓
Instant messaging, video calls, and online meetings	✓	✓	✓	✓
Premium antispam and antivirus filtering (Microsoft Forefront Online Protection for Exchange and Microsoft Forefront Security for SharePoint)	✓	✓	✓	✓
License rights to access on-premises deployment of Exchange Server, SharePoint Server, and Lync Server	✓	✓	✓	✓
Document viewing and light editing		✓	✓	✓

(continued)

Table 1-1 *(continued)*

Office 365 Plan E Family (per user, per month)	E1 ($10)	E2 ($16)	E3 ($24)	E4 ($27)
Complete and full-featured set of office productivity applications (Office Professional Plus)			✓	✓
Publish Access databases, share Excel workbooks, build InfoPath forms, and share Visio business processes and diagrams			✓	✓
Advanced archive capabilities, unlimited e-mail storage, and hosted voicemail			✓	✓
Enterprise voice capabilities to replace or enhance a PBX				✓

Answering the needs of the kiosk workers (K Plans)

If you own a retail chain or run a business with "deskless" workers, you don't have to leave these workers out from the benefits of using Office 365. Deskless workers, shift workers, retail store employees, truck drivers, and similar employees who use shared PCs, have minimal collaboration requirements, and limited communication needs can be signed up with the Kiosk Worker Plans (K1 and K2).

For $4 per user per month, a K1 plan provides users without a dedicated PC access to web e-mail, internal SharePoint sites, and online viewing of Office documents through the Office Web Apps. There is a limit of 500MB of mailbox storage per user for this plan.

For $10/user/month, a K2 plan provides the same features as the K1 plan plus basic editing functionality of Office documents through the Office Web Apps.

Examining the Office 365 for education plan (A Plans)

Office 365 for education provides educational institutions simple-to-use and easy-to-administer cloud-based productivity tools. With the same enterprise class security, reliability, and privacy, educational institutions can have the cloud on their terms backed by the same robust security and guaranteed reliability enterprise customers enjoy.

The family of A (academic) plans offers free subscriptions to students who only need access to Exchange Online, SharePoint Online, Lync Online, and Office Web Apps. For faculty and staff, the fee ranges from $6/month/user to $16/month/user. Table 1-2 below breaks down the cost and key features that come with each plan.

Table 1-2	Academic Plans Pricing Model			
Exchange Online	**Plan A1**	**Plan A2**	**Plan A3**	**Plan A4**
E-mail, calendar, AV/AS, Personal Archive	E-mail, calendar, AV/AS, Personal Archive IM & Presence SharePoint Online Conferencing	E-mail, calendar, AV/AS, Personal Archive IM & Presence SharePoint Online Conferencing Office Web Apps	E-mail, calendar, AV/AS, Personal Archive IM & Presence SharePoint Online Conferencing Office Web Apps Voicemail and Advanced Archive Capabilities Office Pro Plus	E-mail, calendar, AV/AS, Personal Archive IM & Presence SharePoint Online Conferencing Office Web Apps Voicemail and Advanced Archive Capabilities Office Pro Plus Voice

(continued)

Table 1-2 *(continued)*

Exchange Online	Plan A1	Plan A2	Plan A3	Plan A4
FOR STUDENTS				
Free	Free	Free	$2/month	$2.50/month
FOR FACULTY AND STAFF				
Free	$6/month	$10/month	$14/month	$16/month

Chapter 2

Moving to the Office 365 Cloud

- -

In This Chapter

▶ Exploring some of the key benefits and features of Office 365

▶ Working with cloud-enabled Word, Excel, and Outlook

▶ Developing your understanding of cloud-based Exchange and SharePoint

▶ Using Lync to instantly communicate with text, voice, and video

- -

> *There was a time when every household, town, farm or village had its own water well. Today, shared public utilities give us access to clean water by simply turning on the tap; cloud computing works in a similar fashion.*
>
> — Vivek Kundra, Federal CIO, United States Government

*A*s we mention in Chapter 1, cloud computing is simply using a software application over the Internet. Microsoft Office 365 is a grouping of Microsoft products that are hosted and managed by Microsoft. You subscribe to the service on a monthly basis. This model of using software is often called Software as a Service (SaaS).

With the Office 365 offering, Microsoft takes care of all the installation and management of the complicated server products, such as SharePoint and Exchange. Your organization simply signs up, starts paying the monthly fee, and uses the software over the Internet (meaning in the cloud). The burden of the installation, patches, upgrades, backups, and maintenance (among other stuff) is all taken care of by smart Microsoft employees. To make you feel more comfortable, Microsoft has a 99.9 percent uptime guarantee that is backed by a legal contract called a Service Level Agreement (SLA).

In this chapter, you get a high-level view of the software products that Microsoft includes in the grouping of software products known as Office 365 and which are delivered over the Internet. These products include SharePoint, Exchange, Lync, and Office Professional Plus. You also get some of the basics under your belt, including why the cloud and Office 365 in particular are generating such buzz. After all, when Microsoft invests billions of dollars, it must be something worthwhile.

Discovering Office 365 Features and Benefits

Moving to the Office 365 cloud comes with some key features and benefits. Namely, your organization gets to continue to use the software you have been using for years, but you now get to shift the burden onto Microsoft. In addition to shifting the burden to Microsoft, we cover some other key benefits that we describe in the following sections.

Generating greater productivity

Productivity is a great word that management-consultant types love to use. In the real world though, productivity can be summed up in a simple question: Can I do my job easier or not? Microsoft has invested heavily and spent a tremendous amount of time trying to make the user and administrator experiences of Office 365 as easy and simple as possible.

The idea is that increasing simplicity yields greater productivity. Whether it is an administrator setting up a new employee or a business analyst writing policy and procedure documents in Word. When the technology gets out of the way and you can focus on your job, you become more productive. Don't believe me? Try using a typewriter instead of a word processor. Whoever thought copy and paste would be such a game changer?

Accessing from anywhere

Accessing your enterprise software over the Internet has some big advantages. For one, all you need is your computer — desktop, laptop, tablet, or phone — and an Internet connection or phone coverage. Because the software is running in a Microsoft data center, you simply connect to the Internet to access the software, as shown in Figure 2-1.

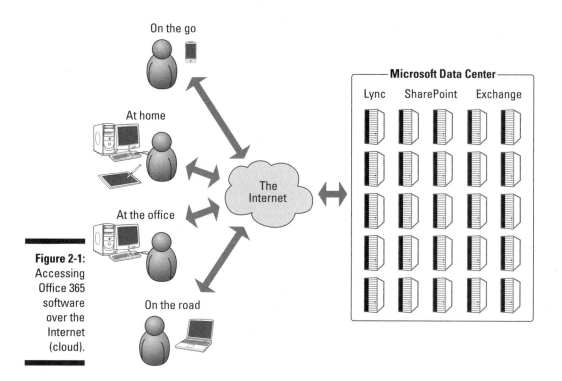

Figure 2-1:
Accessing
Office 365
software
over the
Internet
(cloud).

Another benefit of accessing centrally located data is that you always have a single source of the truth. If you make a change to a document from your tablet at home and then your colleague views the file from their phone, she will see the most up-to-date document. Gone are the days of e-mailing Excel documents between machines with long file names, such as Forecast_ Q1_2011_KW-Reviewed_Jenn-Edited-2-1-11_Revised_2-14-11_KW_final_More_ edits_now-really-FINAL.xlsx.

With SharePoint Online (part of the Office 365 package) a single file, say Forecast_Q1_2011.xlsx, lives out in the cloud (meaning in Microsoft's globally distributed billion dollar data centers). Because the document lives in the cloud, the security permissions can be set up to allow anyone in the organi-zation, regardless of geographic location, to view the document. Security can be as strict or as lenient as desired. For example, you may want everyone in the organization to be able to see a company policy document but only want a select group of individuals to edit the document. In addition, SharePoint takes care of all the versioning and even lets you check out a document to edit so that nobody else can edit it at the same time.

Need to collaborate on the document in real time? No problem. You can do that by using nothing more than your web browser as you find out in later chapters of the book.

Working with what you know

Humans aren't very keen on change. We like to drive the same route to work for years before we figure out there is a better route that avoids all those snarly traffic snafus. Why would it be any different with the software you use on a daily basis?

Microsoft does not always come out with the best software. Remember Windows Vista? Shiver! Instead of running far away and never looking back at Windows again, users simply held their collective breath until Windows 7. And thank you for hurrying Microsoft! Microsoft Word and Excel have been in use for more than 20 years and even though new analysis software comes out all the time, Excel is still the one to beat. You know that you can do what you need to do without much headache.

One thing Microsoft did incredibly right is recognize that users don't want to give up the things that make them comfortable. Don't take away our Word and Excel we shouted! And Microsoft listened. Office 365 hasn't changed our favorites one bit. The only difference is that now they are seamlessly connected to the enterprise software living out in the cloud. In other words, our favorite applications are cloudified.

One of the coolest features about SharePoint 2010 and Office 2010 is that you can work with SharePoint without ever having to leave the Office applications. For example, you can fire up Word, check out a document stored in SharePoint, make some changes, check it back in, review versions, and even leave some notes for your colleagues. All without even having to know that SharePoint is handling the content management functionality behind the scenes.

Robust security and reliability

With Microsoft taking on all the responsibility for security and reliability, your IT team can rest on their laurels. After all, they spent their entire careers keeping the systems up and running. Shouldn't they get a break? All kidding aside, letting Microsoft do the heavy lifting frees up the IT team to do more important things. No, not playing computer games, but helping users get the most out of enterprise software. Ever wonder why nobody could ever find time to implement a company-wide blog and discussion board? Now they can finally be a reality.

Microsoft understands if you aren't fully comfortable about letting them do the heavy lifting. In my opinion, it is the best scenario. After all, who better to handle managing a software product than the same people who built it? To address some of the questions, however, Microsoft has extensive service level agreements to help put your mind at ease.

IT control and efficiency

If you have ever met an IT person, you might have generalized one thing about them. They are control freaks. They like to know exactly what everyone is doing with their systems at all times. If something goes wrong, then it is probably due to user error. Our systems do what they are supposed to do. Microsoft has gone out of its way to create an unprecedented level of control for administrators. But that is not all. Not only do administrators have control over the environment, but it is also actually designed to be simple in nature and, get this, intuitive.

Getting Familiar with Office 365 Products

The Office 365 product is actually a package of products sold on a monthly basis. In particular, these include Office Professional Plus, SharePoint Online, Exchange Online, and Lync Online.

The online part just means that you access these server products over the Internet. If your IT team were to buy these products and install them for your use in the company data center, then they would be called on-premise.

Finding someone who doesn't use some aspect of Microsoft Office on a daily basis is difficult. Whether it is Outlook for e-mail, Word for creating and editing documents, or Excel for manipulating data, these old standbys seem to dominate the life of the modern-day information worker. Office Professional Plus includes much more than these old stalwarts, though. In particular, Office Professional Plus includes the following applications:

- ✔ **Word:** Microsoft Office Word is used for word processing, such as creating and editing documents.

- ✔ **Excel:** Excel is used for data analysis and numeric manipulation.

- ✔ **PowerPoint:** PowerPoint is used to create and deliver presentations.

- ✔ **Outlook:** An application that is used for e-mail, contacts, and calendaring, including scheduling meetings, meeting rooms, and other resources.

- ✔ **OneNote:** An application that is used for capturing and organizing notes.

- ✔ **Publisher:** An application that is used to create and share publications and marketing materials, such as brochures, newsletters, postcards, and greeting cards.

- ✔ **Access:** A database application that is used to collect, store, manipulate, and report on data.

- ✔ **InfoPath:** An application designed to create nifty and useful forms that are used to collect data from people.

- ✔ **SharePoint Workspace:** SharePoint is great but what happens when you aren't connected to the Internet and need to access and work with your website? SharePoint Workspace allows you to take SharePoint sites offline.

- ✔ **Lync:** When you need to connect with other people, Lync is the tool for you. Lync allows you to connect with others by using features such as instant messaging and conferencing, including screen sharing, polling, and shared presentations.

Pay-as-you-go flexibility

With pay-as-you-go licensing, your organization is able to turn on or off licensing depending on the number of users that require Microsoft Office. In addition, Microsoft has added flexibility for you as a user by allowing you to activate the licensing on up to five different computers at a single time. For example, when your organization adds you as an Office Professional Plus subscriber, you can activate the software on your workstation at work, your laptop, your home computer, and your home laptop. When you buy a new computer, you will find a simple user screen where you can update the computers that Office is activated on. This flexibility makes managing your Office Professional Plus applications and licensing as easy and straightforward as possible.

The pay-as-you-go model for Office Professional Plus is only available for Enterprise Office 365 packages. If you are part of a small organization and only need a handful of Microsoft Office licenses, then you will still buy Office the same way as you do now. The difference is that your Office applications are integrated with the server products running in the cloud (SharePoint,

Exchange, and Lync). In addition, you have access to the Office Web Apps, which allow you to work with your Office documents by using a web browser.

Native apps experience integrated into web apps

In addition to running Office applications, such as Word and Excel on your local computer, Office 365 also includes a web version of these applications called Office Web Apps. When working with the Office Web Apps, you simply open your web browser and browse to your SharePoint portal that contains your document. You can then open or edit your document right in the web browser.

Microsoft has gone to great pains to make the Office Web Apps experience very similar to the traditional Office experience. For example, when you are writing a Word document, you expect certain behavior. Microsoft has tried very hard to make the behavior you expect while working in Microsoft Word the same as you will find when using the Office Web App version of Word that is running in your web browser. We cover Office Web Apps in greater detail in Part IV.

Latest versions of the office apps — always

Because Office 365 uses a SAAS model, you are always instantly up-to-date. When Microsoft releases a new version of Office, your licensing is instantly upgraded. You don't need to wait for the IT team to finally get the new product purchased and rolled out. When Microsoft flips the switch, everyone has the latest and greatest instantly available.

Severing Ties to Your Desk

If you are used to using Outlook for your e-mail, then you won't experience any changes when your organization moves to Office 365. The only difference will be that Microsoft, rather than your local IT department, is now hosting your e-mail. Should you decide to look a bit farther, however, you can find a great deal of extra functionality just waiting to make your life easier. For example, the new Windows Phone 7 smartphones are integrated with Exchange in order to push e-mail directly to your phone. Prefer a different mobile smartphone? No problem. Almost every smartphone on the market can be set up to receive Office 365 e-mail.

Using OWA

Outlook Web Access (OWA) provides the ability for you to check your enterprise Exchange e-mail, using nothing more than a web browser. Instead of using Outlook on your local computer you simply browse to a web address, such as `http://mail.myorganization.com` and then log in and check your e-mail. The experience is very similar to other web e-mail services, such as Google's Gmail or Microsoft's Hotmail. What's exciting about OWA, however, is that you finally get access to your enterprise e-mail, calendar, and contacts from any computer with an Internet connection and a web browser.

Outlook and Exchange are both e-mail-related products, but one is for users and the other is server software. Exchange is a server product that sits on a server in a data center and manages all your e-mail. Outlook is an application that you install on your local desktop and then use to connect to the Exchange server to check and manage your e-mail, contacts, and calendaring. With Office 365, you still use Outlook (installed on your local computer) but instead of connecting to an Exchange server managed by your IT team, you connect to an Exchange server managed by Microsoft.

Grouping conversations in your inbox

Like it or not, e-mail has become a primary means of communication for the modern information worker. It is not uncommon for many people to send and receive a truckload of e-mails on a daily, if not hourly, basis. Keeping track of different e-mails on different topics with different people can be a daunting task. Outlook 2010 has a feature geared toward helping you keep track of all those conversations. The feature automatically groups conversations by subject, as shown in Figure 2-2. Notice that Proposal is the subject of the e-mails, and the entire conversation is grouped for easy reading. You can even see your response e-mails and any meetings associated with this conversation. No more digging through your Sent box looking for how you responded to a particular e-mail.

You can turn on the Conversations feature by clicking on the View tab in Outlook and then checking the Show as Conversations check box, as shown in Figure 2-2.

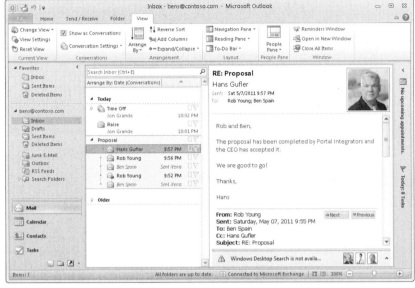

Figure 2-2:
Grouping
conversa-
tions in
Microsoft
Outlook
2010.

Archiving just got personal

Exchange Online gives you access to your own personal e-mail archiving system. Your personal archive shows up as another mailbox right next to your regular mailbox. You access your archive just like you access your regular mailbox. On top of that, when you need to search for an old e-mail, you can choose to search your archive in addition to your regular mailbox.

Collaborating made easy

In the last few years, SharePoint has taken the world by storm. As consultants we had a large-property-management client ask us about SharePoint the other day. We were curious what was driving his decision because he knew very little about SharePoint. Our client told me that when he talks with his peers in the industry, they all tell him that they use SharePoint extensively. When he asks them about their experience using SharePoint, they tell him that they can't imagine running their business without SharePoint. That was enough of a driver for him to find out about SharePoint right away. After all, when the competition moves toward something that increases their advantage, other companies have to move quickly in order to maintain the ability to compete. And thus is the case with the adoption of the technology wave consisting of communication, collaboration, content management, and consolidation, which is all made possible by SharePoint.

With Office 365, your organization gets SharePoint without the hassle of having to work through a complicated deployment. Your IT staff has an administrative interface and can provision sites and set up users with minimal effort. With SharePoint up and running, your organization can spend its resources on solving real business problems with SharePoint rather than working through the technical details of an implementation.

Creating communities for the corporate world

An online community is nothing more than a group of people coming together by using their computers regardless of geographic location. If you have used Facebook or LinkedIn or even AOL or Yahoo Groups, then you have been involved in an online community. SharePoint brings online communities to the corporate world in a secure corporate environment. You can imagine the scenario where you are in the accounting department and the team is working on company financials. The team needs to collaborate with each other, but you wouldn't want to be posting to each other's Facebook walls or Twitter accounts. Some of the online community features that SharePoint provides include Wiki's, blogs, content tagging, document sharing, discussion boards, people search, alerts, and notifications.

In addition to the online community features already discussed, every person who has a SharePoint account also has his own personal SharePoint site. The personal SharePoint site functionality is called My Sites. My Sites lets every user create a personal environment through which others can collaborate and share. You can think of your My Site as your own personal portal that is all about you. You can add your interests, update your profile, view your colleagues, write on your note board, and even see what you have in common with other colleagues.

Sharing information with customers and partners with extranet sites

Because SharePoint Online (one of the components of Office 365) is online, you have the ability to share information with partners that are not part of your local network. These sites that you can make available to people outside your organization are called extranet sites. An example of an extranet site might be a partner network made up of complementary companies. The people in these other companies won't have access to your company network, but you still need to be able to share information and collaborate with them. SharePoint online offers extranet sites for just such a purpose. Chapter 5 covers SharePoint and extranet sites. Microsoft has gone to great lengths to create a secure, safe, and stable SharePoint environment. In particular, Microsoft guarantees the following:

- ✔ The environment is available 99.9 percent of the time.
- ✔ All content and configuration details are backed up regularly.
- ✔ Virus scanning software, called Forefront Security for SharePoint, constantly scans content for threats.
- ✔ File types that can pose a risk to your SharePoint environment are blocked from upload.

Microsoft Office 365 is truly a global product with data center locations distributed throughout the world. The product supports more than 40 languages, including Chinese, Arabic, Spanish, and Portuguese. Need your site to support the Catalan language? No problem, SharePoint Online has you covered.

Going Virtual with Intuitive Communications

Lync Online is the latest iteration of Microsoft's cloud-based communications service. In particular, you can chat through text, talk to people by using voice, and even have face-to-face meetings by using your webcam. In addition, Lync allows you to conduct online meetings by using screen sharing, virtual white boards, electronic file sharing, and even online polling.

Text, voice, and video in a single app and service

You can think of the Lync application as a one-stop shop for instant communication. Because Microsoft has tightly integrated the Office 365 applications, you can move seamlessly between them. For example, you might be reading a post on SharePoint and want to instantly communicate with the poster. You can view the presence icon and if it is green, that means the user is available. You can click on the presence icon by the poster's name and instantly send an e-mail, start a text chat, call by using voice and video, or even schedule a meeting, as shown in Figure 2-3.

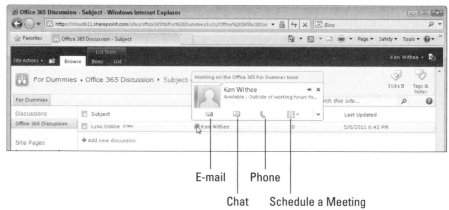

Figure 2-3:
Instantly
communi-
cating with
users by
using Lync
from within
SharePoint.

As you are chatting with the poster, you might decide that you want to share screens and invite others to join the meeting. By using Lync, it is as simple as a couple of button clicks. We cover using Lync for online meetings in Chapters 15 and 16.

From conversations to ad hoc meetings – Yes, it's possible

By using Lync, you can instantly connect with others from multiple locations. You might be reading a SharePoint post but you also might receive an e-mail and want to meet with that person right away if he is available. You can see his status on the presence icon next to his name in your Outlook e-mail message. If you want to communicate with this person, you can hover over his Lync presence icon to access the Lync menu. You may want to send a chat message to the user, so you click the Chat button. A chat session instantly opens, and Lync takes care of pulling in the subject of the e-mail as the subject of the chat so that the person knows what the chat is about. It's almost as good as walking across the hall to talk to someone, only now that someone can be anywhere in the world.

Online meetings unleashed

An online meeting is nothing new. There are many services that offer the ability to share your screen or coauthor documents. What has finally come together with Office 365 is the tight integration between all the different products. You can now see if someone is available for a meeting right from within the applications, such as Outlook and SharePoint, that you use day in and day out. Using Lync, it is also possible to set up meetings with those outside your organization. Lync meetings enable you to conduct meetings by using chat rooms, audio, video, shared white boards, and even polling. Conducting meetings with Lync is covered in detail in Chapter 15.

Interacting with photos and activity feeds

In addition to instant communication, Lync can also contain personal information, such as photos and activity feeds.

Being able to put a face with a name is nice. Just about anywhere you might connect with another person, be it Outlook, SharePoint, or the author information property from within an Office document, you can view information about the person. The name of a person will have a presence icon next to it. Hover over the presence icon or photo and then click the details screen. Figure 2-4 illustrates viewing the details of a colleague from within the Author property of a Word document.

Figure 2-4:
Viewing information about a colleague who authored a specific Word document.

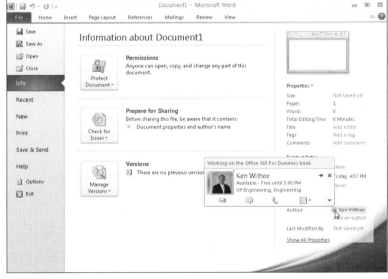

The activity feed is a current status sentence similar to Twitter but on a corporate level. For example, you might be heads down working on a document and update your status with "Working heads down on a document but here if you need me in a pinch!" Other users will see this status message and know that even though you are online at the moment, you are busy working on a document. Of course, another use for the status message could be something along the lines of, "Leftover cake in the break room! Get it while it lasts!"

Part II
Getting Connected with E-mail, Calendar, and Contacts

The 5th Wave   By Rich Tennant

"Your mail program looks fine. I don't know why you're not receiving any personal e-mails. Have you explored the possibility that you may not have any friends?"

In this part . . .

This part explains the Exchange Online component of Office 365. You begin to understand how flexible and reliable the Exchange Online offering can be and how anywhere access can be a true blessing when you need a file or information and are away from your office. You dive into how Exchange Online works with both the Outlook client that installs locally on your computer and how a web version of Outlook called the Outlook Web App provides e-mail from any computer in the world that has a web browser and Internet connection. Finally, you gain some insights into how to manage your mailbox and some of the fringe benefits that come with using Microsoft's most famous e-mail server in the cloud.

Chapter 3

Unleashing the Power of Exchange Online

In This Chapter

▶ Discovering how Exchange Online provides flexibility and reliability

▶ Understanding the value of anywhere and anytime access

▶ Finding out about Exchange Online security and compliance standards

With the cloud, individuals and small businesses can snap their fingers and instantly set up enterprise-class services.

— Roy Stephan

*I*f you are like most people, you couldn't care less about how your e-mail gets into your inbox as long as it does. If your company uses Microsoft products, then chances are that you use an application called Outlook to send and receive e-mail. Outlook also has some other nifty features, including a calendar, the ability to reserve conference rooms, invite people to meetings, store contacts, and even create your to-do lists and tasks. Although you are probably familiar with the Outlook application, you may not know that it has a behind-the-scenes partner. That partner is Exchange, a server application that handles all the heavy lifting. The Outlook application on your desktop is constantly connecting to the Exchange server to find out what information it should present to you.

Because Outlook and Exchange communicate with each other over a computer network, the physical locations of these two hand-in-hand applications are irrelevant. All that matters is that they can communicate with each other. The Outlook software can be installed on your workstation on your desk, and the Exchange software may be installed on a server under your desk or in a data center somewhere out there.

Because Exchange can be located anywhere, a whole bunch of possibilities open up around who is responsible for managing the fairly complicated server software. If Exchange is running on a server under your desk, then it is highly likely that you are the lucky person responsible for it. If it is in your company data center, then you probably have a person, or team of people, responsible for administering Exchange. When you sign up for Office 365, you are letting Microsoft take on all the responsibilities of managing Exchange. Microsoft has Exchange running in their data center, and you simply connect to it with Outlook and use all the nice functionality.

In this chapter, you find out why letting Microsoft take responsibility for Exchange creates a flexible and reliable option for your e-mail, calendaring, contacts, and task needs. You discover that you can access your corporate Exchange system from almost anywhere at any time. You also find out about some of the protection and compliance features that take some of the risk out of letting Microsoft take the lead by managing its Exchange product.

Gaining Flexibility and Reliability

Key traits in any good relationship are reliability and flexibility. You look for these same qualities in computer software. When you deploy software, you want the process to be flexible and predictable. After the software is deployed, you want it to be reliable and dependable. Exchange Online falls into the category of service-based software. With service-based software, you don't have to develop, install, or manage the software. You simply sign up and start using it.

Deployment flexibility

When it comes time to roll out software, you have a number of options. You can pay someone to develop software from scratch, which is known as custom development. You can buy software, install it, and manage it yourself. Or, you can sign up to use software that is installed and managed by someone else. This third option is called Software as a Service (SaaS). You sign up to use the software and pay for it as a service on a monthly basis. Microsoft Office 365 is a SaaS offering by none other than Microsoft. Microsoft has invested billions of dollars building state-of-the-art data centers all over the world. These data centers are staffed by Microsoft employees whose entire responsibility is managing the Microsoft products offered in the Office 365 product.

Because Microsoft is making the service available on a monthly basis, you have the greatest flexibility of all. You sign up for the service and begin using it. No need to go through a deployment phase. Exchange Online is already deployed and ready to go.

The Office 365 product is actually a bundle of products. The products include Office Professional Plus, SharePoint Online, Exchange Online, and Lync Online.

Deployment predictability

Most decision makers cringe when they hear the words custom development. You will hear horror story after horror story when it comes to a custom software development project. If you get really good developers who have been working together for a decade and use a solid agile process, then you might have extraordinary results and the best software available. On the other hand, you may end up with something that doesn't do what you want it to do and costs 12 times what you thought it was going to cost in the beginning. For this reason, many decision makers want to remove the risk and go with packaged software. Because packaged software is already developed and only needs to be installed and managed, the risk associated with adopting the software is greatly reduced.

You will still hear horror stories, however, about the implementation process for packaged software. It generally falls along the lines that someone thought someone else had configured the backups and the person that the other person thought had configured them had already left the company. Oh yeah, and the system was designed to be redundant so that if one key server went down everything would keep working. The only problem is that you only find out if everything works properly when something goes wrong. If the proper procedures were not followed during the implementation, then your organization may find itself in a very bad position.

Those with experience will say that it is often not the fault of any particular person. IT teams are overworked and stretched beyond their capacity to handle everything effectively. For this reason, using a SaaS is becoming increasingly popular. With service-based software, another company specializes in managing the software and keeping it available, reliable, and backed up. You pay on a monthly basis and connect to and use the software over the Internet. This last realm removes the risk for chief technology officer-type decision makers. Not only do they not have to pay someone to develop the software, they don't even have to worry about stretching their valuable IT resources beyond the breaking point. And, should the worst-case event happen, another company is liable for the problem based on the service contract signed.

Because the hosting company is liable for anything that goes wrong with hosted software, making sure that the company is reputable and capable of dealing with a major issue is important. Microsoft is one of the biggest names in the software industry with an established business record and lots of money in the bank. Your cousin's friend who started hosting software in his basement probably doesn't have the same resources that Microsoft has in case something goes wrong.

Flexible provisioning

In addition to the predictability of the deployment costs in both time and resources, Exchange Online offers the ability to easily adjust the number of licenses for people using the software. A hiring manager might plan to hire 45 people but find out later in the year that they need to hire another 30 as the company grows more rapidly than expected. It is easy to provision new users for Office 365 through the simple administrative interface.

Another benefit of SaaS software is that chief financial officer-types can find out exactly what the costs will be now and in the future. The CTO doesn't need to explain why the project was eight times over budget or why four more people were required for the IT team to support the new software. The price in resources, people, and time is very transparent and obvious from the beginning. In other words, the costs are very predictable, which is what accounting people and executives like to see.

Continuous availability

Although it may seem blatantly obvious that software should be available all the time, you may be surprised by how many enterprise systems are only available during certain business hours. Exchange Online is available all day, every day, without interruption. In fact, Microsoft guarantees a 99.9 percent uptime.

Simplified administration

If you have ever spent time talking with someone who is responsible for configuring Exchange Server, you know that it is not for the faint of heart. In fact, many people are so specialized that their entire careers are spent doing nothing but administering the Exchange Server software. If your organization is lucky enough to employ a full-time team of these rock-star administrators, then you have probably not experienced any major e-mail issues. Everything works as expected and nobody really cares why. The problem, however, is that if one critical person leaves the organization, you might not be as lucky with the replacement.

Exchange Online offers a simplified and intuitive administrative interface. You no longer need extraordinary expertise to get the very most out of the Exchange Product. Microsoft handles all the heavy lifting and provides an interface that allows even people with minimal technology skills to administer the company e-mail system by using nothing more than their web browser. The Exchange Online control panel is shown in Figure 3-1.

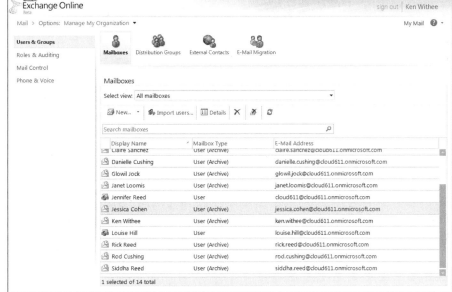

Figure 3-1:
The
Exchange
Online
control
panel
is used
for adminis-
tration.

Accessing from Anywhere

Not all that long ago, e-mail was a relatively new thing. We checked our e-mail like we would check the regular mail, and often we could only e-mail people within the organization. E-mail has come a long way since then. Now you will be hard pressed to find someone who doesn't use e-mail, especially in a work environment. E-mail is tremendously important for the modern workforce.

Exchange Online provides a continuously available service that can be accessed from just about anywhere at any time. All you need is an Internet connection and a web browser. We recently spent time at a firm that didn't have regular e-mail access for those people not in the office. A couple of years ago, this would have been no big deal. In today's connected world, however, we found it almost impossible to cope with my lack of connectivity when not in the office. With modern smartphones, you can carry around instant e-mail access right in your pocket. Exchange Online works great with any of these devices and, of course, with Apple iPhone and Google Android devices. And although Microsoft was late to the party, the new Windows Phone 7 provides complete integration with all of Office 365, including Exchange, Outlook, and Office applications.

From your Outlook e-mail client

The Outlook application that so many people use day in and day out for e-mail, meetings, tasks, and contacts continues to work the same way with Exchange Online but with some added bonuses. In particular, you get an even tighter integration with the other products that are part of the Office 365 offering. For example, you may have a task list that is part of SharePoint. To integrate your SharePoint tasks with Outlook, you navigate to the SharePoint Online list and click a button that says Connect To Outlook. Bingo. Your SharePoint tasks now show up in your Outlook Tasks folder.

From the web

In addition to accessing your Exchange from your Outlook client, you can also use your web browser. When you use your web browser to access Exchange, you are using what has been termed the Outlook Web Application. Office 365 provides a very rich experience for working with enterprise e-mail right from the browser. Using Internet Explorer to access the Outlook Web App is shown in Figure 3-2.

From your phone

Windows Phone 7 has amazing integration with very minimal configuration. The Outlook client for Windows Phone 7 is built right into the device. No need to download or install. Just point your phone to your Exchange Online e-mail and you are good to go.

One of the exciting new features of Exchange Online is the ability to integrate with the Research In Motion BlackBerry cloud service. Microsoft has worked closely with Research In Motion to provide organizations that use the BlackBerry service the ability to integrate with the Office 365 offering.

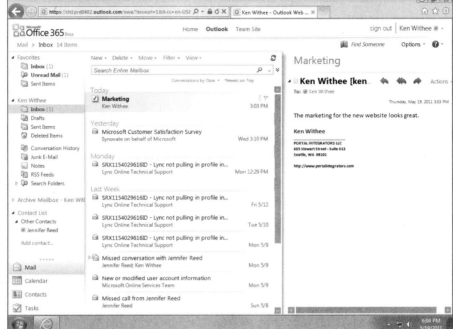

Figure 3-2:
Using the
Internet
Explorer
web
browser
to access
the Outlook
Web App.

From your Mac

In the past, Mac users have faced a difficult decision. Use a Mac and struggle
with compatibility with the corporate e-mail system or use a PC and use
Outlook for full integration. Exchange Online supports the popular Outlook
for Mac 2011, which provides similar integration to Outlook for the PC. By
using Outlook for Mac 2011, you can access your Exchange Online e-mail, calendars, tasks, and contacts.

From any e-mail client

Exchange Online supports all the standard e-mail protocols, including IMAP,
POP, and SMTP. As a result, you can use any e-mail client you like to send
and receive e-mail.

If you want advanced functionality, such as calendaring and meetings, contacts, tasks, and advanced e-mail features, such as presence information for
contacts, then you need Microsoft Outlook as your e-mail client.

Manage inbox overload

The number of e-mails most people send and receive in a given day is amazing! If you are like many office workers, your inbox can quickly become overloaded. Exchange Online attempts to help you manage your e-mail by using a number of different features.

One of the most important features is that you can access your e-mail any time and from any location that has either cell reception for your smartphone or a computer with a web browser and Internet connection. This feature allows you to stay current with your e-mail on your own time and not just when you are sitting in front of your work computer staring at hundreds of unread e-mails. Have some downtime while waiting for the bus? Twiddling your thumbs at the doctor's office? Get caught up on your e-mail and find out whether that important proposal has arrived.

In addition to anywhere access, some powerful productivity features come along with Outlook. For example, you can view all those messages about the same topic in a single e-mail thread known as a conversation. You can also quickly set up a meeting with those involved in the topic of the e-mail with a few clicks of the mouse. Lync Online is closely integrated with Exchange Online and provides even more communication and productivity saving options.

Efficient collaboration

Anyone who works with e-mail on a daily basis has experienced the scenario where an e-mail thread goes on and on, and on some more. People are added to the thread, and those people add more people to the thread. At some point, it would be much easier to just set up a meeting and discuss everything in person. With Outlook and Exchange Online, you can do this with a single click of a button, as shown in Figure 3-3.

A meeting is instantly created, and all the e-mail participants are included in the meeting. The subject of the e-mail thread instantly becomes the subject of the new meeting. This major timesaver increases efficiency on a number of fronts.

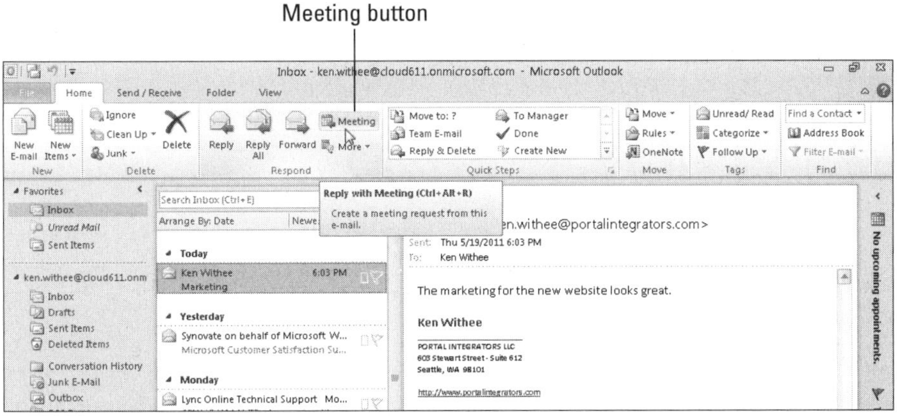

Meeting button

Figure 3-3:
Set up a
meeting with
all the partic-
ipants in an
e-mail thread
by using a
single button.

Enhanced voicemail

A nifty aspect of Exchange Online is that it includes a unified messaging component. Unified messaging means that different types of messaging are tied
together. In this case, we are talking about a physical phone. You remember
when you used to have to actually wait for a dial tone, right? Yep, that is the
type of voice phone we are talking about.

Exchange Online can be used as your voicemail system and automatically
transcribe to text that is then sent to your e-mail or texted to your phone.
Need to check your e-mail but don't have Internet coverage? Exchange Online
has a dial-in interface for callers. All you need to access your e-mail is a
phone. Listening to your e-mail may take longer than glancing at your smartphone but at least it is a possibility. This functionality extends e-mail access
to anywhere with a phone.

Protecting Information

One of the most important aspects of any system is the protection of information and compliance with company and government rules. Exchange Online
is simple to use and administer, but don't let that fool you. Under the covers,
Microsoft has spent a tremendous amount of effort on protecting you from
digital threats and making sure that you are in compliance without
hindrance.

Archiving and retention

Each person has an e-mail box as well as his own archiving system. An archive shows up in Outlook as another mailbox, as shown in Figure 3-4.

Figure 3-4:
The archive
folder
shows up
as another
mailbox in
Outlook.

The intended purpose of the additional archiving folder is to store older e-mail in a permanent storage location. You can think of your archiving folder as your attic or basement. You can go in there to retrieve stuff if you need to, but it is really a long-term storage location.

The size of a user mailbox and archive are dependent on the SaaS plan. Some plans have a maximum mailbox capacity of 25 gigabytes and others have unlimited archiving capacity. For more information about the plans that are available and the resources allocated for each plan, check out Chapter 18.

Information protection and control

The Exchange Online offering includes antivirus and antispam control without needing to install any third-party or external software. When a new message comes into Exchange Online, it is scanned for risks before being delivered to the intended e-mail box.

The technology that makes all this protection possible is called Forefront. It is another Microsoft product that works behind the scenes to make the environment safe and secure. Don't worry though — you don't have to pay extra or even know how it works. As an end user, you just know that someone is looking out for you so that you don't inadvertently receive spam or virus-infested files.

The government has added many rules and regulations around corporate e-mail. Exchange Online provides the ability to meet these rules with features, such as eDiscovery and legal holds.

eDiscovery refers to Electronic Discovery, which simply means that electronic messages can be searched for relevant communications in the event of a legal process. This might not be a big deal but if you are in a heavily regulated industry or government organization, then these features are often required by Uncle Sam.

Chapter 4

Giving Productivity a Boost

· ·

In This Chapter

▶ Appreciating the key productivity advantages of Office 365

▶ Discovering tricks for mailbox management in Outlook Web App

▶ Setting up your calendar

▶ Integrating other e-mail accounts into Office 365

· ·

"Office 365 is more than a new brand. It's a progressive approach to cloud applications. We designed Office 365 to work for a business of one — or a business of one million and one."

— Kurt DelBene, President, Microsoft Office Division

*N*ew web technologies and social media innovations have altered the way everyone does business locally as well as globally. Now more than ever, you can reach a large audience without investing thousands of dollars in marketing and advertising. In today's world, businesses need the right set of productivity tools to support their mission and goals.

With the launch of Office 365, all customers — both big and small — have access to the power of cloud productivity traditionally reserved for large enterprises. For the first time, familiar applications, such as Microsoft Office, Exchange, and SharePoint are tightly integrated with Office Web Apps, the online version of Microsoft Office, and Lync, a new communications application replacing Office Communicator.

In this chapter, you find out how new features of Outlook are powered by Exchange Online.

Understanding the Office 365 Productivity Advantage

Consider Office 365 as a door that is open to organizations of all sizes to take advantage of enterprise-caliber productivity applications, social computing, and unified communications. And all these advantages happen without being trapped behind a firewall or constrained by the cost of implementation and maintenance as in the last decade.

Productivity on the go

With Office 365, you now have access to e-mail, documents, contacts, and calendars on almost any device at anytime from anywhere where there is Internet connection. Whether your platform is on a Mac or a PC, rich desktop Office applications that come with Office Professional Plus in the Enterprise plans, provide you with a familiar Ribbon interface that eliminates the need to master "new stuff."

The familiar user interface that spans across the Office suite (Outlook, Word, Excel, and PowerPoint) is also present in its cloud cousin, Office Web Apps. With web apps, you can view and edit documents in high fidelity by using these supported browsers: Internet Explorer, Firefox, and Safari.

With Outlook Web App, you can access your e-mail, calendar, contacts, and tasks from most browsers. Windows Phone, Nokia, Android, iPhone, and Black-Berry smartphones can access your e-mail, calendar, contacts, and SharePoint sites through your wireless provider's network or a Wi-Fi connection.

Enhanced collaboration

SharePoint Online allows you to create, collaborate, and share large, hard-to-e-mail files in a password-protected portal with team members within or outside your organization. You can coauthor documents with colleagues and simultaneously edit documents online to see real-time updates of the changes being made by your coauthors.

Lync gives you the ability to conduct planned or ad hoc meetings online. Meeting participants can share high-definition audio and video with sup-ported hardware, share their screen or program, whiteboard, do a quick poll, and conduct a PowerPoint presentation (see Figure 4-1).

Other key players in cloud productivity

Understandably, competition is stiff among the software giants to provide a productivity platform in the cloud. In our opinion, Google's Google Enterprise offers the only real competition to Microsoft 365, but the following list covers all offerings:

✔ IBM offers Lotus Symphony as a richly featured set of productivity tools for free, but the multiple platforms these tools come in creates inconsistent user experience. In addition, the suite's interoperability challenges makes integrating on-premises and cloud solutions difficult.

✔ Oracle Corporation is a major sponsor of the OpenOffice.org project, an open-source office suite available in many languages free of charge for any purpose. The completely open development process of the suite allows anyone to enhance the software which, although noble, may be the reason for its reputation as having a cumbersome and visually unattractive user interface.

✔ Google offers an enterprise-grade version of its Apps portfolio with solutions tailored to cover a vast array of industries from aerospace to healthcare to media. Its Apps Marketplace is chock-full of web-based applications ranging from Accounting to Project Management to Sales and Marketing categories. Google Apps provide easy e-mail access across multi-device environments, offers coauthoring capabilities through Google Docs, and internal video collaboration through the corporate version of Google YouTube.

In our opinion, the biggest advantage Office 365 has over Google Apps is the nearly full fidelity-viewing mode of Office Web Apps ensuring that user experience, whether using a desktop software or web-based service, stays the same. In Google Apps, documents lose data, run into styling and formatting issues, and generally just lack fit and finish.

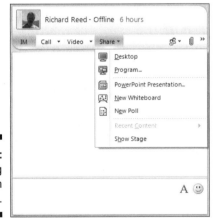

Figure 4-1: Sharing options in Lync.

From either the Outlook Web App or the Outlook desktop client, share your calendar with team members, business partners, clients, and customers. If you subscribe to the Enterprise plan, you can share critical business intelligence, such as Access databases.

Instant Messaging with presence

Presence information in Lync shortens the time it takes to connect with colleagues, partners, and customers. The rich presence indicator gives you real-time status of someone's availability. If you see someone in green, you can immediately start instant messaging or make PC-to-PC voice and video calls.

Managing Your Mailbox

E-mail in Office 365 is powered by Exchange Online, the cloud version of the Exchange Server platform, the world's leading e-mail server for business. Office 365 users are presented with the same familiar Exchange user interface and features, but with the added benefit of anywhere access without the need for a Virtual Private Network (VPN) connection. The user experience stays consistent across PC, web, and mobile devices and matches the look and feel of the desktop Outlook client. The 25GB storage space that comes with each mailbox eliminates the need to constantly delete items to make room for new ones or the need to back up e-mails onto an offline PST file that cannot be accessed from the Internet or smartphones.

Meaningful conversations with the conversation view

One of the most talked about new features of the new version of Outlook (desktop or online) is the conversation view. This view groups together all e-mails with the same subject line or topic into one item. You can then see everyone's replies without hunting for related e-mails in the conversation thread. (Figure 4-2 shows the conversation view.) You can also see your own replies listed in the item. If you move e-mails into a different folder, they are still displayed in the item, including ones that have been deleted.

You can also move the entire conversation with all the e-mails inside it into a different folder in one fell swoop by first collapsing the item so the individual e-mails are not displayed and then dragging and dropping the item into a folder.

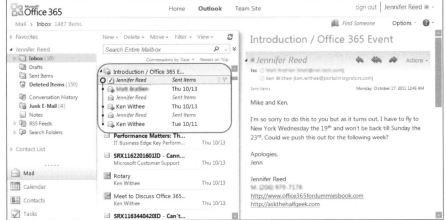

Figure 4-2:
E-mails
displayed in
the conver-
sation view.

By default, Outlook displays your Inbox in the conversation view with
the newest message on top. This view takes a little bit of getting used to,
especially when you've been programmed to scan through e-mails in date
order regardless of the subject line. It can be confusing to see an e-mail on
top of the list on a subject that was discussed yesterday until you expand
the conversation to see that there's a new reply to the conversation. After
you trained yourself to view e-mails by conversation rather than by date of
receipt, you'll quickly appreciate the timesaving feature this view offers.

You can find more options for displaying e-mails in the conversation view.
You can sort the messages displayed in the Reading Pane either by newest
e-mail on top or newest email at the bottom. When you expand the conversation list by clicking on the triangle to the left of the conversation, you can
choose to match the sort order in the list with how the messages are displayed in the Reading pane or show the messages in a conversation tree. In
addition, you can choose to hide the deleted items from the conversation list.
To access these options, click the View link from the menu and then click See
more conversation options, shown in Figure 4-3.

Figure 4-3:
Options for
the conver-
sation view.

Getting deleted items back

It happens. You deleted an e-mail, emptied your Deleted Items folder, and then three days later you need that e-mail.

Not to worry. In both the online and desktop version of Outlook, recovering deleted e-mail is simple. When you delete an item permanently or empty your Deleted Items folder, those items go into the Recoverable Items folder.

To recover an item in Outlook Web App, follow these steps:

1. **Right-click on the Deleted Items folder.**
2. **Click Recover Deleted Items.**
3. **Select the items you want to restore by selecting the boxes that appear when you hover over to the left of the e-mail.**
4. **Click the Recover Selected Items icon (yellow envelope with a blue arrow above the search box).**

Use the search box to look for items in your Deleted Items folder but note that you cannot open an item until you recover it.

You can also purge items from the Recoverable Items folder but when you do so, you will not be able to recover those items again from the Recoverable Items folder.

Accessing other e-mail accounts through Office 365

You can connect up to five e-mail accounts in the Outlook Web App for easy management of those connected accounts in one place. When setting up additional accounts, take note of the following:

- **Hotmail – Windows Live:** There's no need to turn on POP or IMAP access for a Windows Live Hotmail account. If you have folders in your Hotmail account, these folders are copied to your account in Outlook Web App along with the e-mail messages downloaded from your Hotmail account.

- **Gmail**: Set up your account to allow POP access from your Gmail account to download e-mail from the Gmail account to Outlook Web App.

- **Yahoo Mail Plus, Comcast, AOL**: Take note of the POP address provided by these services; IMAP access is not supported.

To set up additional accounts in the Outlook Web App, do the following:

1. **Click Options in the top-right corner.**

2. **Select See All Options to see all the options in Outlook Web App that you can manage yourself.**

   Account on the left navigation is automatically selected and the options to manage your account are displayed on the right pane.

3. **Click Connected Accounts from the right pane.**

4. **Click New under Connected Accounts.**

   The New Account Connection window appears.

5. **Enter your e-mail address and password.**

6. **Click Next and then click Finish.**

Optimizing Your Calendar and Contacts

In the rich Outlook desktop application, displaying multiple calendars side by side is a nifty feature, especially for administrative assistants who manage multiple calendars. That same feature is now available in Outlook Web App in full fidelity as well as other Enterprise-class calendaring features.

Contacts management in Outlook Web App provides the same powerful and familiar collaboration features available in Exchange Server, such as Global Address List, group management capabilities, shared contacts, and shared mailboxes.

Setting up your OOF when you're OFF

When you're off on a vacation or away from the office for any reason, don't forget to turn on your out of office (OOF) notification. Doing so displays an Automatic Reply alert above the sender's message to let him know of your whereabouts before the e-mail is sent out, as shown in Figure 4-4. In the older versions of Outlook, the sender typically does not know your OOF status until she receives an automatic reply e-mail. With this new feature, the sender has an option to cancel the message or send it to someone else. This then reduces the number of e-mails you have to deal with when you get back to the office.

To set up your OOF notification, click Options in the top-right corner of the Outlook screen in Office 365 and click Set Automatic Replies.

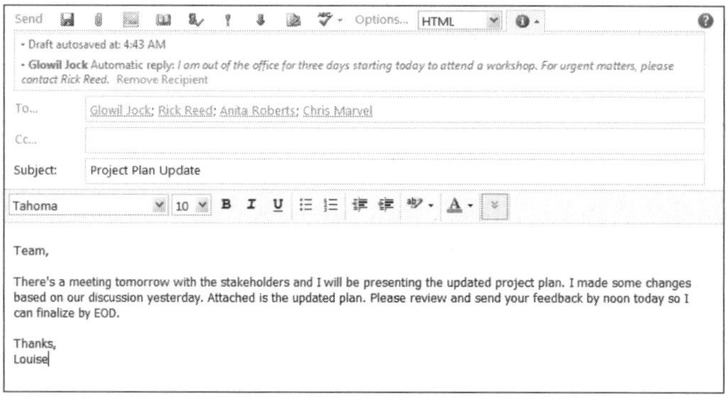

Send | Options... | HTML

· Draft autosaved at: 4:43 AM

· **Glowil Jock** Automatic reply: *I am out of the office for three days starting today to attend a workshop. For urgent matters, please contact Rick Reed.* Remove Recipient

To... | Glowil Jock; Rick Reed; Anita Roberts; Chris Marvel

Cc...

Subject: | Project Plan Update

Tahoma | 10 | **B** *I* U

Team,

There's a meeting tomorrow with the stakeholders and I will be presenting the updated project plan. I made some changes based on our discussion yesterday. Attached is the updated plan. Please review and send your feedback by noon today so I can finalize by EOD.

Thanks,
Louise

Figure 4-4:
Automatic
Reply lets
co-workers
know that
you're out of
the office.

In the desktop version of Outlook 2010, select File on the menu and then click Automatic Replies under the Account Information pane.

One of the nifty things Exchange Online offers is the ability to consistently display your status not only in Outlook Web App but also in SharePoint Online, Office Professional 2010 desktop version, and Lync. So when you set up your OOF, your yellow Away status is displayed alongside your name in SharePoint lists and libraries as well as in your Lync contacts list.

Setting up a conference room

Conference room support provides you with a resource-booking attendant to accept or decline meeting requests. These conference rooms are part of the Exchange Online service and do not require a separate license.

If you have administrator privileges, setting up a conference room is easy. Do the following:

1. **In Outlook Web App, click Options.**

2. **Click See All Options.**

   You see all the features that you can manage on the next screen.

3. **On the right pane, under Shortcuts to administrative tools, click Manage your organization.**

4. **In Mailboxes, click the arrow pointing down next to New and select Room Mailbox (shown in Figure 4-5).**

5. **In the New Room window, enter the required information.**

   This is where you can choose to either automatically accept or decline a booking request or select a delegate to accept or decline booking requests.

6. **When you finish, click Save.**

Figure 4-5:
Creating
a new
Conference
Room
mailbox.

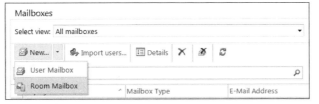

Using the Scheduling Assistant

Setting up meetings and booking conference rooms can be a breeze when you use the scheduling assistant in Outlook Web App. When you select your meeting attendees and conference room, the Scheduling Assistant displays suggested times based on availability on the date and time you selected. This reduces the amount of time going back and forth with team members trying to nail down a meeting time.

To use the Scheduling Assistant, do the following:

1. **In Outlook Web App, click the calendar icon on the left navigation.**

2. **Click the down arrow next to New and then select Meeting Request.**

   A new untitled meeting window appears.

3. **Enter the attendees in the To field and the conference room you want to book under the Resources field.**

4. **Enter the Start and End times.**

5. **Click the Scheduling Assistant tab (shown in Figure 4-6) to display the suggested times.**

6. **Select a suggested time or make adjustments to your time and date to find a time that works for everyone.**

7. **Click Send to send the meeting invitation.**

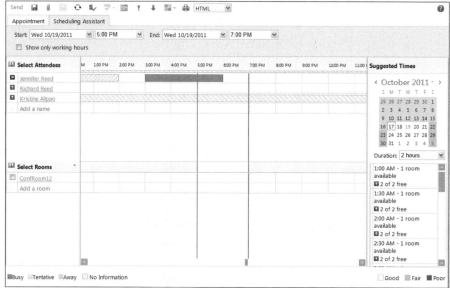

Figure 4-6:
The
Scheduling
Assistant
interface.

Creating a public group

If you constantly need to send e-mail to a group of people, it's a good idea to create a public group or distribution list. This group shows up in the Global Address List (GAL) in Exchange Online so other team members can use it. As the owner of the group, you can restrict membership to the group. You can also join an existing group or leave a group.

To create a public group, follow these steps:

1. **In Outlook Web App, click Options.**

2. **Click See All Options.**

   You see all the features that you can manage on your on the next screen.

3. **Click Groups on the left navigation to see all the public groups you belong to and the public groups you own.**

4. **Under Public Groups I Own, click New.**

5. **Enter the required information and click Save.**

Integrating Social Networking Platforms

Office Professional Plus includes new set of features to help you keep track of your social networks through the Outlook Social Connector. When you connect Outlook to Facebook, LinkedIn, SharePoint My Sites, Windows Live Messenger, Viadeo, and Xing, your friends' and colleagues' current status from their social networking site will auto-magic-ally display right into your Inbox. While you are reading an e-mail from a colleague, glance down at the People Pane in the bottom-right corner to see the picture, name, title, and an aggregated collection of information about the sender, including the current status from social networking sites. (Figure 4-7 shows a contact's social network connections in the People Pane.) You can even "friend" someone on Facebook or add someone to your LinkedIn network right from Outlook.

Figure 4-7: People Pane showing a contact's social network connections.

Installing the Outlook Social Connector requires two downloads for Outlook 2007 and 2003 users: the Outlook Social Connector app, and the social network provider files (Facebook, LinkedIn, and so on).

For Office Professional Plus or Office 2010 users, the Outlook Social Connector app is already installed.

To integrate social networking into Outlook, follow these steps:

1. **Go to the View tab and click the People Pane icon.**

2. **From the drop-down menu, select Account Settings.**

3. **Click Next on the window that pops up.**

4. **Click the link to View social network providers available online.**

5. **Select the provider files by clicking on the icon (Facebook, LinkedIn, and so on) from the browser that opens up and follow the instructions outlined on the web page to install the provider file.**

    After you install the provider files, you will be asked to restart Outlook.

6. **After Outlook is restarted, repeat Steps 1 through 3.**

    The Social Network Accounts window appears.

7. **Select the accounts you want to connect to, enter your user information for each of the social networks (shown in Figure 4-8), and then click Connect.**

Figure 4-8:
Social
networking
in Outlook.

8. **If the connection was successful, you see a green check mark to the left of the social networking icon. Click Finish.**

Part III
Exploring SharePoint Online

The 5th Wave   By Rich Tennant

"The funny thing is he's spent 9 hours
organizing his site directory."

In this part . . .

This part explores one of the most exciting aspects of Office 365, SharePoint Online! SharePoint Online is nothing more than SharePoint hosted by none other than Microsoft. This part takes you through how to use SharePoint Online to collaborate with colleagues, add and manage content, and integrate with your trusted Office applications. In addition, you find out how to whip SharePoint into shape to meet your specific business needs by creating sites, pages, lists, and libraries.

Chapter 5

Collaborating Has Never Been This Easy!

In This Chapter

▶ Using social computing in the workplace

▶ Showcasing your background and skills in My Site

▶ Managing content across intranets and websites

▶ Setting up a team collaboration site with versioning and workflows

▶ Creating an intranet by using the SharePoint Online Publishing template

In the long history of humankind (and animalkind, too) those who learned to collaborate and improvise most effectively have prevailed.

— Charles Darwin

Undoubtedly, many workers collaborate online every day by using e-mail, Instant Messaging (IM) web conferencing, Wikis, and a slew of collaboration tools. Recent studies, however, have shown that 20 to 50 percent of collaborative activities result in wasted effort caused by poorly planned meetings, unproductive travel, and redundant e-mail communications.

This chapter helps you turn those inefficiencies into sizable gains simply by applying the out-of-the-box features of SharePoint Online. If you are one of the 100 million Microsoft SharePoint users whose experience with a collaboration tool is limited to document libraries, then you're in for a treat. And if you've never used Microsoft SharePoint before, get ready to be wowed!

Using SharePoint Online At Work

SharePoint Online as a collaboration tool is a great way for people to share ideas while incorporating social computing practices. It is one of the cloud services offered in Office 365 but is also available as a stand-alone subscription service.

If your company subscribes to the Office 365 Enterprise plan, you will have access to SharePoint Online social features, including

- ✔ My Site is a personal site assigned to a user in the organization.

- ✔ Wiki (Hawaiian word for "quick") is a SharePoint feature where users as a community can freely create, edit, alter, and contribute to online pages by using a web browser.

- ✔ Blogs (short for web logs) are structured content designed for sharing knowledge. A blog can be set up so readers can leave a comment about the blog.

- ✔ Social tagging allows users to "tag" or categorize content with a word or a phrase that makes the most sense to them. This feature improves collaboration and increases discoverability of content for the organization.

Working with My Site

My Site is a public page designed to let you share information about yourself with others who visit your site. The My Profile page in My Site is a great place to market your skills and expertise. It also serves as a central repository of information you can easily access.

Think of My Site as Facebook in the workplace. Just like on Facebook, you enter your status in the status balloon above your profile photo in the My Profile page, as shown in Figure 5-1.

Your colleagues can leave notes and messages for you on the Note Board just like your Facebook friends can post on your Wall. The idea behind using the status updates and notes is not just to bring social computing into the workplace. Entries in the status update end up in your What's New feed under My Site, which then shows up in your colleagues' pages, if they have added you as a colleague. Notes you post show up in the Recent Activities feed under My Profile. The What's New and Recent Activities feeds become your team's collaboration tool for notifications, side conversations, quick questions and answers, and basically function as a virtual hallway conversation.

What does this mean for your organization? It means fewer e-mails going back and forth between you and your colleagues on things that may already be outdated by the time either of you get around to reading them. As your e-mails gets focused on action items and in-depth conversations, you may find that you spend less time sorting through and cleaning up your inbox.

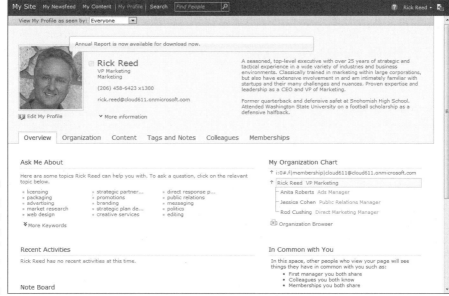

Figure 5-1:
Your status
appears
above your
profile
photo.

Viewing and editing your profile

Take the time to update your profile — it will pay off. I know someone who worked in an organization of more than 60,000 employees who became the "Visio Guru" by virtue of his listing Microsoft Visio as one of his areas of expertise. He eventually left the company and started his own consulting firm specializing in — you guessed it — Visio!

To edit your profile, follow these steps:

1. **From the Microsoft Online Services Portal, click Visit SharePoint Home under the Team Site link or click Team Site from the top navigation.**

   A new window opens, displaying your team site.

2. **Click your name at the top-right corner of the page to display the drop-down menu.**

3. **Select My Site to leave the Team Site and go to your own personal site.**

4. **From the top navigation, select My Profile.**

5. **Click Edit My Profile under your photo.**

6. **Enter your basic information and change your picture.**

If you don't have a photo associated with your contact information, a silhouette of Bill Gates' 1975 arrest photo (see Figure 5-2) for speeding and driving without a license is displayed — with his approval of course!

7. Click Save and Close.

Figure 5-2:
Silhouette
of Bill Gates'
arrest
photo.

Danielle Cushing
Engineering Manager
Engineering

(206) 458-6423 x 1503

danielle.cushing@cloud611.onmicrosoft.com

Add as colleague

SharePoint Online is designed to help users find content and people faster by using a combination of relevance, refinements, and social cues. Therefore, the more frequently you update your profile with new skills, just-launched projects, recently added colleagues, and tagged content, the quicker you'll show up in relevant searches. This search feature allows organizations to capture knowledge about you outside of documents you've authored and posted. With that knowledge, you and your colleagues can share ideas and expertise to solve problems and come up with innovative solutions.

Tagging and noting

A *tag* allows you to label content or web pages with words or phrases that make sense to you. When you share your tags with colleagues, you improve collaboration by allowing others to find out more about your interests and the projects you are working on.

If you are working on a confidential project, make sure to mark your tags "private."

Notes are the equivalent of posting something on your friend's Facebook Wall. You can ask a question, congratulate someone for a job well done, or comment on a project. Depending on the user's preferences, the person you left a note for may also be notified of your note by e-mail.

Notes are visible to everyone in your organization; people can see notes you leave for a colleague whether they follow you or not. When you share your thoughts about an article, a page, or a person, be mindful of the potential impact. Just as you would not post photos on Facebook that you don't want to come back to haunt you, don't post notes that violate your company's policies.

Content and pages you tag and annotate are displayed in the Tag and Notes tab in the My Profile page. Within that tab, you can refine the display alphabetically, by type, or by size.

Your tags and notes are also displayed visually in a tag cloud. The size of the tag is displayed according to the usage frequency.

If you are viewing an internal site that has open permissions and you'd like to visit it later, click the I Like It button at the top right to quickly tag the page. If the I Like It button doesn't quite do it for you and you want to include additional information about the page you're viewing, use the Tags and Notes button instead. Here's how:

1. **On the page you want to tag, click the Tag and Notes button at the top right.**

   The Tags and Note Board window appears.

2. **Navigate to the Note Board tab and enter your notes in the text box, as shown in Figure 5-3.**

3. **Click Save.**

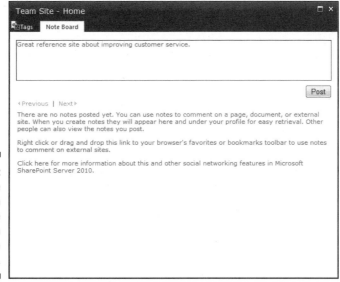

Figure 5-3:
Add more information about the content with the Note Board.

Adding tags and notes to web pages

Tags and notes are not limited to just your internal SharePoint sites. You can also use this feature for any website. You can install the Tag and Note tool into your Favorites toolbar for easy access whenever you come across an interesting site. The easiest way to use the tool is to add it to your browser's Favorite bar. Instructions for adding the tool are in the Tag and Notes tab in the My Profile page. When installed, click the tool whenever you come across a web page you want to tag. The tool behaves as if you were tagging an internal SharePoint site with the Note Board.

Managing content in your personal site

When you create a personal site, you essentially create your own SharePoint site collection). This site collection is automatically created under the My Site host as specified by your organization's network admin. As with any SharePoint site, you can create document libraries, maintain a blog, set versioning control for your documents, and set permissions for your documents and lists. These libraries, lists, and blogs are then aggregated and displayed in the Content section in My Profile (see Figure 5-4).

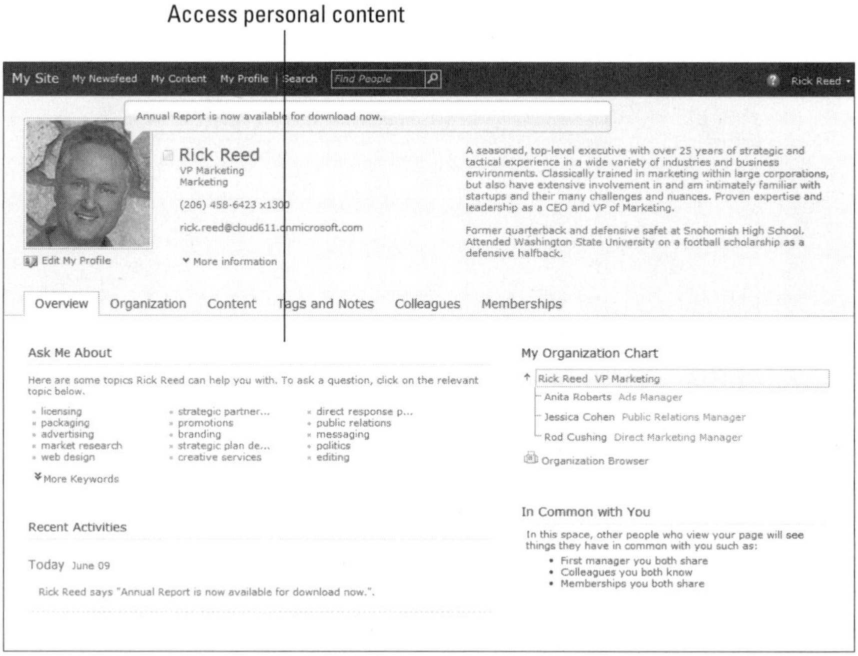

Access personal content

Figure 5-4: Easily access your personal site's content from the Content section.

Adding files to your document libraries

When you set up your personal site, SharePoint Online automatically creates a shared document library with open permissions and a separate personal document library with no access for anyone other than yourself. As the name implies, you put files in the shared document library that you want others to access. Conversely, the personal document library will house files you don't want to share with others.

The traditional way of adding files to your library is to upload documents by using the Add document icon below the document library from the My Content page.

However, to add multiple documents, you can use the familiar drag-and-drop method by following these steps:

1. **Select the document library from the left navigation of the My Content page to display the library.**

2. **On the Ribbon, click Library tools and then click Documents.**

3. **Select Upload Document and then select Upload Multiple Documents under the Name box from the window that appears.**

4. **Drag and drop files from your computer to the Upload Multiple Documents dialog box.**

5. **Click Done.**

Creating a Personal Blog

A blog is a great way to share your ideas and get feedback from others. It's also ideal for documenting step-by-step instructions for a variety of topics. This is handy when co-workers ask for instructions to add a YouTube video, for example, to a SharePoint site. Instead of repeating and resending the same information, you write the instruction up as a blog so you can share the information more than once.

SharePoint Online's personal site comes with a personal blog already pre-configured. You can access the blog from the Content section on the My Profile page.

Here's how to create your first blog:

1. **Click the Content tab from your profile page.**

2. **Under Recent Blog Posts, click Create Blog.**

    You are taken to your blog site, which is a subsite or child site in My Site.

3. **Click Create a Post from the links below Blog Tools on the right-hand side of the page (see Figure 5-5).**

   The New Item window appears.

Creating a blog

Figure 5-5:
Creating
your first
blog from
the Blog
tools.

4. **From the Posts – New Item window that appears, enter the title of your blog, add your blog content under Body, select one or more Categories (optional), and enter under Published the date you want your blog published.**

5. **Click either Save as Draft (if you want to finish it later) or Publish.**

After your blog is published, others can share your blog, send it as a e-mail, and leave a comment.

SharePoint Online lets you set permissions on libraries, lists, blogs, and items within your libraries, lists, and blogs. This means that you can set permissions on your shared documents library for 50 people and, within that document library, restrict permissions to a file to just10 people.

Using Team Sites for External Sharing

Good collaborators are those who contribute, take responsibility, cooperate, and listen. Great collaboration happens when you provide good collaborators the tools and techniques to automate and simplify their work. Organizations are starting to harness the power of using collaboration tools. Over 17,000 companies in the U.S. actively use SharePoint as an intranet. Of those 17,000 installations, we are certain that SharePoint Team Sites is the most widely used feature of the software.

And why not?

Team Sites keep teams in sync with shared document libraries, task lists, calendars, and a lot more. With the integration of mobile connectivity, anytime, anywhere access is no longer just an empty marketing pitch — it's real.

Setting up the Team Site

Your Office 365 subscription automatically provisions a default team site for your organization. If you need a separate site for your team, you can easily create a subsite with its own unique permissions. You need to have at least Full Control privileges on the Team Site to be able to do this. Follow these steps:

1. **From the Microsoft Online Services Portal, click Visit SharePoint Home below the Team Site link or click Team Site from the Top navigation.**

2. **At your Team Site, click Site Actions at the top-left corner and then select New Site.**

    The Create window appears.

3. **Select Team Site from the templates available in the Silverlight carousel (see Figure 5-6).**

4. **Enter the site's title and URL on the boxes below the selected template and click Create.**

That's it! Your Team Site is ready to go with a shared documents library, a team calendar, a task list, a discussion forum, and a Wiki.

When you share links to files from a SharePoint document library, please note that spaces are converted to %20 in the links. Use underscores rather than spaces as separators because, as you can see from the examples below, underscores enhance readability. This is true for site names, libraries, lists, and documents. You can always edit the title to remove the underscore from your sites, libraries, and lists through the Settings section.

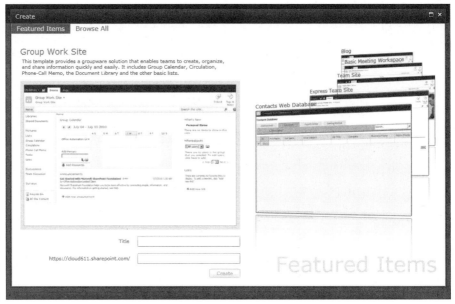

Figure 5-6:
Choosing
a site
template
from the
Silverlight
carousel.

Example: Underscores as separators

```
https://cloud611.com/ Puget_Sound_Farmers_Online/Shared_Doucments/Project_
                       Plan.mpp
```

Example: Spaces as separators

```
https://cloud611.com/ Puget%20Sound%20Farmers%20Online/Shared%20Doucments/
                      Project%20Plan.mpp
```

Restoring a previous version of a document or item

When versioning is turned on in a SharePoint Online list or library, any changes you make to an item in a list or a file in a document library is stored as a version, allowing you to manage content as it goes through various iterations. This is especially helpful when you have multiple users editing a document. If you run into a scenario where you have to roll back to an older version of the file, all you have to do is select a version from the version history that you want to restore.

To turn on version control for any document library, follow these steps:

1. **Go to your Shared Documents library.**
2. **On the Ribbon, click Library.**
3. **Click Library Settings.**
4. **Below General Settings, click Versioning settings to view all available options from the Versioning Settings page.**
5. **Below Document Version History group, select Create major versions.**
6. **Click OK to complete the versioning control process.**

Now that you've turned on version control, you can view the history of a document and restore a previous version as follows:

1. **In your document library, click Library below Library Tools and then click Library Settings on the Ribbon.**
2. **Hover over the name a file in the library until you see the down arrow.**
3. **Select Version History.**

   The Version History window appears with a list of the versions stored for the file.
4. **Hover over one of the dates until you see the down arrow on the right.**
5. **Click the arrow to bring up the View, Restore, and Delete options for the version (see Figure 5-7).**

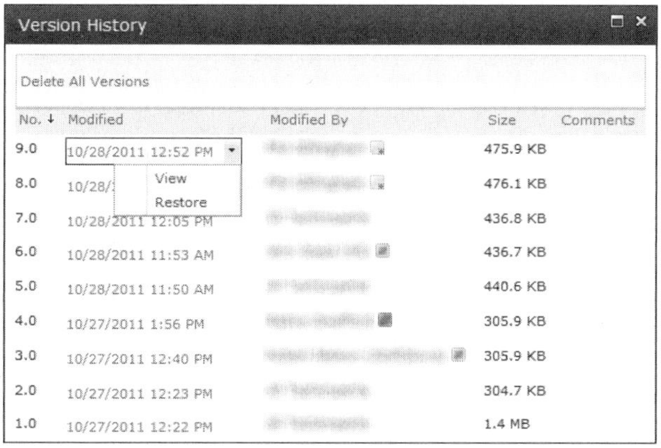

Figure 5-7: Restoring a previous version.

6. **Click OK after you make your selection.**

Instructions for restoring an item in a list is similar to how you restore a file in a document library.

Staying in sync with team calendars and tasks

As more organizations move their operations to the cloud and outsource some of their work to companies in other countries, it's inevitable that teams are going to be comprised of members from different parts of the country and the world. With seemingly endless streams of meetings, tasks, and deliverables, how can teams stay connected and coordinated?

The SharePoint Online calendar and task lists provide a great solution to keep team members in sync, regardless of their location and time zone. SharePoint calendar and task lists can be shared with others, downloaded into Outlook, and even provide a quick view of a team member's online status.

You can immediately start using the calendar list that comes preconfigured with Team Sites.

To add a new event in the calendar, double-click on the date to open the Calendar – New Item window. Enter information as you would in Outlook calendars and then click Save.

Similarly, you can also quickly get up and running with tasks for your team. Enter tasks for yourself and your team members by clicking the Add new item button.

If e-mail notification is turned on when an ownership is assigned to a task, an e-mail automatically goes out to the Assignee. When a task approaches its due date, the Assignee receives a reminder. When the due date passes without the task being completed, the Assignee continues to receive *nag* e-mails until the task is marked complete.

If your account includes access to Office 2010 applications, you can keep track of all your SharePoint tasks and events in Outlook by connecting the lists to your Outlook client.

To make the connection, go to your team calendar, click Calendar from the Ribbon and then select the Connect to Outlook icon. You can do the same thing for the task list (substituting calendar for list in the instructions).

Sharing Team Sites with external users

SharePoint Online provides a unified infrastructure for organizations to share documents not only with colleagues, but also with external partners. A site collection owner can enable external sharing and then invite external users to collaborate on sites, lists, and libraries. To address security issues, the infrastructure is designed so that external users will only have access to sites to which they are invited. And the best part? Every Office 365 customer will get 50 external partner access licenses (PAL) free! Additional PAL licenses can be purchased at a minimal cost.

To turn on external sharing and invite partners to your site, ensure first that your system administrator has turned on external sharing for the whole Office 365 tenancy. If you are the system administrator, here's how to do it:

1. **On the Microsoft Online Services Portal, click Manage below SharePoint Online.**

2. **From the Administration Center, click Manage Site Collections.**

3. **On the SharePoint Online Administration Center dashboard, click Site Settings below the Site Collections toolbar.**

4. **Click Manage External Users and then click Manage External Users.**

5. **Select Allow and then click Save (see Figure 5-8).**

Figure 5-8: Turning on external sharing for site collections.

After external sharing is turned on, you can grant access to external user to your team site as follows:

1. **On your team site, click Site Actions and then select Share this site from the drop-down menu.**

2. **Enter the e-mail addresses of the external users you want to invite either as a visitor or a member.**

   Any valid e-mail address can be used for the invitation. The external user, however, needs either a Hotmail or Windows Live account to log in.

3. **Enter your message and then click Send.**

When the external user successfully logs in, an Office 365 account is then created and this account becomes their signin name and password credentials.

Setting up the Intranet with the Publishing Template

SharePoint Online's publishing template is designed for organizations with authorized team members with no programming skills that are charged with keeping the intranet's content current through the web browser. The default starter publishing site template includes a home page, a press releases subsite, a Search Center, preconfigured document libraries and lists, and tagging tools (I Like It and Tags and Notes). Workflows are preconfigured for the template to route content for approval prior to publication.

To set up the intranet with the publishing portal template, you need to have Global Administrator privileges. If you don't have the right privileges, ask your system administrator to do the following steps:

1. **On the Microsoft Online Portal, click Manage below SharePoint Online.**

2. **Click Manage site collections at the Administration Center page to display the dashboard.**

3. **Click New under the Site Collections menu and select Private Site Collection.**

4. **In the New Site Collection dialog box, enter the title and URL of your intranet site (see Figure 5-9).**

5. **Below Select a template, click the Publishing tab and select Publishing Portal.**

6. **Enter the time zone, the primary administrator's name (you), the storage limit, and the resource usage quota (4GB maximum).**

7. **Click OK.**

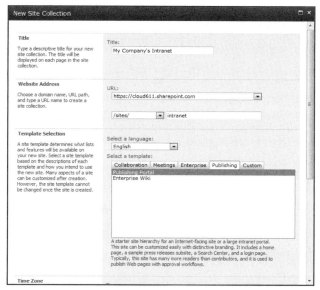

Figure 5-9:
Creating
your
intranet by
using the
Publishing
Portal
template.

SharePoint Online comes with a preconfigured SharePoint site, which serves as the default Team Site. If you have the authority to do so, you can set your newly created intranet as the default Team Site with the following steps:

1. **On the Microsoft Online Portal, click Manage below SharePoint Online.**

2. **Click Manage site collections at the Administration Center page.**

3. **Select the site from the list of site collections in the SharePoint Online Administration Center.**

4. **Select Settings and then select Set as Default Site.**

Configuring the permissions for your site

When you create a site collection in SharePoint online, you automatically get several SharePoint groups. View these groups and their associated permission levels by going to Site Actions, Site Settings, and Site Permissions in the Users and Permissions area.

Users in the Approvers group can publish pages, images, and documents in your intranet site.

Users in the Members group can create and edit pages as well as upload images and documents. They, however, cannot publish the pages, images, or documents.

The publishing portal template comes with workflow enabled in the pages library. Content approval is enabled in the documents and images libraries. Therefore, content is not visible to all users until they are approved and approval is routed through the workflow.

Before you create pages or update the home page of your intranet, add users to the appropriate groups to ensure that content for approval is routed and approved by the right people. This step also ensures that unapproved and unpublished content remains hidden from the rest of the organization until the content is ready for general consumption.

To add users to any of the groups, go to Site Actions⇨Site Settings⇨Site Permissions. Select any of the groups, click New from the menu, enter the user's name, and click OK.

Changing the logo

To change your intranet's logo, first prepare a 60-x-60 pixels image and then upload the image into a document library in your site. You can use the Images document library created by the Publishing feature to store images that are used on pages in the site, or create your own library to store the logo. Display your logo by going to Site Actions⇨Site Settings⇨Title, description, and icon Under Look and Feel. Enter the URL of where your logo is located and then click OK.

Creating additional pages

Your intranet is a repository for content created and published by a few and consumed by all members of your organization. To increase the relevance and optimize the distribution of information, create site pages to focus the delivery of the information. Figure 5-10 is a wireframe that serves as a guide for creating the Human Resources page. The page has five web parts: Welcome, Announcements, Document Library, Training Schedule, and Helpful Links. Add as many pages as needed for your intranet by following the instructions outlined in this section to build the page.

The following table shows the libraries and lists you first need to create in SharePoint Online in order to build the Human Resources page. You need to do this because you will be displaying web parts on the page, which pulls information from the libraries and lists on the table.

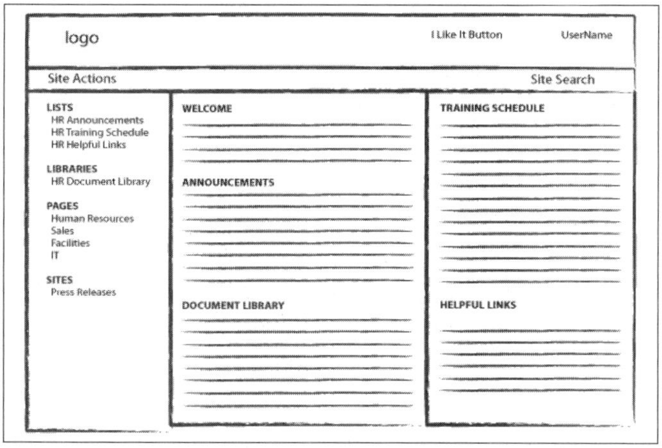

Figure 5-10:
Wireframe
for the
Human
Resource
Pages.

In the table, the column on the left is what you will be naming the SharePoint template type on the right column.

Library or List Name	SharePoint Template Type
HR Announcements	Announcement
HR Document Library	Document Library
HR Training Schedule	Calendar
HR Helpful Links	Links

By default, the publishing portal template does not include all the handy document libraries and lists available in Team Sites. To activate these features, do the following:

1. **Go to Site Action⇨Site Settings.**

2. **Below the Site Actions Group, click Manage Site Features.**

3. **Scroll down to find the Team Collaboration Lists feature and then click the Activate button.**

To create the HR Announcement lists shown in the earlier table, do this:

1. **Go to Site Actions⇨More Options.**

2. **Click the Announcements icon from the list of templates on the right pane.**

3. **Enter** HR Announcements **in the Name text box and then click Create.**

Follow the same instructions to create the HR Document Library, HR Training Schedule, and HR Helpful Links lists and libraries by using the specified template on the right column of the table.

After you set up the libraries and lists, build the HR page as follows:

1. **Go to Site Actions ➪More Options.**

2. **Below Filter By, select Page.**

3. **Select Publishing Page and click Create.**

4. **On the Create Page page, enter Human Resources below Title.**

5. **Leave the default URL name or enter your own.**

6. **For the page layout list of choices, select (Welcome Page) Blank Web Part page.**

7. **Click Create.**

    A new page displays in Edit mode.

8. **To add the Welcome message web part for the page (refer to Figure 5-10), enter text below Page Content. Use the Ribbon commands to format the text.**

    The text you enter here will show up in the Welcome web part from the sample wireframe shown in Figure 5-10.

9. **Add the HR Document Library web part:**

    1. Below Header, click Add a Web Part.

    2. Select HR Document Library and click Add.

    Add the web parts in reverse order because the last web part you add is the web part that shows up on top.

10. **Add the HR Announcements web part:**

    1. Below Header, click Add a Web Part.

    2. Select HR Announcements and click Add.

11. **Add the HR Helpful Links web part:**

    1. Below Right (next to Header), click Add a Web Part.

    2. Select HR Helpful Links and click Add.

12. **Add the HR Training Schedule web part:**

    1. Below Right (next to Header), click Add a Web Part.

    2. Select HR Training Schedule and then click Add.

    3. Hover over the right of the HR Training Schedule web part title and click the down arrow.

    4. Select Edit Web Part to display the Tool Pane on the right.

    5. Below Selected View, choose Current Events.

    6. Below Toolbar Type, select No Toolbar.

    7. Click OK on the web part editing pane.

13. On the Ribbon, click Check In, enter your Comments, and click Continue.

    If you do not see the Check In icon, click Page on the menu.

The page is now saved, but it is not visible to everyone yet. The next step is to submit the page for approval so that it can be published and become visible to everyone in your organization.

You may find that the default views for lists and libraries do not quite meet your needs. They either have too much or too little information. You can easily create a custom view. Just go to the list or library, select List or Library from the Ribbon, and click Create View. Choose a format or select one of the existing views that closely match what you are looking for. In the Create View page, enter the view name, select the columns you want displayed, and deselect the columns you want to hide. Click OK. That's it!

Publishing pages

The publishing portal template used for the intranet site in this example is preconfigured with a workflow that routes content pages for approval before they are published.

Follow these steps to make the Human Resource page visible to all:

1. With the Human Resources page displayed on your browser, click Publish on the Ribbon.

    The publish icons are displayed on the toolbar.

2. Click the Submit icon.

3. From the form that displays, enter all the necessary information.

4. Click Start.

An e-mail is sent to all users belonging to the Approvers SharePoint group. When the page is approved, it will become visible to all the users of the site.

Updating the home page

To update the home page requires Contribute permissions at a minimum. If you meet that requirement, you can update the home page by following these steps:

1. **Go to Site Actions and select View All Site Content.**

2. **Click Pages to display all the site pages with publishing workflows.**

3. **Hover over default below Name and click the down arrow.**

4. **Click Check Out.**

   You are taken back to the Pages list.

5. **Click on default below Name to open the page.**

   When the page opens, the menu items display.

6. **Click the Edit icon (see Figure 5-11).**

   The publishing menu appears.

Figure 5-11:
Edit icon
opens the
publishing
menu.

7. **Update the page by adding or removing content.**

8. **On the Ribbon, click Check In, enter your comments, and click Continue.**

   You are taken back to the home page.

9. **Back on the home page, click Publish on the Ribbon and then click Submit.**

10. **On the form that displays, enter all the necessary information.**

11. **Click Start.**

An e-mail is sent to all users belonging to the Approvers SharePoint group (refer to instructions in the "Configuring the permissions for your site" section, earlier in the chapter). When the page is approved, it will become visible to all the users of the site.

The home page includes a Press Release Content Query web part in the Top section that automatically displays the five most recent pages from the Press Release subsite. If you intend to use the Press Release subsite that comes configured with the portal publishing template, you may not want to delete this web part.

Displaying site pages in the navigation

For quick access to site pages with focused content in your intranet (for example, HR, Sales, and IT pages), modify your site's left navigation by following these steps:

1. **Go to Site Actions⇨Site Settings.**

   The Site Settings page appears.

2. **On the Site Settings page, below Look and Feel, click Navigation.**

3. **In Current Navigation, select the check box next to Show pages.**

4. **Click OK.**

Managing the Press Release Subsite

Technically, your organization's press releases can reside in a document library at the parent intranet site. There are, however, advantages to creating a subsite to house your organization's press releases. One of them is the ability to create special permissions for the subsite so that users outside of the organization can have access to press releases without gaining access to confidential company information.

Creating and editing press release pages is done through your browser by using the HTML Editor to format your content. You can select links and images for your pages from your site's libraries.

To create new press releases, follow these steps:

1. **Go to Site Actions⇨New Page.**

2. **Enter the name of the page (example: New Product Release).**

3. **Click Create.**

4. **Add content to the page by using formatting tools on the Ribbon.**

5. **Click the Check In icon on the Ribbon.**

6. **Enter your Check In comments and then click Continue.**

   Your new press release page displays without the editing tools and boxes.

7. **Click Publish from the top Menu and then click the Submit icon.**

8. **On the form that displays, enter all the necessary information.**

9. **Click Start.**

An e-mail is sent to all users belonging to the Approvers SharePoint group. When the page is approved, it will become visible to all the users of the site.

Note that a Content Query Web Part in your intranet's parent site home page displays the five most recent press releases. If you want to replicate that content query into your Press Release subsite's home page, follow these steps:

1. **Edit the home page.**

   Refer to the instructions in the "Updating the home page" section, earlier in the chapter.

2. **In the Top section, click Add a Web Part.**

3. **Below the Content Rollup category, select Content Query.**

4. **Click the Open the Tool Pane link in the newly added web part.**

5. **Expand the Query section by clicking on the + sign.**

6. **Select Show items from the following list and then click Browse.**

7. **Select Press Releases and then click OK.**

8. **Below Content Type, select Page Layout Content Types from the drop-down choices in the first box and select Article Page from the drop-down choices in the second box. Select Include child content types.**

9. **Click the + sign to expand the Appearance section.**

10. **Under Title, enter Recent Press Releases or your own title.**

11. **Scroll all the way down and click OK.**

If you decide not to use the Press Release subsite, you can delete by going to Site Actions⇨Site Settings, and clicking Delete this Site under Site Actions.

Chapter 6

Going Beyond Websites: SharePoint Scenarios

In This Chapter

▶ Exploring some of the features SharePoint offers beyond websites

▶ Understanding the Search feature

▶ Finding out about some of the services available in SharePoint Online

> *I used to think that cyberspace was fifty years away. What I thought was fifty years away, was only ten years away. And what I thought was ten years away . . . it was already here. I just wasn't aware of it yet.*
>
> — Bruce Sterling

*F*inding out what people think about SharePoint is always interesting. Ten different people will often give ten different answers. One thing most people have as a common understanding is that SharePoint focuses on websites. SharePoint definitely handles websites with ease, but there is a whole lot more under the covers.

In this chapter, we explain some of the features SharePoint has beyond websites. In particular, you discover how adept SharePoint is at managing digital content and unlocking the wealth of information contained in that content through the Search feature. Search is the ability to find the digital content you are looking for when you are looking for it. In addition, you find out about the services available in SharePoint Online.

Managing Digital Content

Imaging a business that functions without using computers is nearly impossible. Computers are used for everything from communication to accounting. Computers definitely speed up business, but this speed has a consequence.

The result is that mountains of digital content are produced on a daily, if not hourly, basis. Managing all this content is one of the areas in which SharePoint shines. In the next sections, we examine some nifty SharePoint Online features, including special online libraries for documents and other media, lists for managing data and tasks, and specialized features, such as Document Sets for working with groups of documents as a single block.

Document libraries

A *document library* is a special folder that you can access through your web browser or directly from within Office applications, such as Word or Excel. If you have ever used SharePoint, then you are familiar document libraries. With SharePoint Online, these document libraries work the same way they do had you spent the time, energy, and resources of implementing SharePoint yourself. With SharePoint Online, however, you just sign up in the morning and begin using SharePoint in the afternoon.

A document library used to store Word documents is shown in Figure 6-1.

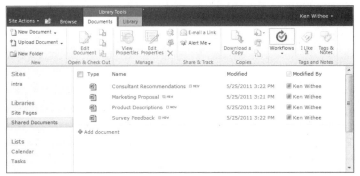

Figure 6-1: A document library in SharePoint Online.

A SharePoint document library takes care of the heavy lifting of managing content, such as the capability to check in and check out a document, versioning, security, and workflow. Each document in a library has a context menu that can be accessed by hovering over the item and then clicking the drop-down menu that appears in the right-hand corner, as shown in Figure 6-2.

A familiar theme in Office 365 is integration between products. In addition to working with document library functionality, such as check in and check out by using the browser, you can also do so from within the Office documents, as shown in Figure 6-3.

How the cloud is creating a level playing field worldwide

Notice in Figure 6-1 that presence information with Lync Online is displayed next to the author of the document. In this case, the presence icon is green (even though you can't see it) which means that Ken Withee is online and available. A SharePoint user can instantly communicate with Ken by clicking on the green presence icon to open Lync information and then click a button to send an e-mail, start a text chat, call directly, or even schedule a meeting. This tight integration between the different products of Office 365 creates a tremendous value. If you work for a very large enterprise, you might already be familiar with this type of integration with Microsoft products. It takes a small army of consultants and specialists to deploy enterprise software. With Office 365, you sign up and begin using the products as a service.

Microsoft has already invested heavily in the required data centers, servers, and well-paid professionals. With Office 365, small mom-and-pop shops all over the world are instantly thrust into the advantages that enterprise software provides. No longer is it only the deep-pocket larger firms that get to experience technological advantages. In this manner, Office 365 is a leapfrog technology. The developing world has not been able to build up the computer infrastructure and expertise required to implement technology like SharePoint and Exchange. Now, all of a sudden, no data center and minimal expertise is required to leverage game-changing software. As long as a company has Internet access, employees have access to Microsoft's enterprise software in Office 365.

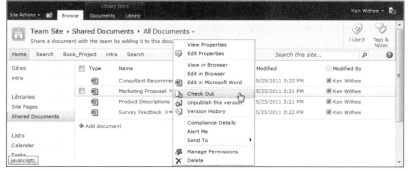

Figure 6-2: Accessing the content management functionality for a document in a document library.

WARNING!

As you can imagine, it takes a lot of space in the database to store multiple versions of documents. For this reason, versioning is turned off by default on new SharePoint document libraries.

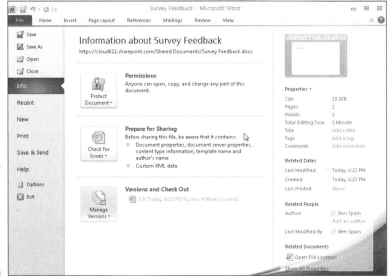

Figure 6-3:
Checking in
a document
from within
Microsoft
Word 2010.

To turn on versioning, follow these steps:

1. **On the Ribbon, click the Library tab and then click the Library Settings button.**

   The Library Settings page appears.

2. **Click the Versioning Settings link.**

   The Versioning Settings page appears, as shown in Figure 6-4.

3. **Select the versioning settings that are required for your scenario.**

   • You can choose to have No Versioning, Major Versions, or Major and Minor versions. Major versions are created when you check in a document and Minor versions are created when you save a draft.

   • You can also configure a number of other settings, including requiring content approval, the number of versions to retain, the number of draft versions to retain, the level of security, and whether the library should require users to check out the document before they can make changes.

4. **Click OK to save your settings.**

Figure 6-4:
Turning on
versioning
for a
SharePoint
document
library.

Slide library

As you see in the previous section, SharePoint does a great job of handling and managing documents. In addition to working with documents, a number of other features are designed to make you more efficient.

People give presentations on everything from sales to accounting. If information needs to be presented in a meeting, PowerPoint is often the tool of choice.

SharePoint Online includes a special library that is specifically geared for PowerPoint slides. Think of a *slide library* acting as a slide headquarters. You have probably experienced the problem of looking for a company slide that you know you saw in the past. You might blast an e-mail out asking if anyone has the particular slide deck that you saw presented last year. You may get a reply, but how do you know that is the most recent version of the deck? After you track down the owner of the deck, you might get the right slides you need for your presentation. The SharePoint slide library provides a one-stop shop for slides.

To create a PowerPoint presentation by using the slide library, you can follow these steps:

1. **Open Internet Explorer and browse to the SharePoint Online slide library.**

   The library contains all the slides anyone in your organization has uploaded to this library, as shown in Figure 6-5.

To upload additional slides, you simply click the upload button at the top of the library.

2. **Select the slides you want in your presentation by clicking the selector next to each slide and then clicking the Copy Slide to Presentation button, as shown in Figure 6-5.**

   Your slide presentation is built instantly in PowerPoint and ready for your presentation.

Figure 6-5:
Working with the slide library in SharePoint Online.

In addition to building presentations from the slide library, you can manage and monitor your slides. You can select a particular slide in the library by clicking on its preview to open up the management page for that particular slide. The management page lets you edit a slide, manage its permissions, or even set up alerts for the slide, as shown in Figure 6-6.

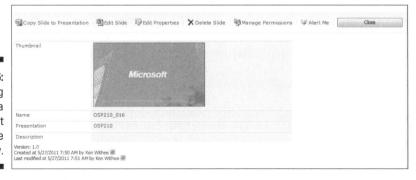

Figure 6-6:
Managing a slide in a SharePoint Online slide library.

An alert allows you to be notified through either e-mail or a text message whenever changes are made to the slide. You can set up alerts to

✔ Cover any changes to any slide.

✔ Cover any changes to a single slide you select.

✔ Cover any changes to any slide you have created.

✔ Cover any changes to any slide that you were the last to modify.

Because the slide library is just a specialized SharePoint library, it still has all the rich content-management features available to other libraries, such as check-in and check-out, versioning, security, and workflow.

In addition to the specialized slide library, SharePoint also has a specialized library for managing rich media files, such as images, video, and audio files. You can create one of these media libraries by selecting the Asset Library template on the Create screen, as shown in Figure 6-7. You can access the Create screen by clicking Site Actions from your SharePoint Site and then selecting Other Options.

Figure 6-7:
Creating a media library by using the Asset Library template in SharePoint Online.

Adding tags and notes

A SharePoint site often grows over time to include lots of pages and content. Keeping track of all this content can be a daunting task. SharePoint includes a couple of features to help navigate and search a site based on the tags and notes left behind by yourself and others. To add a tag or note to a page, click on the Tags and Notes icon in the upper-right corner of the page, as shown in Figure 6-8.

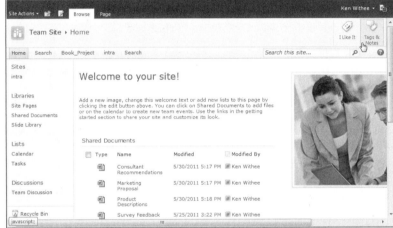

Figure 6-8:
Adding a tag
or note to a
SharePoint
page.

The Tags & Notes page lets you enter your own tags and leave notes about the page. SharePoint keeps track of all the tags throughout the system and automatically recommends tags that are similar to the tag you are starting to spell, as shown in Figure 6-9. To leave a note, you simply click on the Note Board tab.

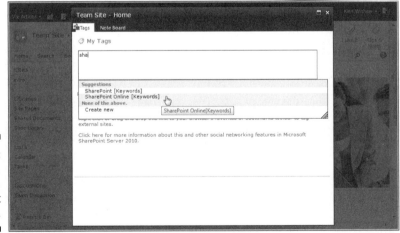

Figure 6-9:
Adding a
tag to a
SharePoint
page.

A popular way to visualize tag data is a utility known as a tag cloud. A tag cloud is a cloud-shaped image with keywords, also called tags, located throughout the cloud. The physical size of the keyword is a direct relation to how popular that particular tag is in the keyword collection. Figure 6-10 shows a typical tag cloud. Notice that SharePoint is the largest word, which indicates that "SharePoint" is used the most frequently out of all the words that make up the tags.

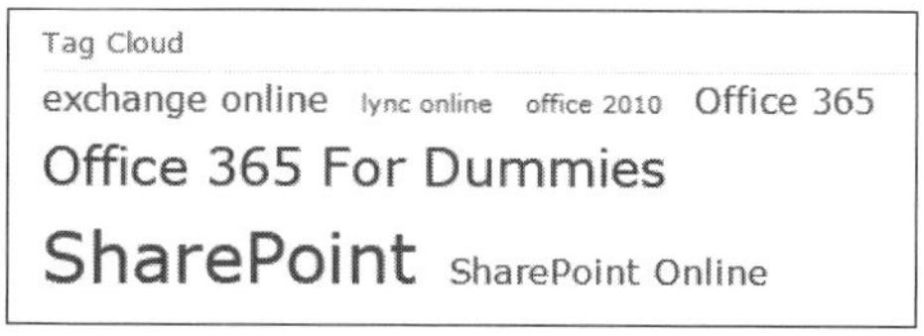

Figure 6-10:
A tag
cloud in
SharePoint
Online.

Tag Cloud

exchange online lync online office 2010 Office 365

Office 365 For Dummies

SharePoint SharePoint Online

You can view others tags and notes as a feed similar to Twitter. If you want to keep your tags private, you can select the Private check box on the page where you enter the tag.

Document Sets

A new feature in SharePoint 2010 is the ability to work with documents in a group rather than individually. In a given day, you might be working on documents for a number of different projects. In SharePoint a Document Set allows you to group documents together based on some criteria and then work with the group of documents as a single entity. For example, you may have a project you are working on for marketing and a project you are working on for accounting. You can group your marketing documents together and group your accounting documents together. You can then interact with the accounting or marketing documents as a single group rather than individually. Using Document Sets, you can send all your marketing documents through a workflow in a batch simultaneously or view versioning for all the documents as a set at a given point in time. Versioning is covered earlier in the chapter and also in Chapter 5.

To begin using Document Sets, first you need to activate the feature for your Site Collection. To do so, follow these steps:

1. **Click the Site Actions button and then click Site Settings.**

   The Site Settings page appears showing you all the settings for this particular SharePoint site.

2. **Go to the Site Collection Administration grouping and click the Site Collection Features link.**

    The features page for this specific Site Collection appears.

3. **Click the Activate button next to the Document Sets feature.**

After the Document Sets feature is activated, you can add the functionality to any library. The Document Set takes the form of a Content Type in SharePoint. A Content Type is the grouping of metadata fields into a single group. For example, you may have a recipe that has a content type that includes metadata, such as ingredients, cooking times, and required seasonings. The SharePoint Document Set content type includes all the functionality required to group multiple documents into a single entity.

A common document library in SharePoint is the Shared Documents library. You can add the Document Set functionality to the Shared Documents library by following these steps:

1. **Navigate to the library in which you want to add the Document Sets functionality.**

    In this example, we add it to the Shared Documents library.

2. **Click the Library Settings button located on the Library tab.**

    In order to add a Content Type to this library, you first need to enable editing.

3. **On the Library Settings page, click the Advanced Settings link.**

    The Advanced Settings page appears and lets you perform advanced configuration for this library.

4. **On the Content Type section, select Yes to allow the editing of content types.**

5. **Click OK to return to the Library Settings page.**

    Notice that a new section appears on the page now called Content Types.

6. **Click the Add from existing site content types link to add an existing site content type.**

7. **Select the Document Set content type, click the Add button, and then click OK.**

Now that the Document Set functionality has been added to the library, you can create a new document set. To create a new Document Set, click on the Documents tab of the Ribbon and then under the New Document drop-down menu, select Document Set, as shown in Figure 6-11.

Figure 6-11:
Creating
a new
Document
Set in
SharePoint
Online.

A Document Set shows up in the Shared Documents library just like another document. You can interact with a document set just like you interact with a single document in the library. The difference, however, is that when you click on a Document Set, you open up the grouping of documents rather than a single document. When the Document Set is opened, a new Document Set tab will appear on the Ribbon. This tab allows you to manage the document set with features, such as editing the properties, changing security permissions, sharing the documents, capturing versions, or pushing all the documents through workflow in a batch. Figure 6-12 shows the Document Set tab in the Ribbon.

Figure 6-12:
The
Document
Set ribbon
tab, which
is used to
manage a
Document
Set.

Using Search Functionality

The rich content-management features of SharePoint may be what often garner the most press, but SharePoint is not a one-trick pony. The search functionality of SharePoint is very robust and brings a Google or Bing-type experience to the corporate documents.

Search is one of those things that doesn't seem important until you really need to find something. You may vaguely remember seeing a presentation done by your colleague a few months ago but have no idea where to even start to look for it in the shared folder. You could e-mail him, but what if he is not available and you need it right away. Search solves the problem of needing to find specific information in a sea of digital data.

SharePoint Online includes the ability to search across multiple sites. As your organization grows and you have an increasing number of sites, it would sure be a pain to have to navigate to each site in order to perform your search. With SharePoint Online, you can search in a single location and the search will span across multiple sites.

Sometimes, it can be difficult to get the exact terminology just right to return the content for which you are searching. SharePoint Online includes the ability to refine a search based on a number of configurable refiners. For example, you might be searching for that presentation that Bob presented to a client a while back. You type in the search term "onboarding employees" but receive hundreds of pages of content back. You remember that the presentation was a PowerPoint presentation so you narrow the search to only PowerPoint slides. You still do not see the presentation right away, so you narrow the search down again farther to only those presentations where Bob was the author. Bingo! The presentation you were looking for is right at the top of the list. Use the refiners to narrow a search, as shown in Figure 6-13.

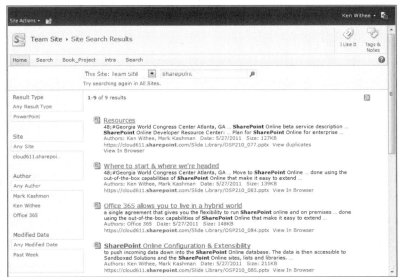

Figure 6-13:
Using
refiners to
narrow a
search.

You can think of a search refiner as a filter. Your search for a broad topic might return hundreds of possible results. The refiner allows you to filter this information down based on the configured criteria.

Another key aspect of search is finding someone you just met but are not sure how to spell his name. For example, you might meet a co-worker in the hall and he mumbles to you that his name is Kain. You register the name as Kain but when you go to search for him online, you wouldn't normally find him if you type in *Kain* because his name is actually Ken. SharePoint phonetic search allows you to still type *Kain* and SharePoint recognizes that this is phonetically very similar to Ken. SharePoint is smart enough to show Ken in the search results, as shown in Figure 6-14. Because SharePoint also shows Ken's mug shot, or should we say company profile picture, in the search results, you can see that you have found the right person you just met in the hall.

Figure 6-14:
Using
SharePoint
phonetic
search
to find a
colleague.

In addition to Search, SharePoint also includes business intelligence functionality and the ability to develop business solutions without writing a single line of code. Business intelligence covers such things as reports, scorecards, dashboards, and key performance indicators. Business intelligence features in SharePoint fall into a marketing bucket called *Insights*. All the nifty tools and features that provide business users with the ability to create applications without programming are called *Composite*s. These aspects of SharePoint require their own books, but for now you should know that they are important pieces that make SharePoint so valuable.

For more information about business intelligence by using SharePoint, check out *Microsoft Business Intelligence For Dummies* by Ken Withee (Wiley 2010). For more information about developing business solutions for SharePoint without writing code, check out Chapter 9. To dive deeper, check out *SharePoint 2010 Development For Dummies* by Ken Withee (Wiley 2011).

Using SharePoint Online Services

SharePoint Online includes a number of services that organizations adopting SharePoint OnPremise have enjoyed for some time. In particular, SharePoint Online includes Excel Services, Access Services, Visio Services, and InfoPath Forms Services. These services enable the tight integration between products in the Microsoft Office productivity suite and SharePoint.

Excel Services

The Excel application is a component of Microsoft's productivity suite called Office. Excel is geared toward numbers, lists, and analysis. Excel is widely adopted in the business world and many users probably wonder how they could function in business life without this tool. Excel Services is a service provided by SharePoint that provides integration between the Excel application and SharePoint. In particular, Excel Services lets you embed your Excel data in a SharePoint site. Using Excel Services, you could have one analyst responsible for the management of the Excel document but share the summary page, graph, or entire document with the rest of the organization. The rest of the members of the organization might not even realize they are looking at an Excel document as the driving force behind the data. From their perspective, they just see a web page on a SharePoint site with graphs, charts, grids of data, and summary data (or whatever part of Excel you decide to embed in the page). The person that manages the Excel document doesn't need to learn a new tool. If she has used Excel, then she can simply continue to use Excel with the difference being that her hard work is displayed to the rest of the organization without the involvement of the IT department, developers, or anyone else.

Access Services

Access is another application that is part of the Microsoft Office productivity suite. Access is a data management application that allows you to create databases, forms, and reports in one single file. The issue that Access files have run into in the past is that they are not easily shared among multiple people. For example, you may create a contact-tracking Access application consisting of a database, data entry forms, and reports. If you need to share this application (it is a file with the extension .accdb), you may either e-mail it to someone or put it out on a shared folder. To limit access, you may need to mess with folder permissions or only send it to trusted individuals. This scenario may be fine for a handful of users, but what happens when you need to share the application with hundreds of people throughout the organization?

Access Services is a component of SharePoint that allows you to publish your Access application to a SharePoint site. All the forms, data, and reports that you created in Access are imported into SharePoint, and the application instantly becomes a multiuser web-based application that is hosted in the SharePoint environment.

Visio Services

Microsoft Visio is a component of the Office productivity suite designed for creating process flows and diagrams. By using Visio, you can create everything from org charts to manufacturing processes. Visio Services lets you embed your Visio documents directly in a SharePoint page. The result is that anyone in the organization can view Visio diagrams by simply navigating to a SharePoint page — assuming that you have given them permission.

InfoPath Forms Services

InfoPath is a component of Microsoft Office designed for data collection. In particular, InfoPath creates forms that can submit data to a multitude of sources. By using InfoPath, a form developer can create rich forms that include functionality, such as data validation.

InfoPath Forms Services provides integration with InfoPath and SharePoint. By using InfoPath Forms Services, the forms that have been developed with InfoPath can be used to collect data in SharePoint. In fact, when you create a SharePoint list or library, you are unknowingly creating associated InfoPath forms for these components. You are creating forms to add new items or edit existing items. When you add or edit an item in a list or library, you need to work with a form. These forms are using InfoPath under the hood and can be customized by using the InfoPath application. To customize a SharePoint form by using InfoPath, you can click the Customize Form button located on the List tab, which is part of the List Tools tab of the Ribbon, as shown in Figure 6-15.

Figure 6-15:
Editing a
SharePoint
list form in
InfoPath.

Chapter 7

Microsoft Office Integration

· ·

In This Chapter

▶ Getting familiar with Microsoft Office integration

▶ Using SharePoint Workspace

▶ Understanding how Microsoft Access integrates with SharePoint Online

· ·

> *"With just one click, I can show my co-worker a document I'm working on and make suggested changes while in a videoconference; we can even use a virtual whiteboard. My co-worker might be in Ohio, while I'm in Seattle, but we're drawing on the same whiteboard, just like we're sitting in the same room. That is just really, really cool."*
>
> — David Kroenke, Technology Textbook Author

*M*icrosoft Office 2010 reached the phenomenal level of selling one copy of the software every second (that's about 31.5 million copies sold as of June 2011). This success was hard won. Bundled programs, such as Microsoft Word, lagged behind WordPerfect, a word processing program that dominated the industry in the 1980s.

The allure of Office 1.0 in the 1990s, with its bundled suite including Word (with its intuitive graphical interface), Excel, and PowerPoint, eventually won over most of the last WordPerfect holdouts. Over the years Microsoft Office continued to evolve with the addition of more applications to the suite, including: Mail, Access, Schedule +, Outlook, Photo Editor, and Publisher, to name a few.

The investments Microsoft made to architect a powerful design that enables Microsoft Office and Microsoft SharePoint to work better together in the cloud means that you — the business owner or end user — have the opportunity to leverage this productivity tool to advance your organization's mission and goals.

In this chapter, you find out how you can save time and gain efficiencies simply by having the ability to save Office documents directly to SharePoint Online document libraries.

You also discover how you can access documents stored in the cloud while you're offline and understand the basics of integrating an Access database with SharePoint.

Integrating Office 2010 with SharePoint Online

For most users, Microsoft Outlook serves as the core application for integrating Microsoft Office and SharePoint. Since Office 2003, the integration between the two programs has so greatly improved that in Office 2010, features crucial to effective collaboration, such as simultaneous document coauthoring, are now enabled. Calendars in Outlook and SharePoint can now be overlaid and plug-ins that connect Outlook to Facebook, LinkedIn, and SharePoint social features are now available. Synchronizing data to and from the server became a one-click task, and Visio 2010, a stand-alone diagramming software part of the Office 2010 wave of products, now allows for a direct publish to Visio Web Services in SharePoint 2010 from the desktop application.

Getting a Backstage view

The Microsoft Office Backstage view is your one-stop-shop feature to see all the things you can do to any document you create. You access the Backstage view from the File menu. From there, various commands give you one-click access to more information about your document. You can see your document's properties with Info (see Figure 7-1), view the most recent documents you worked on with Recent, create a new document from scratch or from a template in New, preview your document with Print, access a whole new world of options for saving and sending your document with Save & Send, and much more!

If you are editing a document from a SharePoint document library with versioning settings enabled, you can check the document back in to SharePoint or discard your checkout right from the application in the Info section of the view. It's also easy to find the exact location of your document from the same section and quickly know whether it came from a SharePoint site or a website, your hard drive, or from an e-mail attachment (see Figure 7-2).

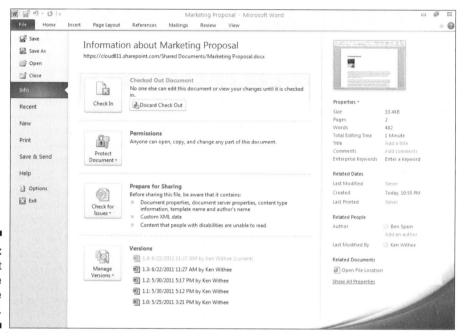

Figure 7-1: Microsoft Office Backstage view.

If you've ever been distraught from not being able to find a file you were just working on, try going to the Backstage view. Check the list of recent documents under Recent and take note of the path right below the filename.

Figure 7-2: Viewing the path of your document.

The story behind the Backstage view

The thinking behind the final design for the nifty features you find in the Backstage view started back in 2003 when the Microsoft Office User Experience (UX) Team started designing the Ribbon. In his blog post at technet.com, Clay Satterfield (Senior Program Manager, Office UX team) relates how his team spent a lot of time looking into the entire Office feature set to come up with a user interface that would accommodate the volume of commands in the mature Office application. They were able to identify two distinct types of features within the applications: the ones most people are familiar with (IN) and the ones that help people *do something with* the content they create (OUT). Based on the planned feature set for Office 2007, the team tackled the IN features first,

including Smart Art, Conditional Formatting, and Themes. As planning for Office 2010 began, the team could see that they were sorely lacking the WYSIWYG equivalent for the OUT features, such as saving, printing, permissions, versioning, and collaboration, and the Office Menu wasn't going to cut it. Knowing that usage of the OUT features was growing rapidly as the need for efficient collaboration becomes critical, they came up with a solution to address the problem: the Backstage view.

You can read Clay's blog at this link:

```
http://blogs.technet.com/b/
office2010/archive/2009/07/15/
microsoft-office-backstage-
part-1-backstory.aspx
```

Using the PowerPoint Broadcast feature

PowerPoint has come a long way since Forethought Inc. developed the software for Apple in 1984 to provide businesses with a program for slide shows and presentations. It's hard to imagine that there was once a time when PowerPoint slides were created in black and white (and shades of gray) only! We never imagined then that the program would offer not only color slides, but the ability to also lightly edit photos and videos. Beyond that, we never imagined that someday you would be able to break geographical limitations and be able to present to audiences in different locations, on a computer or a phone with an Internet connection, and without the need for the software to be installed in our audiences' computer. As it turns out, some genius at Microsoft came up with PowerPoint broadcasting. Here's how it works with your Windows Live ID account (go to http://live.com if you don't have one).

1. **Open your PowerPoint presentation.**

2. **When you're ready to broadcast your presentation, choose Slide Show from the menu.**

3. **Click the Broadcast Slide Show icon on the Ribbon.**

   The Broadcast Slide Show window, shown in Figure 7-3, opens.

Figure 7-3:
Broadcast
Slide Show
window.

4. **Click the Start Broadcast button.**

5. **Enter your Windows Live ID and click OK.**

   You are presented with three options for sharing the link to your broadcast: Copy Link, Send in Email, and Send in IM. Select one of them.

6. **Start the Slide Show.**

After your recipients follow the link to your broadcast, they see exactly what you're seeing on your screen in Slide Show mode. Supported browsers for this feature are Microsoft Internet Explorer 7 and above, Firefox 3.5, and Safari 4 on the Macintosh.

You can escape out of the Slide Show mode while broadcasting without changing that last slide displayed on the screen for your audience before you press the Esc button. Doing so allows you to make quick edits/updates or send additional invitations in the middle of the broadcast. When you're ready to go back to your broadcast, just select the appropriate slide and then click the Slide Show icon.

The enterprise subscription plan for Office 365 allows any organization to set up its own private broadcast service, using a site collection on SharePoint Online created with the PowerPoint Broadcast service.

Follow these steps to set up the service if you have administrator permissions:

1. **From the Microsoft Online Services Portal, click Manage under SharePoint Online.**

2. **From the Administration Center, click Manage Site Collections.**

3. **Under Site Collections on the right pane, click New and then select Private Site Collection.**

4. **Give your site collection a title, an address, and select the language.**

5. **Under Select a template, click the Enterprise tab and then select PowerPoint Broadcast Site.**

6. **Select the time zone, enter the Administrator name, the storage limit, and the resource usage limit.**

7. **Click OK.**

When you're ready to conduct a private broadcast, just add the URL of the site collection as a new broadcast service when the Broadcast Slide Show window pops up. You are prompted for your Office 365 credentials before you can share the link to members of your PowerPoint Broadcast SharePoint site.

Coauthoring documents

In Office 2010, you can coauthor documents in Word, PowerPoint, and OneNote or a collection of documents with others simultaneously. If you use the Excel Web App (not the desktop version), you can also conduct real-time coauthoring with others. This feature is made possible with the use of SharePoint technologies.

For Word and PowerPoint, we recommend enabling both major and minor version tracking in the document library before you start coauthoring. Doing this lets you keep a history of the document as it goes through the editing phase, roll back to an older version if necessary, and indicate milestones reached in the collaboration process by marking the document as a major version.

Ideally for OneNote notebooks, you should only enable major versions because too many minor versions may cause synchronization errors that can result in lost data. The one drawback to that, however, is that you need to create a separate document library for your OneNote notebooks. As an alternative, you can limit the number of versions saved to prevent errors. Ultimately, we recommend taking into consideration your business needs to determine whether or not both major and minor versions for OneNote note-books need to be turned on.

When you turn on versioning for a document library, you have the option to enable the Require Check Out feature. If you select Yes under Require documents to be checked out before they are edited?, you are basically saying no one else can edit the document while you have it checked out. Other users can still view a read-only copy of the document, but they won't be able to make edits to it and save it back to the document library. Because this is contrary to what you want to achieve when you are coauthoring documents, do not enable this feature. By default, SharePoint libraries do not have this turned on. Even so, you still have the ability to check out a document from the library and when you do that, no one else will be able to work on the document while you have it checked out.

The Excel Web App 2010 is a cloud version of the desktop application viewable from a web browser in high fidelity, resulting in a visually familiar look and feel as its desktop counterpart (see Figure 7-4). The technology for mathematical computations is the same in web app as it is for the desktop app. Therefore, regardless of whether you entered the formula in your spreadsheet from the web app or the desktop client, you can get the same results.

Coauthoring in Excel Web App is like magic. You see edits made by your coauthor *auto-magically* pop up on your screen as soon as your coauthor moves to a different cell. You can see who is editing the spreadsheet by clicking the coauthoring status bar on the lower-right corner of the screen, as shown in Figure 7-4.

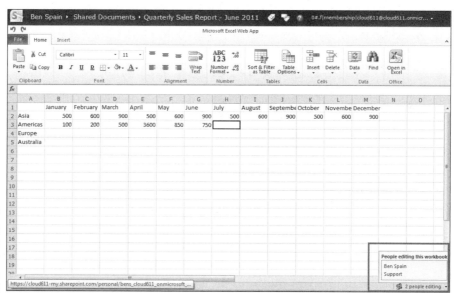

Figure 7-4: Excel Web App user interface.

Enabling versioning control

Turning on versioning control for your SharePoint libraries (or lists) is as easy as a few mouse clicks. Here's how you do it:

1. **From your document library, click the Library tab on the Ribbon and go to Library Settings.**

2. **Under General Settings, click Versioning Settings.**

3. **From the Content Approval group, select either Yes or No to indicate whether or not a document needs to be approved first before it comes visible to the site users.**

4. **From the Document Version History group, choose from one of the options for tracking version history.**

5. **From the Require Checkout group, select either Yes or No.**

   Select No if you are going to use the library for coauthoring.

6. **Click OK.**

After versioning is enabled, you can view the version of your document by selecting the check box to the left of the document name and then clicking the Version History icon from the Ribbon.

From the list of version histories, you can view or restore previous versions by clicking on the down arrow to the right of the date and then selecting either View, Restore, or Delete.

Outlook and Outlook alerts

With Outlook 2010 and SharePoint Online integration, you can synchronize document libraries with Outlook and view the documents in the Outlook built-in viewer. You can also pull lists, such as calendars, tasks, and contacts into Outlook and even work on them offline, knowing that when you reconnect to the Internet, your updates will be synced back to SharePoint.

For both libraries and lists, click the Connect to Outlook option on the Ribbon and follow the prompts to sync them to Outlook (see Figure 7-5). You have to do this for each of the libraries and lists you want to pull into Outlook.

Connect to Outlook

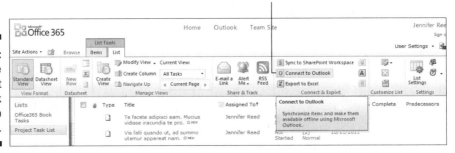

Figure 7-5: Use the Connect to Outlook option to sync.

If you use Outlook to manage your own tasks separate from your team tasks in SharePoint, you can now aggregate both your Outlook tasks and SharePoint tasks to ensure that you don't forget to pick up milk from the grocery store on your way home while you're busy delivering great work for your team. Just pull your SharePoint task list into Outlook and you'll see that all tasks assigned to you from the SharePoint list now show up in your To-Do list along with the tasks you created for yourself in Outlook. You can view the To-Do list two ways:

- ✔ From the Outlook navigation pane on the left, click Tasks and then select To-Do List under My Tasks.

- ✔ From the To-Do bar in Outlook on theright-hand side, look for your To-Do List below the calendar. If you can't see the To-Do bar, it's probably hidden. Display it by clicking View from the Menu, click on the To-Do Bar icon from the Ribbon, and then select Normal.

If you rather receive e-mail alerts to stay on top of SharePoint document libraries and lists, set up Outlook alerts instead. Follow these steps:

1. **From your Team Site on a professional and small business subscription (P plan), click the User Settings menu at the top-right corner of your screen (see Figure 7-6). If you have an enterprise subscription (E plan), click on your name at the top-right corner of your screen.**

Figure 7-6: Accessing the User Settings.

2. **Choose My Settings from the drop-down menu.**

3. **Click My Alerts.**

4. **Click Add Alert.**

5. **Select the list or library you want to be alerted to.**

   You can only select one at a time.

6. **Enter your options for the alert.**

   The options include frequency, who to send it to, delivery method, when to send the alert, and so on.

7. **Click OK.**

Yet another way to set up alerts is to go to your document library or list, go to Library Tools on the Ribbon, and click Alert Me. Follow the prompts.

You will be notified by e-mail that you have successfully set up your alert.

Offline Access with SharePoint Workspace

Microsoft SharePoint Workspace is the artist formerly known as Microsoft Office Groove, a desktop application geared for people who want to collaborate on documents online and offline. It comes bundled with Office 2010 and provides a user interface similar to Windows Explorer for viewing and editing files and lists from a SharePoint site (see Figure 7-7). SharePoint Workspace is easy to set up, provides immediate access to the latest version of documents in a library, and delivers a robust search functionality. You can perform basic SharePoint tasks, such as check documents in and out, copy links to files, drag and drop documents between folders (including folders from your local drive), quickly access the version history of a file, and much more!

Setting up SharePoint Workspace

Synchronizing your SharePoint site with SharePoint Workspace is quick and easy. Follow these steps:

1. **From your SharePoint Online site, go to Site Actions⇨Sync To SharePoint Workspace (see Figure 7-8).**

2. **Click OK on the Sync to SharePoint Workspace window that opens.**

   SharePoint Workspace starts syncing your site to a local cached copy on your hard drive.

3. **After the syncing is done, click the Open Workspace button for an Explorer-like view of your SharePoint site content.**

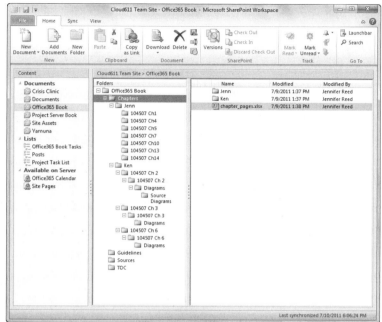

Figure 7-7:
Navigating
the
SharePoint
Workspace
user
interface.

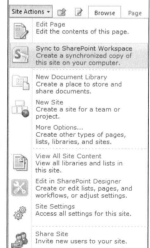

Figure 7-8:
Sync your
SharePoint
site to
SharePoint
Workspace.

SharePoint Workspace does not yet support SharePoint Online calendars, Wiki page, and Survey as of this book's printing. A Gantt view of project task lists is not supported either. Also note that you can only open attachments to list items in read-only. Lastly, lists and libraries protected by Information Rights Management (IRM) will not display.

If you prefer to sync individual lists or libraries rather than the whole site, simply go to your list or library, click Library or List under Library Tools on the Ribbon, and then click the Sync to SharePoint Workspace button, as shown in Figure 7-9.

Figure 7-9:
Sync to
SharePoint
Workspace
button on
the Ribbon.

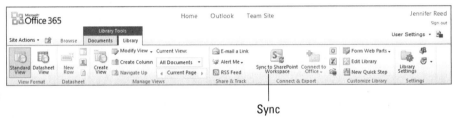

Sync

Synchronizing documents libraries and lists

SharePoint Workspace provides two-way direct synchronization for your libraries and lists between your computer and your SharePoint site. Synchronization happens every 15 minutes, or at any time with a manual refresh.

To perform a manual sync, click the Sync menu and then click the green Sync button on the left.

If you need to free up storage on your hard drive and want to disconnect a list or library from SharePoint Workspace, simply click on the list or library, select Change Sync Settings from the Sync menu, then click Disconnect "[library or list]" from Server.

Clicking Sync Status from the Sync menu gives you more details of the sync status for your libraries and lists.

Integrating SharePoint Online with Access 2010

One of the scenarios you may encounter, as the number of site collections for your organization grows, is the need to aggregate data from various lists to glean business intelligence and run reports. SharePoint Online's integration with Microsoft Access 2010 (Access) allows a non-programmer to work around current SharePoint Online limitations to solve this problem.

Or, if you are a growing small business with an existing web database in Access, you can leverage SharePoint Online to allow members of your organization whose subscription plans do not include Office Professional 2010 to interact with your database through the browser.

MS Access 2010 is bundled with Office 2010 and comes with an array of web database templates compatible with the Publish to Access Services feature. Office 365 subscription plans include Access Services, a feature that lets you publish any of those Access templates to your SharePoint sites.

Understanding Access databases

In very simplistic terms, an Access database is a relational database that organizes your data in tables. The tables in the database are comprised of rows or records and the attributes of those records are defined in the columns or fields (see Figure 7-10). The database becomes relational when attributes from the table form a relationship or dependency on another table.

For example, you can have a Contacts table that contains the contact information for all your customers. You can then have a separate Orders table that contains the order history of all your customers in the Contacts table.

Figure 7-10:
Creating a
simple data-
base table.

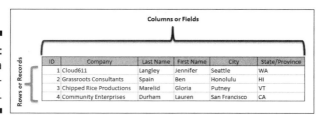

ID	Company	Last Name	First Name	City	State/Province
1	Cloud611	Langley	Jennifer	Seattle	WA
2	Grassroots Consultants	Spain	Ben	Honolulu	HI
3	Chipped Rice Productions	Marelid	Gloria	Putney	VT
4	Community Enterprises	Durham	Lauren	San Francisco	CA

The beauty of tracking all this data in separate tables rather than one long flat list is not lost on Access users who catapulted the software to fame when Microsoft shipped its millionth copy of MS Access 1.1 in September 1993, just ten months after announcing its release.

Translating Access lingo into SharePoint terms

Before embarking on an integration project between SharePoint Online and Access, it's best to understand some geek terminologies to ensure success and, of course, to impress your co-workers.

In Access, you have fields and records. In SharePoint, fields translate as columns, and records are rows.

If you are using the desktop application of Access 2010, take note that an Access database contains forms, reports, queries, macros, and tables. These are called objects. Each of these objects can either be a Web Object or a Client Object. As the name implies, Web Objects is web compatible and, therefore, what you see in your desktop application translates well when you view it from a web browser. Client Objects can only be used in the client or desktop application.

An object can only be either a web object or a client object. You can't convert one into the other. You can, however, save a web object as a new client object.

An Access database can only contain either web tables or client tables — not both. It can, however, contain both web and client forms, queries, and reports.

Knowing this is important because if you plan to publish a database to your SharePoint site, you need to create a web database (as opposed to a client database) to ensure data integrity and compatibility.

Exporting an Access table to a SharePoint List

If you have tables in an existing Access database that you want to make available to members of your team who don't have the MS Access 2010 application, the best way to do this is to export those tables into a SharePoint list. Follow these steps:

1. **From your database, right-click on the table on the left pane and select Export.**

2. **Select SharePoint list from the drop-down menu (see Figure 7-11).**

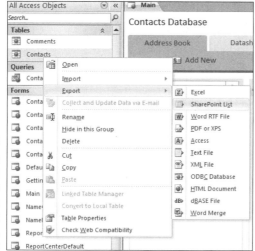

Figure 7-11:
Exporting an Access table to a SharePoint list.

3. **In the Export data to SharePoint list window, enter the URL of your SharePoint site and specify the name for the new list.**

4. **Click OK.**

5. **Unless you deselected the check box next to the Open the list when finished option, the new SharePoint list will open when the export is successful.**

From your SharePoint list, members of your organization can now add new items and modify or delete existing items. Take note that this SharePoint list is now a stand-alone list that is not connected to your Access database. If you want to manipulate this list in Access, however, you have to open the SharePoint list into a new Access file by clicking the Open with Access button from the Ribbon (see Figure 7-12) and following the prompts. If you choose to link the data from the SharePoint site to your Access file, updates that you make on Access will be reflected on the SharePoint list and vice versa.

Figure 7-12:
Opening a
SharePoint
list in
Access.

You can have multiple SharePoint lists pulled into one Access file, giving you the ability to create client object queries and reports that can pull data from multiple SharePoint list sources.

Using the Publish to Access Services feature in Access 2010

Access 2010 comes with a bunch of cool web database templates, some with instructional videos for using and configuring them. Before you create your own web database from scratch, you may want to check these templates out for ideas. Who knows? You might find one that meets your needs or just requires minor tweaking.

After you have your web database built — complete with forms, queries, and so on — publishing it to your SharePoint site as a subsite requires only a few mouse clicks.

Follow these steps:

1. **Click File from the menu to go to the Backstage view of the application.**

2. **In the Backstage view, select the Publish to Access Services option on the middle pane.**

3. **On the right panel, enter the URL for your SharePoint site where you want the subsite for the database to be created.**

4. **Click the Publish to Access Services icon to the left of the URL boxes (see Figure 7-13).**

   Depending on how your account is set up, you may or may not need to log in with your Office 365 credentials.

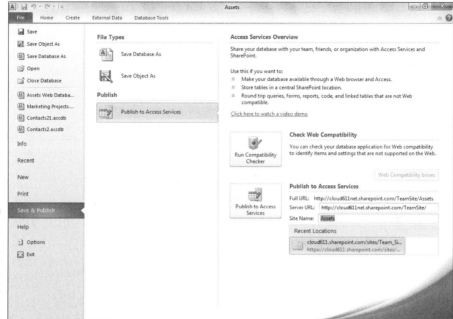

Figure 7-13:
Publish a
web data-
base to
SharePoint
site.

5. **If there are no errors, you get the Publish Succeeded dialog box with a link to your new site.**

Your newly created site is now connected to the Access database running from your desktop application. Changes you make to your database from the desktop application will be reflected at the SharePoint site, and the changes you make at the SharePoint site appear in your database.

Chapter 8

Demystifying SharePoint Online Administration

In This Chapter

▶ Getting familiar with SharePoint geek-speak

▶ Understanding external sharing

▶ Looking at various admin roles and responsibilities

"Organizations buy SharePoint because, out-of-the-box, it provides them with the ability to aggregate their information and content, sharing it through a companywide portal, allowing them to then drive day-to-day productivity. They often see it as a single web application, with many optional features. With SharePoint, there are many accessible features that enable end-users to do much of what they need for themselves without necessarily involving IT."

— Derek Miers, SharePoint as a Strategic Weapon Author

*I*f you are working for a small business or a nonprofit organization, or you are a sole proprietor, you likely wear many hats. It's not easy to function as your organization's CEO, CMO, COO by day and at the same time be the IT department also by day! Getting bogged down with data security and protection, patch management, network stability, and a host of other IT-related daily tasks takes time away from your efforts to move your business forward and achieve your goals.

The folks at Microsoft understand those issues and as a result, they've made it so that administering Office 365 and SharePoint Online is not an onerous task.

Office 365 administration is easy, intuitive, and even fun! Setting up a globally distributed organization with a dozen people can be done in 20 minutes. For $24 a month per user on an E3 plan, your business will get Exchange Online,

SharePoint Online, Lync Online, Office Web Apps, and a public facing website. Best of all, you get premium antivirus and antispam security, 99.9 percent uptime guarantee, and 24/7 support from the Microsoft IT department.

In this chapter, you find out how to share the workload with other team members by delegating some administrative tasks, such as enabling access for external users and allowing site collection owners to configure and manage their sites. You explore the similarities and the difference of the roles and responsibilities between the SharePoint Online Administrator and the Site Collection Administrator.

In case you're ever in a SharePoint conference or gathering, we also include some basic information about SharePoint-speaklike farms, tenancies, and multitenancies. The intent is not to turn you into a SharePoint geek, but rather to make you a knowledgeable SharePoint technology user.

Appreciating the Concept of a SharePoint Farm

For the end user, the SharePoint Online experience centers around using the technology to collaborate effectively, secure and share information, upload and download files, track tasks, manage content, and outlines other ways to stay connected with the team. Although you may not think much about what happens to create the SharePoint Online experience, a series of services and applications are running on multiple servers on the backend to give you just the right experience.

Servers are similar to desktop computers but with a lot more power. These powerful computers *serve* up requests from network users either privately or publicly through the Internet, hence the term "server." When SharePoint servers and SQL (a programming language used to communicate with data-bases) servers come together, they provide a set of services, such as serving up HTML so you can view formatted text on your browser (Web Server), or executing search queries (Query Server), or performing calculations on Excel workbooks (Excel Calculation Services), and much more!

In essence, the infrastructure responsible for your experience as the end user is supported by a collection of servers, each responsible for a set of tasks. That collection of servers is what makes up a SharePoint farm. Everything that happens in SharePoint is administered at the highest level in a SharePoint farm.

Don't let SharePoint jargon deter you from exploring and using the great benefits that this technology has to offer. At its core, SharePoint Online is what allows your organization to round up most — if not all — of your organization's data collection and storage efforts, business processes, collaboration activities, and much more in one web-based application. After you get past the confusion of how farms, tenants, and silos ended up in this technology's dictionary, you'll be on your way to a successful SharePoint co-existence.

Administering the SharePoint Farm and why you don't want to do it

SharePoint farm administration is not for the faint of heart. If you look at the list of typical SharePoint farm administration tasks, your eyes will probably glaze over. Don't fret though. In Office 365, Microsoft manages SharePoint farm-level administration. This is the value of having SharePoint Online as a service hosted in the cloud. In a sense, "putting up the farm" in SharePoint is a risk-free exercise.

The following list covers the SharePoint farm administration tasks:

- ✓ **Backup and recovery:** A backup is a copy of a set of data as insurance in case of system failure. You use a backup to restore and recover lost data. Recovery in SharePoint farms enables administrators to quickly restore the farm in the event of a disaster.

- ✓ **Database management:** This administration task includes adding, attaching or detaching, and moving content databases, moving a site collection between databases, and renaming or moving service application databases.

- ✓ **Security and permissions:** Your organization's SharePoint sites most likely will contain data that you don't want to be publicly available. To restrict access, security and permissions need to be configured. At the highest level, this configuration is done in a SharePoint farm.

- ✓ **Service application and service management:** When resources are shared across a SharePoint farm, service applications are deployed. Services that are deployed are named service applications. Service applications are tied to web applications by service application connections. Some services can be shared across farms.

- ✓ **Web application management:** In order to create a site collection, such as My Site, a web application must be created first. A web application isolates a site's content database from another. It also defines the authentication method for connecting to the database.

✔ **Health monitoring:** As with any IT systems, it is important to monitor how the SharePoint server system is running in order to determine issues, analyze problems, and repair those problems. The monitoring feature in SharePoint collects data in a log, which in turn is used to create health reports, web analytics reports, and administrative reports.

✔ **Farm administration settings management:** Configuring and customizing the default SharePoint farm settings are part of the farm administration settings management tasks. In addition, these tasks include enabling some key features that are turned off at the initial installation, such as diagnostic logging, e-mail integration, and mobile account connections.

✔ **Farm topology management:** At some point, a SharePoint farm will need to be updated to address current needs. Farm topology management tasks include adding or removing a web or application server, adding a database, renaming a server, and managing the search topology.

Multitenancy explained

In a multitenancy environment, a SharePoint farm is architected in such a way that it serves the needs of multiple client organizations. This means that the farm is sliced into subsets and deployed individually for clients and tenants who then manage their own tenancy. As a business owner, this model gives you the ability to run your business the way you want to and leave the IT-related tasks to Microsoft.

For example, as a tenant, you have full control to manage how your content, product, service, marketing collateral, and anything else that you want to manage on the Tenant Administration level (see Figure 8-1), are categorized or classified. In SharePoint-speak, this process defines your taxonomy. Defining your taxonomy upfront establishes naming standards to achieve consistency and content discoverability. After you enter your taxonomy in the Term Store, tagging content becomes easy and intuitive. For example, if you're tagging a content from a SharePoint site and you type in the letters *pro*, terms listed in your taxonomy starting with *pro* (for example, program, project, prospect, and so on) appear, giving you the ability to select the one that fits your needs. The great thing about this is that all the site collections under your tenancy can now consume company-approved, corporate-driven keywords from your taxonomy. This doesn't mean, however, that tagging is limited to the keywords in your taxonomy. Users can always add new tags, which the admin can then add to the Term Store, if appropriate.

In a multitenancy environment, each tenant is separated from all the other tenants with secure "walls" so that one tenant cannot access another tenant's assets. Therefore, if you do a keyword search from any of your site collections, the search results will only pull data from within your tenancy. For this reason, FAST Search, Microsoft's enterprise search product that uses deep linguistics and text analytics technology to add tags to content, is not included in SharePoint Online. FAST Search is not multitenant aware, so if you do a search with FAST, FAST goes up to the farm level and returns results from other tenants or companies on the same farm.

Figure 8-1: Breakdown of SharePoint Online Administration levels.

Delegating administration tasks

Delegated administration is pervasive throughout Office 365 and bodes really well for businesses knowing that their cloud solution is not hinged on one person. Can you imagine what it would be like if only one person had the power to grant access, enable features, and block users and then one day that person is somehow not available?

With Office 365 and SharePoint Online specifically, you can delegate administration up and down. By delegating administration and sharing the workload, you can empower the person who knows his business unit best to control who gets access, how much storage to have, and what custom solutions to install in his site collection.

At the top level, the Tenant Administration level, Office 365 enterprise plans offer the following administrator roles in the Microsoft Online Administration Center:

✔ **Global Administrator:** This role is the top-level administrator for your company who has access to all the features in the administration center. Global administrators can assign other administrator roles, including granting someone a global administrator role.

- ✔ **Password Administrator:** This role can reset passwords for users and other password administrators, manage service requests, and monitor service health.

- ✔ **Service Administrator:** This role is limited to managing service requests and monitoring service health.

- ✔ **User Management Administrator:** This role can do everything password and service administrators are empowered to do plus the ability to manage user accounts and user groups. The exception is that this role cannot create or delete other administrators or reset passwords for billing, global, and service administrators.

- ✔ **Billing Administrator:** This role is limited to making purchases, managing subscriptions, support tickets, and service health.

From the Microsoft Online Administration Center, the Global Administrator can go down one more layer to the SharePoint Online Administration Center where further tasks can be delegated. The SharePoint Online Administration Center is where site collection administrators are assigned, who in turn can go down one more layer to assign site collection owners.

Understanding SharePoint Online Administrator Responsibilities

The SharePoint Online Administration Center is the hub of activities for the SharePoint Online Administrator, who may be the same person as the Global Administrator.

To get to the SharePoint Online Administration Center, click the Manage link below SharePoint Online in the Microsoft Online Administration Center.

As a SharePoint Online Administrator, you have control over site collections, InfoPath forms, user profiles, and the Term Store (see Figure 8-2).

Turning on external sharing

If you anticipate that any of your site collections or business units that use SharePoint Online have a need for external sharing, the first step as a SharePoint Online Administrator is to turn on external sharing. By turning on this feature, users outside of your organization can be invited to SharePoint Online. This one-time action enables the site collection administrators to grant external access to their individual sites without going through the SharePoint Online administrator.

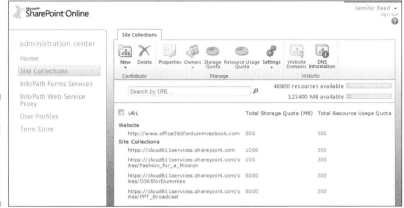

Figure 8-2:
SharePoint
Online
Admini-
stration
Center.

Enabling external sharing turns on the feature for all existing and future site collections within your tenancy. This does not mean that all your SharePoint sites are now publicly accessible. The site collection administrator has to grant someone outside of the company access to a SharePoint site.

To enable external sharing, follow these steps:

1. **Click the Manage link below SharePoint Online in the Microsoft Online Administration Center.**

2. **Click Manage site collections from the Administration Center window that displays.**

   You are taken to the administration center dashboard.

3. **Click Settings from the action icons (see Figure 8-3) on the menu and then click Manage External Users.**

   The External Users window appears.

4. **Select the Allow radio button and click Save.**

Figure 8-3:
Site
Collection
action
icons.

Creating a new site collection

A site collection contains a single top-level site and multiple subsites below it that share common navigation, template galleries, content types, web parts, and permissions.

To create a new site collection, follow these steps:

1. **Click the Manage link below SharePoint Online in the Microsoft Online Administration Center.**

2. **Click Manage site collections from the Administration Center window that displays.**

   You are taken to the Administration Center dashboard.

3. **Click New from the action icons on the menu and then select Private Site Collection.**

   The New Site Collection window appears.

4. **Enter the required information.**

5. **Click OK to go back to the SharePoint Online Administration Center dashboard.**

When you create a new site collection, you are prompted to enter a value for the Resource Usage Quota, as shown in Figure 8-4. The value you enter in the box represents resource points that measure the effectiveness of custom applications running inside your site collection. For example, say you uploaded a custom web part that does a lot of calculations and uses up a lot of computing power. SharePoint Online monitors how many resources your custom web part uses. The resource points that you assigned will authorize SharePoint Online to either leave it alone if it's performing within the quota, throttle it if the code is poorly written and starts to hog all the resources, and ultimately kill the web part or make the application stop running if it goes haywire and starts to cause problems. Fortunately, the killing only happens within the affected site collection and has no impact in other site collections within the tenancy.

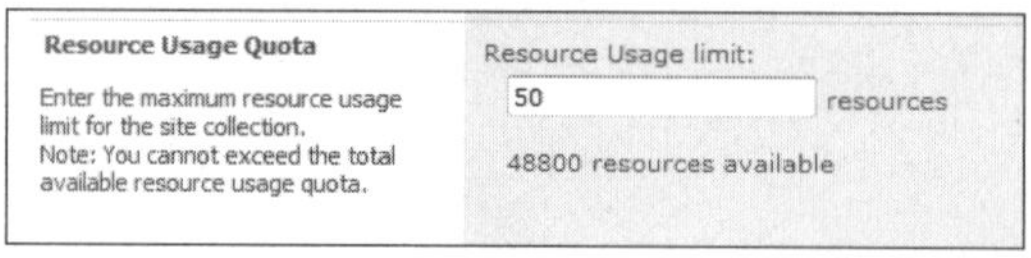

Figure 8-4:
Adding a
Resource
Usage
Quota.

Resource Usage Quota	Resource Usage limit:
Enter the maximum resource usage limit for the site collection. Note: You cannot exceed the total available resource usage quota.	50 resources 48800 resources available

Assigning a new site collection owner to the new site collection

The idea behind delegated administration is to share power so that you, as the SharePoint Online Administrator, can be relieved of business-unit-specific tasks while at the same time, empowering members of your organization to make the call on tasks related to SharePoint for their business unit.

To assign one or more site collection administrators to your site, follow these steps:

1. **Click the Manage link below SharePoint Online in the Microsoft Online Administration Center.**

2. **Click Manage site collections from the Administration Center window that displays.**

   You are taken to the Administration Center dashboard.

3. **Select a site collection by hovering over the URL to display a check box to the left of the URL and then clicking the box.**

4. **On the menu, click the Owners action icon and then select Manager Administrators.**

5. **Enter the name or names of the site collection administrators.**

6. **Click OK to go back to the SharePoint Online Administration Center dashboard.**

Managing the user profiles

As a SharePoint Online Administrator, you may need to edit a user profile to identify the relationship between one user and another, to encourage or enhance social collaboration. Or you may need to edit a user's profile on behalf of someone having trouble updating his or her profile from My Sites.

To edit a user profile, do the following:

1. **Click the Manage link below SharePoint Online in the Microsoft Online Administration Center.**

2. **Click Manage User Profiles from the Administration Center window that displays.**

   You are taken to the Administration Center dashboard.

3. **In the People group, click Manage User Profiles.**

4. **Enter a name in the Find profiles search box and click Find.**

5. **On the name you want to edit, hover over to the right of the entry and click the down arrow to display additional commands.**

6. **Select Edit My Profile (see Figure 8-5).**

7. **Enter your edits in the page that displays and then click Save and Close to go back to the SharePoint Online Administration Center dashboard.**

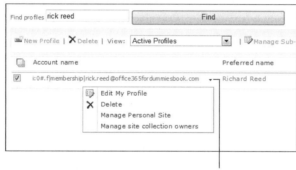

Figure 8-5:
Editing a
user profile.

Display commands

Importing a new custom taxonomy into the Term Store

As a content management system, SharePoint Online provides great out of-the-box metadata management capabilities through the Term Store. If your organization uses taxonomy to organize data, then you can simply use what you have by importing your custom taxonomy into the Term Store.

If you are a small business, using taxonomy to tag content could mean better governance of how things are described in your company, as well as help build the social fabric or your organization.

For example, say that you require SharePoint users to enter certain information about files they upload to the document library. They have to enter the title, author, business unit, audience, and subject for each file. You can leverage taxonomy so that when a user enters metadata in the Audience field, they can choose from keywords already in the Term Store, such as Internal or External. If the user selects Internal, additional options display to choose from, depending on whether the internal audience is for executives or managers. Under Subject, users can select from keywords, such as HR, Legal, or IT. You can also allow users to enter their own keywords to describe the subject. As you see a pattern emerging of frequently used keywords, it may signal you, as the SharePoint Online Administrator, to move those keywords into the main term set. Not only that, but it may prompt your organization to start thinking about creating a new name for a product according to what words best describe it to your people and what those words mean to them.

To import a custom taxonomy to the Term Store, follow these steps:

1. **Click Term Store from the left navigation in the SharePoint Online Administration Center.**

   Make sure that your name is listed under Term Store Administrators.

2. **Under Sample Import on the right pane, click View sample import file.**

3. **Download the comma-separated values (.csv) file and make edits to it in Excel to fit your taxonomy.**

4. **In Excel, arrange the terms in hierarchies up to seven levels deep.**

5. **Save the file in its original .csv format.**

6. **Back at the Term Store from the SharePoint Online Administration Center, hover over the group where you want load the term set and then click on the arrow that appears on the right (see Figure 8-6) to display additional commands.**

7. **Select Import New Term Set.**

8. **From the Term set import window, click Browse.**

9. **Navigate to the .csv file you saved in Step 5, select the file, and then click Open.**

   You are taken back to the Term set import window.

10. **Click OK.**

    You are taken back to the SharePoint Online Administration Center portal where you'll see the term set you just imported listed under the group you selected in Step 6.

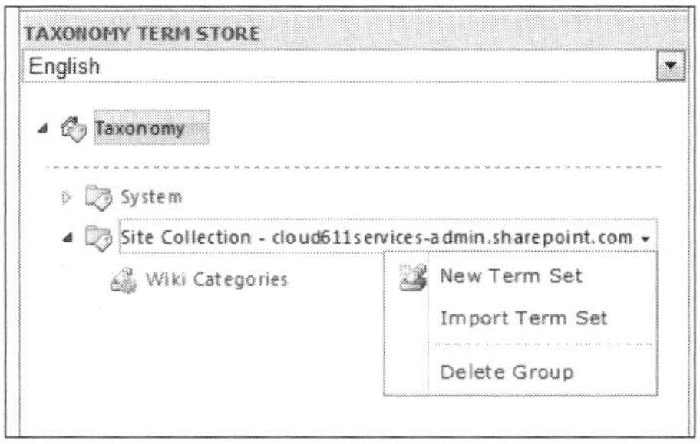

Figure 8-6: Importing a custom term set.

Exercising the Powers Vested on the Site Collection Administrator

As a Site Collection Administrator, you have the highest level or permission in your site collection that allows you to perform tasks, which may have routed to your IT team in the past. You also have the power to enable or disable features that are used in subsites within your site collection. Moreover, you have access to all the subsites regardless of whether you've been added as user to the site.

Sharing your site externally

When the SharePoint Online Administrator enables external sharing from the SharePoint Online Administration Center, this does not mean that all site collections are automatically shared externally. You, as a Site Collection Administrator, have two more steps to take before you can start inviting external users.

1. **Activate the site feature.**

    1. From the top-level site in your site collection, go to Site Actions⇨ Site Settings.

    2. Below Site Collection Administration, click Site Collection Features.

    3. Click the Activate button to the right of External user invitations.

2. **Share the site (or any subsite).**

    1. Go to Site Actions⇨Share Site.

    2. Enter the e-mail address of the external user you want to invite to the site and then click Share.

If the external users you invited to your site already have an Office 365 account, they can log in by using that account. If not, they will be asked to log in with a Hotmail, MSN, or Live account.

Creating a new team subsite and/or new document libraries

A subsite is merely a SharePoint site under a site collection. It uses the same navigation as the top-level site and has the capability of using all the site collection features that have been activated at the site collection level. Sometimes, it is referred to as the child site, whereas the top-level site is called the parent site.

To create a subsite, follow these steps:

1. **Go to Site Actions⇨New Site.**

   The Create Window appears.

2. **From the Silverlight carousel displayed in the Featured Items tab, choose a template by clicking on the images in the carousel.**

3. **Enter the title of your site in the Title box and enter the URL for your site in the box below if you want a URL different from the title.**

4. **Click Create.**

   After the request is processed, you are taken to your new site.

About content and content types

One of the many cool features SharePoint Online offers is the ability for users to not only upload documents but also to create a new Word document right from the document library by clicking Documents from the Library Tools on the Ribbon and then clicking New. This action opens a new blank document in Microsoft Word that will be saved online after you give it a filename.

What most new SharePoint users don't know is that you can actually "upload" a link to a document in another library or create new Microsoft Office documents other than Word. In the case of the former, this eliminates duplicate documents that could become a nightmare to sync. For the latter, it streamlines creation of form-based documents.

Uploading a link instead of a file is made possible by SharePoint content and content types features. Think of content as the Word document you uploaded or the new file you created from the document library. The way you defined the settings for your documents is the content type. The geek way of defining content type according to Microsoft Tech Net is as follows.

To fully understand content type, the next two sections cover scenarios that you're likely to encounter.

Keeping one version of a document in multiple sites

You manage two separate SharePoint sites and you have a document you want to share between the two sites. If you create two documents to upload one for each site, you have to update two documents when something changes. To avoid the extra work, you can upload one document in one site, and "upload" a link to the document in the other site. To do so, follow these steps:

1. **In the document library where you want to add the link to, click the Library tab from the Library Tools menu on the Ribbon.**

2. **Click Library Settings on the Ribbon.**

3. **Under General Settings, click Advanced Settings.**

4. **Under Allow Management of content types, select Yes. Scroll down and click OK.**

5. **Under Content Types you see that Document is already listed as the default content type.**

6. **Click the Add from existing site content types link below the Document content type.**

7. **On the Add Content Types page, select Link to a Document below the Available Site Content Types: box.**

8. **Click the Add button in the middle to add the selected content type into the Content types to add: box on the right.**

9. **Click OK.**

   You are taken back to the Document Library Settings page.

Now that you've added Links as a content type, let's see it in action. Exit out of the library settings view and go back to your document library. To do so, follow these steps:

1. **Click the Document tab from the Library Tools menu on the Ribbon.**

2. **Click the New Document icon to display the available content types. Select Link to a Document.**

3. **On the New link to a document window that appears, enter the document name and the URL.**

4. **Click OK.**

   You are taken back to your document library.

Viola! Now you can see the link listed as if it were a real document in the library. When you update the original file, the link will always open the latest version of the file it's linked to.

Adding an Excel template in the content type

You want to be able to create not just Word documents from your library but also Excel files. The Excel file you want to use when you create new Excel files is a form template for an Invoice that you created. To achieve this, first you need to add your invoice template as a new content type in the site collection. The second step is to then add this new content type to your document library following Steps 1 through 9 in the preceding section, but replacing Link to a Document with the new Excel form template.

To add your invoice template as a new content type in the site collection, follow these steps:

1. **At the parent site, go to Site Actions⇨Site Settings.**

2. **Under Galleries, click Site content types and click Create.**

3. **Give it a name (Invoice Template), enter a description if needed, and select Document Content Type under Select parent content type from.**

4. **Select Document under Parent Content Type and choose from one of the existing groups or create a new group for your new content type and then click OK.**

5. **Click Advanced under Settings, select Upload a new document template, browse for your template, and then click OK.**

Your new template now displays as an option when you create new documents at your document library.

Managing the look and feel

Sometimes the default look and feel of the site may not suit your needs for one reason of another. You can easily customize your site with out-of-the box features that do not require coding. You can edit the title, description, and icon for your site, give it a new theme, reorder the left navigation, and customize the top link bar (or the horizontal navigation). Go to Site Actions⇨Site Settings. The commands are available under Look and Feel.

Managing the galleries

As a site collection administrator, you have the ability to manage the galleries in your site collection. These galleries include site columns, site content types, web parts, list templates, master pages, themes, and solutions. You access the galleries by going to Site Actions⇨Site Settings.

As with content types, you can create a new site column to represent an attribute or metadata for a list item or content type. When created, the site column can be reused in multiple lists, and in multiple sites within the site collection.

One of the handy links in the Galleries group is List templates. When you see a SharePoint list that you like and may want to reuse, save the list as a template and then add that template in the gallery. After the template is added, an icon for the list will be displayed as one of the options when you create a new list.

To save an existing list as a template and add to the gallery, follow these steps.

1. **Go to an existing list.**

2. **Click the List tab under the List Tools menu on the Ribbon.**

3. **Click List Settings.**

4. **Under the Permissions and Management group, click the Save list as template link.**

5. **In the Save as Template page, enter the file name, template name, and description.**

   If you want to include the content of the existing list in the template, check the Include Content box. Note that the more data you have in your template, the bigger the file size will be and may cause issues loading the template. We recommend leaving this option unchecked.

6. **Click OK.**

   When the saving process is complete, a notification will be displayed confirming successful completion of the operation.

7. **Click OK.**

   You are taken back to the List Settings page.

When you go to Site Settings⇨More Options, you will see the new template you added under the List templates.

If for some reason you do not like the master page template that's applied to your SharePoint site, you may need to hire a designer to create a new master page. You then load the new master page into the Master Page Gallery as if it were a document in a document library.

Web parts, themes, and solutions require technical know-how to create but after you have them, you can easily add them to the Gallery as if they were list or document items.

Managing permissions and groups

To maintain security and integrity of your site, assign the right level of permission or privilege to the users of your site. As a best practice, create a SharePoint group first, assign a permission level to the group, and then start adding users to the appropriate groups.

An example of a SharePoint group could be the "Executive" group with Contribute access where all your C-level executives are members. Another example is a "Site Owners" group with Full Control privileges, comprised of a few members of your team who are technically advanced.

Grouping your users with similar access needs minimizes the administrative burden of individually adding or removing users from sites, libraries, and lists. Doing this allows you to use those groups in workflows, such as assigning tasks to a group rather than an individual.

In SharePoint 2010, you can assign permissions on the site collection level and have those permissions be inherited or not inherited on the subsite level. You can also further customize the permission on document libraries or lists so even if users may have access to the site, they may or may not have access to certain contents within the site. You can take it even farther down to the granular level by customizing the permission for items in a list or contents in a library so that even though a group may have access to a document library, only certain individuals have access to certain files. Do the following:

✔ To manage your site's permissions, go to Site Actions⇨Site Settings and then follow the links under User and Permissions.

✔ To manage permissions on a list, library, or item, hover over the list, library, or item, click the down arrow on the right, and then select Manage Permissions.

Chapter 9

Understanding SharePoint Online Development

In This Chapter

▶ Using your web browser to develop SharePoint solutions

▶ Understanding how to develop sites

▶ Developing your knowledge of lists, libraries, and pages

▶ Discovering how to develop by using SharePoint Designer

The first 90 percent of the code accounts for the first 90 percent of the development time . . . The remaining 10 percent of the code accounts for the other 90 percent of the development time.

— Tom Cargill

After get the hang of SharePoint, you may want to dive deeper into the technology. SharePoint is a web-based product (meaning that you use it with your web browser). Being a user of SharePoint is just the beginning, however. You can develop real-world business applications by using nothing more than your web browser. You don't need to be a programmer and you don't even need to be very technical. You just need some time to find out how to drag and drop components and enter content. When you need a little more power, you can fire up a tool called SharePoint Designer. SharePoint Designer provides a powerful and intuitive user interface designed specifically for SharePoint development.

In this chapter, you walk through SharePoint development by using your web browser. You find out about key SharePoint development concepts, such as sites, lists, libraries, and pages. You also take a look at SharePoint Designer and explore how you can develop solutions without needing to write a single line of programming code.

Going Over SharePoint Development

SharePoint development does not mean you need to be a programmer or have any understanding of programming. If you can tweak your Facebook page or update your LinkedIn profile, then you can be a SharePoint developer. SharePoint development begins with nothing more than your web browser. When you are ready to move beyond your browser to more advanced functionality, you have a tool called SharePoint Designer at your disposal. Even though SharePoint Designer provides advanced development functionality, almost no programming is involved. If you can use Microsoft Office Word, then you can use SharePoint Designer.

For a more thorough look at SharePoint development by using your web browser, SharePoint Designer, and other development tools, check out *SharePoint 2010 Development For Dummies* (Wiley 2011) by Ken Withee.

Using a Web Browser As a Development Tool

To a user, browsing a SharePoint site looks like a regular website — with some fancy SharePoint capabilities. Those SharePoint capabilities enable easy collaboration, access to business information, and a boost to business intelligence, all though the Web. In SharePoint terms, a site is a container for SharePoint pages. This entire ball of functionality, also called a *platform* (because you can build on it), is the Microsoft product called SharePoint. One of the things that makes SharePoint so exciting is that you don't even have to drop out of your web browser to tell SharePoint what to do. As long as you have access to SharePoint and a current browser, you are ready to start developing a site.

When you are first starting out with SharePoint development, you need a site that you can use to practice. When you create a new site, you can start with a blank site or a *template site* that already has some stuff built into it — such as lists, libraries, and web parts developed and configured to do particular tasks. Those templates are available on the Create screen when you create a new site. For example, you may get a request to create a Document Center site in order to manage documents from a central location. Rather than start from scratch, you can use a template specifically designed for this task. In this scenario, the template site you would use is called the Document Center and is shown in Figure 9-1.

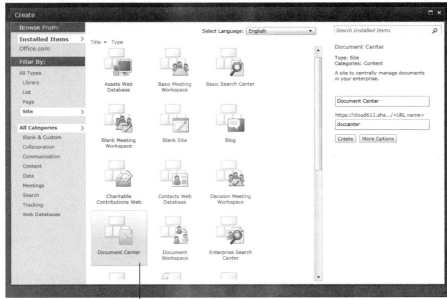

Figure 9-1:
The
Document
Center site
template.

Document Center template button

Developing SharePoint sites

When you need to develop a SharePoint site to solve a problem, be sure that you start with a solid understanding of the available site templates. It's often much easier to start with a site template that almost does what you want and then develop it from this starting point than to develop everything from scratch.

Before you start building custom applications for SharePoint, having a solid working knowledge of its various components is a good idea. (After all, you wouldn't try to design a house without having some knowledge of how the plumbing works, right?) The best way to get to know SharePoint is to start with a blank site and develop it from scratch so you understand what the templates are doing. Then you can more easily start with a template as a baseline and develop your site from there.

Creating a new site is as simple as clicking Site Actions➪New Site from the parent site and then clicking through the templates to find the site you want to create. A parent site is simply a site that holds another site.

Table 9-1 lists the available site templates in SharePoint Online — along with the description of each site.

Table 9-1	SharePoint Online Site Templates
Site Template	*Description*
Assets Web Database	Create a database to keep track of your organization's information assets (valuable information), including the details and owner(s) of each asset.
Basic Meeting Workspace	A site on which you can plan, organize, and capture the results of a meeting. It provides lists for managing the agenda, meeting attendees, and documents.
Basic Search Center	This site provides SharePoint search functionality, including pages for search results and advanced searches.
Blank Meeting Workspace	You can use this blank meeting site to customize to your meeting's requirements. The difference from a Blank Site is that a Blank Meeting Workspace has the components available that you need to build out a site geared toward meetings.
Blank Site	A blank site has no built-in features; customize it to match your requirements. It sounds funny to create a blank site by using a blank site template. What you are actually doing is creating a container for SharePoint stuff, a site, without actually putting any of the SharePoint stuff in there at the time of creation.
Blog	This site works like an Internet blog; a person or team can post ideas, observations, and expertise that site visitors can comment on.
Charitable Contributions Web Database	By using this site, you can create a database that keeps track of information about fundraising campaigns — including donations, contributors, campaign-related events, and scheduled tasks.
Contacts Web Database	By using this site, you can create a database to manage contact information from customers, partners, and other people who work with your team.
Decision Meeting Workspace	You can use this site at meetings to track the status of projects or make decisions. The site includes lists you can use to create tasks, store documents, and record decisions.
Document Center	You can manage documents centrally for your entire enterprise from this site.

Site Template	Description
Document Workspace	Colleagues can use that famous SharePoint collaborative capability to work together on a document. The site provides a document library for storing the primary document and supporting files, a list for to-do tasks, and a list that can hold links to resources related to the document.
Enterprise Search Center	This site provides the SharePoint search capability. The Welcome Page includes a search box that has two tabs: one for general searches and another for searches for information about people. You can add tabs, delete them, or customize them with different search scopes or specified result types.
Enterprise Wiki	You can use this site for publishing knowledge that you capture and want to share across the enterprise. Use this site to edit, coauthor, and discuss content, as well as to manage projects.
Express Team Site	This site is for teams to quickly create, organize, and share information. It provides a document library and a list for managing announcements.
Group Work Site	This template provides a site that teams can use to create, organize, and share information. It includes the Group Calendar, Circulation, Phone-Call Memo, the document library, and the other basic lists.
Issues Web Database	Create an issues database to manage a set of issues or problems. You can assign, prioritize, and follow the progress of issues from start to finish.
Multipage Meeting Workspace	You can use this site to plan a meeting and make note of the meeting's decisions and other results. The site provides lists for managing the agenda and meeting attendees, as well as two blank pages you can customize to your requirements.
Personalization Site	You can use this site to deliver personalized views, data, and navigation from this site collection to My Site. It includes Web Parts that are specific to personalization and navigation that is optimized for My Site sites. This template is available only at the site level.
Projects Web Database	You can create a project-tracking database to track multiple projects and assign tasks to different people.

(continued)

Table 9-1 *(continued)*

Site Template	Description
Publishing Site	This template offers a starter site hierarchy (grouping of SharePoint sites) for an Internet site or a large intranet portal. You can use distinctive branding to customize this site. It includes a home page, a sample press-releases site, a Search Center, and a logon page. Typically, this site has many more readers than contributors; it's used to publish the Web pages by using a process for approving new content known as an approval workflow.

By default, this site enables content-approval workflows to provide more control over the publishing process. It also restricts the rights of anonymous users: They can see content pages but not SharePoint Server 2010 application pages.

This template is available only at the site-collection level. A site collection is a special SharePoint site that allows you to separate key aspects of the sites contained within the site collection. For example, you turn on features at the site collection level, which makes those features available to all sites within the site collection. On a technical level, SharePoint separates site collections by using different databases. This allows for separation of security and users because two different site collections use two different databases. |
Publishing Site with Workflow	A site for publishing web pages on a schedule by using approval workflows. It includes document and image libraries for storing web-publishing assets. By default, only sites that have this template can be created under this site.
Social Meeting Workspace	A site on which you can plan social occasions and use lists to track attendees, provide directions, and store pictures of the event.
Team Site	A site on which a team can organize, generate, and share information. It provides a document library as well as lists for managing announcements, calendar items, tasks, and discussions.
Visio Process Repository	A collaborative site on which teams can view, share, and store Visio process diagrams. It provides a document library (with version control) for storing process diagrams as well as lists for managing announcements, tasks, and review discussions.

Adding lists, libraries, and pages

In order to develop a SharePoint site (using your browser no less!), you need to understand some of the key components. In particular, these include lists, libraries, and pages.

Knowing your list options

SharePoint Online comes with a collection of standard lists and libraries. Microsoft has already taken the time to develop these in order to make your life as a developer easier, so you may as well use them. The following list introduces the standard SharePoint lists and provides brief descriptions:

- **Announcements:** This list is for brief news items, quick status checks, and other quick-and-informative stuff.

- **Calendar:** This calendar is strictly business — deadlines, meetings, scheduled events, and the like. You can synchronize the information on this calendar with Microsoft Outlook or other Microsoft-friendly programs.

- **Circulations:** This list is for sending information around to team members via an e-mail notification; the list includes confirmation stamps, so members can indicate that they've seen what you wanted them to see. An example would be an important new company policy. You can use the Circulations list to track that everyone has read and accepted the policy. Note that in order to see this list template, you must have the Group Work Lists feature activated.

- **Contacts:** If you're a regular Outlook user, you may have developed a list of contacts. If you haven't, here's your chance to list the people relevant to your team (such as partners, customers, or public officials). You can synchronize the SharePoint Contacts list with Microsoft Outlook or other programs that play nice with Microsoft products.

- **Custom List:** If you're trying to develop a list but none of the standard list types does what you have in mind, you can start from scratch with a blank list and drop in the views and columns you want.

- **Custom List in Data Sheet View:** Here's a familiar twist on the blank list: SharePoint shows it as a spreadsheet, so you can set up a custom list as easily as you would in Excel, specifying views and columns as needed. Note that this list type requires an ActiveX control for list datasheets; fortunately, Microsoft Office provides such a control. (Coincidence? I think not.)

- **Discussion Board:** If you're a seasoned netizen from the heyday of the newsgroup, this list will be a familiar place for online discussions. Naturally, you want to keep the discussion businesslike, so this list type helps you manage those discussions (for example, you can require posts to be approved before everybody can see them).

✔ **External List:** Use this list type to create a list of data identified as an External Content Type. An External Content Type is a term used to describe groupings of data that live outside of SharePoint. An example might be data that lives in a backend system, such as SAP.

✔ **Import Spreadsheet:** If you have data contained in an existing spreadsheet (created in Excel or another Microsoft-compatible program) that you want to use in SharePoint, you can import it into a list of this type. You get the same columns and data as the original spreadsheet.

✔ **Issue Tracking:** If you want to organize your project team's responses to a problem associated with (say) an important project, this is the type of list you use to set priorities, assign tasks, and keep track of progress toward resolving the issue.

✔ **Languages and Translation:** SharePoint offers a Translation Management workflow that helps assign translation tasks. This list type is for creating a list of the languages used in those tasks — and of designated translators for each language.

✔ **Links:** This list type helps you organize links. The user can consult a list of web pages and similar online resources — and simply click to go to any of them.

✔ **Microsoft IME Dictionary List:** Create a Microsoft Input Method Editor (IME) dictionary list when you want to use data in a SharePoint list as a Microsoft IME dictionary. Microsoft IME is a system that allows you to enter characters, such as Japanese or Chinese, not found on your keyboard. When an application that supports these characters is running, a small virtual keyboard appears on your screen that allows you to enter the characters. The Microsoft IME Dictionary List allows you to store the various character values in SharePoint. Note that in order to see this list template, you must have the Group Work Lists feature activated.

✔ **Project Tasks:** If you're a veteran of Microsoft Project 2010 (especially if you have Project — or a compatible equivalent — running in your organization), this list type is probably familiar. It's essentially a big to-do list organized as a Gantt Chart (which you can, in fact, open with Project): a place to track team or individual progress on tasks and keep your eye on allocated resources and deadlines.

✔ **Status List:** This list type offers a big-picture perspective of a project's status. It's a place to display goals for (say) a project and show how close you are to reaching them.

✔ **Survey:** This list type is for gathering information, specifically by crowd-sourcing. Here's where you put a list of questions you want people to answer. A survey list helps you formulate your questions and can summarize the responses you get back. The responses to the survey are stored in the list and can then be analyzed, charted, or exported.

✔ **Tasks:** This list type is essentially a to-do list for a team or individual.

Checking out the available libraries

When you need a way to organize files so that they're accessible via a SharePoint site, you find a selection prebuilt for the most common types of libraries in SharePoint Online. Take a gander at these standard libraries and the brief descriptions of what they do:

- ✔ **Asset Library:** Here's where you store information assets other than documents — ready-to-use information in the form of images, audio files, video files — to make them available and regulate their usage.

- ✔ **Data Connection Library:** This library type is where you can put and share files that specify and describe external data connections. For example, you might want your users to be able to pull data from a data warehouse. Setting up a connection to the data warehouse and getting all the server names, usernames, and connection information just right can be tedious. Using a Data Connection Library, an administrator could set up the connections and store them in the library. The users would then just use the connection to the data warehouse whenever they want to pull data and analyze it.

- ✔ **Document Library:** You run across — and create — a lot of these in SharePoint. Such libraries are for storing documents, organizing them in folders, controlling their versions, and regulating their usage with a check-in/check-out system.

- ✔ **Form Library:** Here's where you store and manage electronic versions of blank business forms for everyday documentation, such as purchase orders and status reports. To create and maintain libraries of this type, you need a Microsoft-compatible XML editor. As it happens, Microsoft provides one — InfoPath. (Coincidence? Well, no, not really.) Keep in mind, however, that the form library is just a place to store the data that has been entered into the form. To build the actual form, you need to use InfoPath.

- ✔ **Picture Library:** This library type is for storing and sharing digital images. The difference between the Assets Library and the Picture Library can be subtle because they both store images. The key distinction lies in the name. The Picture Library is designed specifically to store pictures, and the asset library is used to store images. If you think of a picture as a photo and an image as something like a logo or graphic, the differences start to emerge. For example, the pictures in a Picture Library show a thumbnail image when they show up in searches, but the images in an image library do not.

- ✔ **Record Library:** You store business records in this library. When you create a Record Library, you are adding some functionality that allows SharePoint to create record management and retention schedules. This type of functionality is important when you want to make sure that you are doing your due diligence in keeping track of your business records by letting SharePoint do the heavy lifting.

✓ **Report Library:** This library type is dedicated to web pages and documents that keep track of performance (and other such metrics), progress toward business goals, and other information used in business intelligence.

✓ **Slide Library:** You can use this type of library to display Microsoft PowerPoint slides (or those created in compatible similar applications) to multiple viewers through the SharePoint system. You can also use this library type to find, organize, and reuse existing slides.

✓ **Wiki Page Library:** Libraries of this type have interconnected web pages containing content, such as text or images and functionality in the form of Web Parts that multiple users can edit easily.

Paging through the available pages

You can create and develop three primary types of SharePoint pages (in your browser, no less!) — each with a distinct function:

✓ **Content page:** Also known as a *wiki page*, this is the Swiss Army knife of SharePoint pages. A content page provides not only a place to put content but also a kind of workshop for collaboration, development, and customization — multiple users can wield a full-featured text editor built right into the browser. A content page is easy to develop and is an extremely powerful and intuitive tool for collaborative authoring, data capture, and documentation. For example, if you are in the business of manufacturing consumer products, then you might have a content page that allows customer service reps to capture common questions that users have regarding your products. The page could be dynamically updated as the reps encounter new questions without the need to call in a programmer.

✓ **Web Part page:** This type of SharePoint page provides Web Part zones where you can drag and drop various Web Parts (reusable pieces of functionality) right onto your pages from the SharePoint Web Part gallery. Although a set of Web Parts comes standard with SharePoint, you can also custom develop Web Parts to meet your specific business needs. Imagine developing a Web Part for your company that ventures forth to become an everyday tool for nearly all the users in your organization — on their own sites — and to get the tool, all they have to do is simply drag and drop the Web Part right onto their pages. For example, you may have Web Parts that you have developed for your call center reps. When new Web Part pages are developed, the Web Parts that are used by the call center can be added to the page. This lets a programmer package up web functionality into a reusable component (Web Part) that can be reused on multiple pages.

✔ **Publishing page:** This type of SharePoint page is designed to serve two functions: managing content and managing the look and feel of the page. A publishing page lives in a document library that provides version control and the SharePoint workflow feature. It's designed for the management and distribution of content — the essence of publishing content to SharePoint.

For more information on developing in the SharePoint environment, check out *SharePoint 2010 Development For Dummies* by Ken Withee.

Cracking Open SharePoint Designer

SharePoint Designer provides an intuitive interface for the underlying SharePoint platform and a staggering range of development possibilities. You can, of course, develop and configure sites, pages, lists, and libraries, but you can also go deep into advanced functionality that is beyond the scope of this section, including building custom page layouts, developing workflows, and creating branding (just to name a few). Aside from using the browser, SharePoint Designer is one of the most useful tools for developing on the SharePoint platform — and a place you are likely spend a great deal of time.

Peering into the looking glass with SharePoint Designer

To exercise all its well-muscled capabilities, SharePoint relies heavily on another Microsoft product: SQL Server, a database application that's designed to store data.

In the case of SharePoint Online, you don't need to worry about this product, but you should at least be aware that SharePoint is using a database to store content and configuration data. Microsoft takes on the burden of supporting the infrastructure to SharePoint (including SQL Server). All you have to do is use the final product.

The SharePoint platform stores its content and configuration information in a number of SQL Server databases. Because those databases hold all the crucial goods, you can't just crack open Windows Explorer and start looking at files in SharePoint. You need a tool that allows you to peer into the databases and work with the SharePoint platform. SharePoint Designer is just such a tool.

You can download, install, and use SharePoint Designer for free. After you install SharePoint Designer, use one of the following methods to open the tool:

- ✔ Press the Windows key and type **SharePoint Designer** into the search box.
- ✔ Click Start⇨All Programs⇨SharePoint ⇨Microsoft SharePoint Designer 2010.

When you open SharePoint Designer, the Backstage View appears, as shown in Figure 9-2. Because SharePoint Designer is designed to work only with SharePoint, you must connect SharePoint Designer to an existing site or create a new site in an existing SharePoint environment. If you've already connected to a site, then that site shows up in the Recent Sites section — you can simply click the name of the site to connect and start developing.

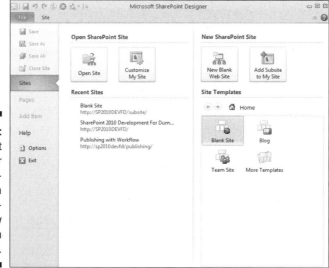

Figure 9-2: SharePoint Designer must connect to a site or create a new site when opened.

After you connect to a site, the Ribbon activates, the navigation comes to life, and you have all the SharePoint Designer capabilities at your disposal, as shown in Figure 9-3.

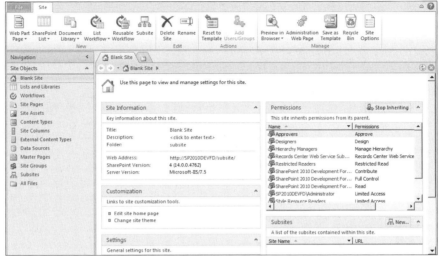

Figure 9-3:
When
SharePoint
Designer is
connected
to a site, the
Ribbon and
site naviga-
tion become
active.

If you're a newcomer to SharePoint Designer, check out the following tips on what SharePoint Designer can do:

- ✔ **You can use SharePoint Designer to work with SharePoint.** Because SharePoint stores all of its content and configuration information in a database, it would be very difficult to modify the database directly. What you need is a logical window into the database in order to work with SharePoint. SharePoint Designer is a tool specifically for the task of connecting to the SharePoint database to provide you with the ability to perform development tasks.

- ✔ **You can develop a horde of SharePoint components.** Develop pages, lists, libraries, data sources, content types, views, forms, workflows, and external content types — all without having to write any code. SharePoint Designer spans a large swath of development capabilities.

- ✔ **You can keep using SharePoint Designer when you go deeper into SharePoint development.** You can work on masterpages, page layouts, CSS, and JavaScript.

And here's what you can't do:

- ✔ **You can't use SharePoint Designer as a more general web-development tool.** If you don't have a SharePoint site to develop, then you have no need for SharePoint Designer (or, really, anything for it to work on). If you need a more general web-development tool, check out Microsoft Expression Web. Expression Web is similar to SharePoint Designer, but it isn't tied to SharePoint sites.

- ✔ **You can't write .NET code.** When your SharePoint site calls for .NET code, switch to Visual Studio, which is covered in Chapter 10.

SharePoint Designer 2010 works only with SharePoint 2010. If you are using Office 365, then you are in luck because SharePoint Online in Office 365 is based on SharePoint 2010. If you're working with SharePoint 2007 (and not SharePoint Online, which is part of Office 365), install SharePoint Designer 2007 instead.

Taking a spin around SharePoint Designer

Any piece of software can be overwhelming at first glance, and SharePoint Designer is no exception. Microsoft has gone to great lengths to make the tool as intuitive and user friendly as possible — but it still helps to take a spin around the user interface. The screen is divided into three main sections: the Ribbon across the top of the screen, a navigation window on the left side of the screen, and a design surface at the right of the screen, as shown in Figure 9-4.

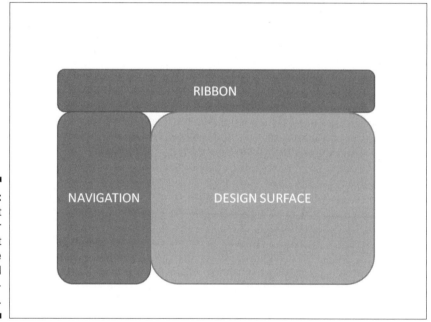

Figure 9-4: SharePoint Designer is split into three functional components.

Finding site-creation tools

You can use SharePoint Designer in several different ways to create a site. The easiest way is to use the SharePoint Designer File tab, also known as the Backstage View. The Backstage screen is what appears when you open SharePoint Designer for the first time; after all, you have to either create or connect to a site or Designer has nothing to work with. The base templates that are available include a blank site, a blog site, and a team site. Depending on which features you activate for a particular site collection, additional templates are available. Clicking the More Templates button enables you to connect to a site collection in order to view the range of templates you have available (based on the activated features).

SharePoint Designer cannot be used to create new site collections. In order to do that, you need to use the Office 365 administrative interface.

Unwrapping the Ribbon

SharePoint Designer incorporates the visual arrangement of controls that you find in other Office applications in a feature known as the Ribbon. The Ribbon runs across the top of the screen; it's where you go to activate the commands you use as you develop your custom programs in SharePoint. The following Ribbon features come in handy as you begin using it:

✔ **The Ribbon is dynamic.** The Ribbon changes to match the component of SharePoint you're using. For example, if you're working on a workflow, the Ribbon displays options for developing workflows (as shown in Figure 9-5). If you're developing a page, the Ribbon displays the commands you need for page development, as shown in Figure 9-6.

Figure 9-5:
The
SharePoint
Designer
Ribbon
when a
workflow
is being
developed.

Figure 9-6:
The
SharePoint
Designer
Ribbon
when a
page
is being
developed.

> ✔ **You can customize the Ribbon.** You can add new Ribbon sections that
> are your own creations. All you have to do to customize a Ribbon tab —
> or add a new one — is right-click anywhere on the standard Ribbon and
> choose Customize the Ribbon from the menu that appears.

Steering the navigation features

In addition to the Ribbon across the top of the screen, a navigation window
occupies the left side of the screen, as shown in Figure 9-7. The Navigation
window provides a quick display of the Site Settings page, lists and libraries,
workflows, site pages, site assets, content types, site columns, external content types, data sources, Master Pages, page layouts, site groups, and subsites. In addition, it offers an All Files view that shows you all the files in the
site (which is similar to the behavior of SharePoint Designer 2007).

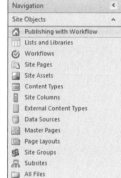

Figure 9-7:
The
SharePoint
Designer
navigation
window.

The page layouts navigational menu is only displayed if the site is a *publishing
site* — a site that has the SharePoint Server Publishing Infrastructure feature
activated.

The Design section of SharePoint Designer is dynamic — what you're working
on provides the context that determines which commands are displayed. For
example, the Design section displays everything from the settings screens to
the editors to the Workflow Designer.

The top of the Design section includes a navigational component similar
to a web browser. The Design section's navigational component includes a
Home button and Forward and Back buttons to move through the history
of windows that have been opened. For example, if you clicked the Settings
page, and opened an editor, and then clicked to a different list altogether,
you can click the Back button to retrace your steps back through the various
windows. In addition, a *breadcrumb* component (*Hansel and Gretel*, anyone?)
shows the location of the current component in the overall hierarchy of the

site. For example, if you're editing the columns in a calendar list, you see a breadcrumb "trail" to show that the location is the site, the List and Libraries galleries, the calendar list, and then the editor. SharePoint Designer allows multiple design windows to be open at the same time — say, an editor, a gallery screen, and/or a settings page. Each window is represented by a tab. The Design section's navigational components are shown in Figure 9-8.

Figure 9-8:
The Design
section's
navigational
component.

You can change the order in which the tabs are displayed across the screen by clicking them and dragging them either left or right. This is helpful when you want to see the tabs in a particular order as you work. For example, you may want to keep the tab that contains your style sheet always to the left of the tab that contains the page editor.

The breadcrumb feature is also a handy way to navigate to a specific window in the same context as the window you're viewing. For example, if you're viewing the settings window of a page, you may want to do a quick click to the editor window for this page without having to move the cursor down to the Edit File link. You can see the available windows that you can move to from the current window by clicking the drop-down arrow on the rightmost breadcrumb, as shown in Figure 9-9.

Figure 9-9:
Using the
breadcrumb
feature to
launch
context-
specific
windows in
the location
of the
current
window.

Configuring with settings windows

A *settings window* provides configuration details and controls for a particular component of SharePoint. Components such as sites, pages, lists, libraries, and workflows all have settings pages associated with them. If you need to configure a list, for example, you don't have to open the list in the browser and then navigate to the settings page. You can view and configure the settings for the list right from SharePoint Designer — in a settings window like the one shown for a Calendar list in Figure 9-10.

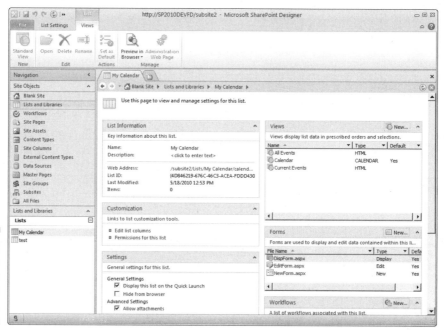

Figure 9-10:
The settings window for a Calendar list.

When you first create a site by using SharePoint Designer, the initial screen that appears is the settings window for the new site.

Viewing gallery windows

A *gallery* is a grouping of SharePoint artifacts displayed in a window. For example, when you click Lists and Libraries in the navigation window, you're presented with all the lists and libraries on the site. Whenever you click any navigation button in the navigation window, SharePoint Designer pulls all the artifacts from the site for that navigation button (for example Content Types) into one grouping and displays that group in a gallery window.

You can view a gallery of the following types of SharePoint artifacts by clicking the corresponding navigation item for each one:

- ✔ Lists and Libraries
- ✔ Workflows
- ✔ Site Pages
- ✔ Site Assets
- ✔ Content Types
- ✔ Site Columns
- ✔ External Content Types
- ✔ Data Sources
- ✔ Master Pages
- ✔ Page Layouts
- ✔ Site Groups
- ✔ Subsites

Many of these items may be unfamiliar to you and are beyond the scope of this chapter and book. For an in-depth look at these items and other development tasks, check out *SharePoint 2010 Development For Dummies* by Ken Withee.

Each gallery has a corresponding SharePoint Designer Ribbon tab where you can find the commands specific to that gallery. For example, the Master Page Gallery has a Ribbon tab called Master Pages that offers functionality, such as creating, editing, and managing your site's Master Pages.

Developing in editor windows

SharePoint Designer contains a number of different editor programs that are used for SharePoint development. For example, when you develop a page, you're using a Page Editor (as shown in Figure 9-11). If you're developing a workflow, you use the Workflow Editor. The tool fits the job.

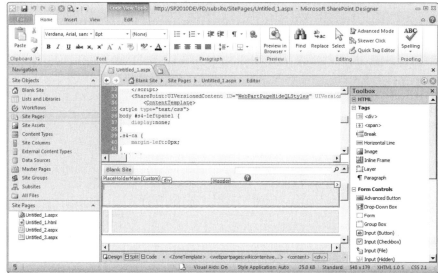

Figure 9-11:
Developing
a page
by using
the Page
Editor in
SharePoint
Designer.

The following editors are available in SharePoint Designer:

- ✔ **Page Editor:** Use this editor to develop pages. For example, when you want to develop a new content page, you use this editor.

- ✔ **Workflow Editor:** This editor is designed to develop workflows. Do you need to create a workflow that sends a new proposal off to your 15 executives for approval and tracks their feedback? This is the editor you use to do it.

- ✔ **List and Library Editor:** Use this editor to work with lists and libraries. When you need to work with the views, forms, workflows, and content types that are attached to a list or library, this is the editor you use.

- ✔ **Content Type Editor:** Developing content types often takes patience as you figure out exactly which columns for metadata you want to include. When you need to develop a content type, however, this editor is the one you use.

- ✔ **Column Editor:** The column editor lets you develop metadata columns for your SharePoint libraries in a single interface. When you need to configure the columns on your site, this is the editor you use in SharePoint Designer.

- ✔ **Script Editor:** When you need to develop code, such as Cascading Style Sheets (CSS) or HyperText Markup Language (HTML), you use this editor to get the job done. The editor is actually nothing more than a glorified text editor with some nifty features, such as turning key words different colors, to help you identify key words syntax.

✔ **Image Editor:** The image editor is an image manipulation program that you can use to modify your images. You can change the brightness, contrast, and color or even crop, rotate, or flip the image.

✔ **Text Editor:** This editor is similar to using Wordpad or Notepad but without having to leave the SharePoint Designer application. Need to edit a text file on your SharePoint site? You can use this editor.

✔ **XML Editor:** The XML editor is similar to the script and text editor but provides some nifty functionality for getting the syntax and formatting of eXtensible Markup Language (XML) documents correct.

✔ **External Content Type Editor:** Just like the Content Type editor is used to work with content types, this editor is used to develop content types that are external to your SharePoint environment. An example of an external content type might be a grouping of metadata that is stored in your backend Line Of Business (LOB) system that you want to interact with in SharePoint. The external content type would contain the connection information, the details of the metadata, and how SharePoint should use it.

Part IV
Diving into the Office Web Apps

The 5th Wave   By Rich Tennant

"The odd thing is he always insists on using the latest version of Office."

In this part . . .

This part explores the Office Web Apps and guides you through the power of using Office with nothing more than your web browser. You begin with an overview of the Office Web Apps in order to gain fundamental knowledge about what a Web App is and how it differs from the traditional Office product. You then dive into each component individually by looking at the Word Web App, Excel Web App, PowerPoint Web App, and finally the OneNote Web App.

Chapter 10

Introducing the Office Web Apps

In This Chapter

▶ Discovering the various environments Office Web Apps comes in

▶ Comparing the Office Web App services to Office Professional Plus applications

▶ Understanding the user experience and the engine the runs Office Web Apps

> *"For over two decades, millions of people have been using Microsoft Office to power their businesses. As we move into the cloud computing age, people expect to share and collaborate with their customers and colleagues with the same level of confidence whether they are using desktop software or web-based services. We believe a document should look exactly the same in the cloud as the original copy on the desktop."*
>
> — Tony Tai, Senior Project Manager, Office 365

Office Web Apps is the cloud version of Microsoft Word, Excel, Power-Point, and OneNote. The apps allow users to create high-quality documents, simultaneously make changes to the documents with coauthors, and share these documents from a browser without the need for the desktop application. Therefore, you are no longer tethered to your office desk to be productive. In the past, your documents were stored where you last saved them — on a hard drive or on a server. If you need that document, but you're not at your office, tough luck. With Office Web Apps and Office 365, you can be working from home, at your favorite coffee shop, or even on vacation (not that we recommend that!) and still be just as productive as your co-workers in the office.

You don't have to give up beauty when you create documents on Office Web Apps — your visual-rich documents look identical to documents created with the Office 2010 desktop application. Formatting styles, graphs, charts, and data are retained when you open and share documents from Office Web Apps. Flat, boring documents have no place in Office Web Apps.

In this chapter, you find out about the three environments Office Web Apps come in and understand why the Office 365 environment is the most suitable option for businesses and organizations. We explain the options for Office Professional Plus available to one-man-show professionals and small businesses who do not subscribe to the enterprise plan.

Exploring Office Web Apps Environments and Benefits

For the end users, Office Web Apps mean any time, anywhere to their documents where there is an Internet connection — even on a mobile device! You don't need Office 2010 installed to create, view, and edit documents because Office Web Apps is browser based.

Office Web Apps are available in three environments:

- ✔ **Windows Live SkyDrive,** a free online storage service accessible through the Internet. The service is geared for personal use with 25GB of storage. There is a file size limit of 50MB for Word, PowerPoint, and OneNote files. For Excel files, the limit is 2MB. As is common practice with online providers, there is advertising for this environment; that is, the service is free, but it is not ad free.

- ✔ **On-premises,** where customers with Microsoft Office 2010 licenses run Office Web Apps, on their own servers, as a tightly integrated service with SharePoint 2010 products. Pricing, storage, and file size limitations are configurable in this environment.

- ✔ **Office 365 as part of the license included in SharePoint Online.** This section focuses on this environment.

The nice thing about using the Office 365 subscription plan to access Office Web Apps is that you can scale up or down depending on your business needs without investing a lot of capital upfront. You can assign a plan with basic features, including Office Web Apps with a lower monthly fee for kiosk workers, and simultaneously assign a full pledge plan (with higher fees) for other workers.

Working on your documents in Office Web Apps is almost the same as working on them in the Office 2010 application. The high-fidelity rendering ensures consistent formatting so you will see your content as intended. Images, charts, table of content, even cross-references in documents created in the desktop application are retained when you open and make light edits to them in Office Web Apps.

Office Web Apps broke the platform barriers by enabling users on a PC or a Mac with a supported browser to have the same experience when creating, viewing, and editing documents. This means better collaboration, increased efficiency, and reduced cost, especially for small businesses.

Supporting Office Web Apps with the right browser and devices

Although Office Web Apps run on most browsers we've tested, the following list is the official Microsoft-supported browsers and their requirements.

- ✓ Internet Explorer 7 and later on Windows operating systems
- ✓ Safari 4 and later on Mac operating systems
- ✓ Firefox 3.5 and later on Windows, Mac, and Linux operating systems

As of this book's writing, Chrome is not officially supported but plans are underway to support it soon.

You can view and make light edits to Word, Excel, and PowerPoint files by using Office Web Apps on most smartphones running on various operating systems. What follows is Microsoft's official list of supported mobile devices.

- ✓ Internet Explorer on Windows Mobile® 5/6/6.1/6.5
- ✓ Safari 4 on iPhone 3G/S
- ✓ BlackBerry 4.x and later
- ✓ Nokia S60
- ✓ NetFront 3.4, 3.5, and later
- ✓ Opera Mobile 8.65 and later
- ✓ Openwave 6.2, 7.0, and later

In addition to smartphones, you can also view Word and PowerPoint documents on an iPad.

Comparing Office Web Apps and Office Professional Plus

Office Web Apps is the online version of Microsoft Word, Excel, PowerPoint, and OneNote that allows users to create, edit, and collaborate on documents by using a browser. Users get a consistent look and feel for Office Web Apps regardless of the environment in which it is used (Windows Live SkyDrive, On-premises, or Office 365).

Office Professional Plus for Office 365, on the other hand, is a flexible, pay-as-you-go, per-user licensing of Office applications as part of the Office 365 enterprise plans (E3 and E4). It is not bundled in the professional and small businesses plan (P plan) but it can be purchased separately, either as a monthly or an annual subscription. With Office Professional Plus, businesses and organizations have access to the latest version of the same Office 2010 applications (Figure 10-1 shows a list of included applications), connected and delivered through the cloud.

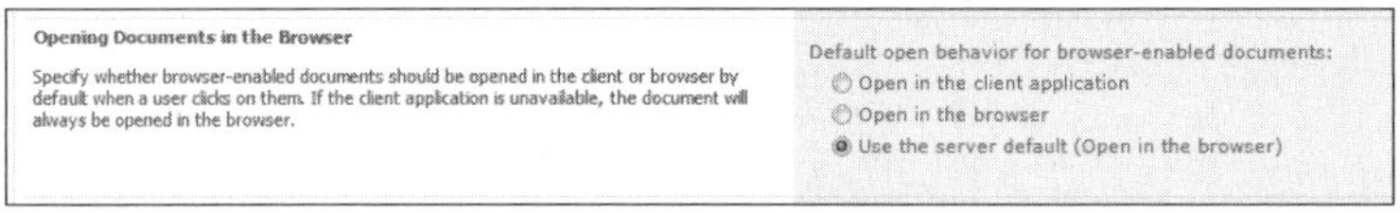

Figure 10-1: Applications included in Office Professional Plus subscription.

Opening Documents in the Browser

Specify whether browser-enabled documents should be opened in the client or browser by default when a user clicks on them. If the client application is unavailable, the document will always be opened in the browser.

Default open behavior for browser-enabled documents:
- ○ Open in the client application
- ○ Open in the browser
- ⦿ Use the server default (Open in the browser)

Experiencing Office Web Apps Front and Back

By default, when you open a Word, Excel, PowerPoint, or OneNote document from a SharePoint document library, the file is opened directly in the browser by using Office Web Apps. Although you're viewing the document through a browser, you will experience the same look and feel as if you were to open them in a desktop application. Office Web Apps is designed for light editing with many commonly used editing features, such as clipboard, fonts, para-graph, styles, and spelling. You can insert tables, pictures, clip art, and links directly from the web app, as well as toggle between the Editing view and the Reading view. If you need to use the full set of features of your Office desktop application, open your document with your desktop application by clicking the Open in [Office App] icon on the Ribbon.

Supported file types and oddities

New files created in Office 365 are based on Office Open XML file formats — think of the four-character extensions, such as docx, .xlxs, .pptx, and so on. Not to worry, SharePoint online is configured with Word, Excel, and PowerPoint templates that are compatible with Office Web Apps. The OneNote web app on the other hand, will open a blank OneNote 2010 note-book when you create a new file. Unlike the other web app files, a new OneNote notebook file is actually a folder with another file named Untitled Section.one inside of it. This is the default name until you change the name of the section.

Supported file types for Office Web Apps are as follows:

- ✔ **Viewing and editing:** .docx, .xlxs, .xlsb, .pptx, .ppsx, .one
- ✔ **Viewing only:** .doc, .dotm, .dotx, .ppt, .pps, . pptm, .potm, .ppam, .potx, .ppsm

Macro files for Word (.docm) can be edited in Office Web Apps, but the macros will not be run. For macro Excel files (.xlsm), Office Web App will strip the macros and prompt the user to save a copy of the file with macros removed.

Coauthoring in Office Web Apps versus Office 2010 is not the same. In Office Web App, you can have multiple users editing a document simultaneously only in Excel and OneNote (not Word or PowerPoint). In Office 2010, coauthoring works in Word, PowerPoint, and OneNote only (not Excel).

Understanding the engine behind the user experience

When you open a document in Office Web App, a whole series of processes and services occur behind the scenes, all within the few seconds between the time you click on the file and when the browser renders the file for you to view. Images, HTML, JavaScript, and Silverlight all come together to give you the best viewing experience for your document. These are your native browser objects, and how they come together to represent your document is based on what web application is started and what feature of Office Web Apps is activated.

HTML (Hyper Text Markup Language) is the wrapper that gives your candy or package the right look and feel. In the world of websites and web pages, HTML is what makes text appear in bold or a picture align left or right. For example, if you want to have the phrase "Office 365" appear bold on a web page, you would use the following HTML tags.

```
<b>Office 365</b>
```

JavaScript, on the other hand, is a scripting language that helps put inter-activity to web pages. It's what gives HTML glamour by making text or graph-ics behave in certain ways in response to an event.

Silverlight enhances your web experience by loading pages faster, improved text fidelity, smoother animations in PowerPoint, presentation slides that grow or shrink depending on the size of the browser, and much more. Silver-light is not required to run Office Web Apps, but it would be a mistake not to take advantage of this free web browser plug-in.

So the next time you use Office Web App, think of all the processes, services, events, and instances happening in the background to provide you with the best viewing pleasure. Actually, you probably won't think about it because the geniuses behind Office Web Apps designed it to go so fast you're not supposed to notice it.

Chapter 11

Getting into the Word Web App

In This Chapter

▶ Finding out how the Word Web App differs from the regular Word

▶ Wrapping your head around some of the basic features of the Word Web App

▶ Exploring some of the advanced features of Word Web App

I have an almost religious zeal . . . not for technology per se, but for the Internet which is for me, the nervous system of mother Earth, which I see as a living creature, linking up.

— Dan Millman

*W*ith the release of Office 365, a new version of Word is available that runs as a web application in your web browser. This development may not sound very spectacular, but it has some nifty benefits that we explore in this chapter.

In this chapter, we go over some of the basic concepts of the Word Web App, such as using the web interface to create, read, edit, and delete documents. We also look at some of the advanced features of the Word Web App, including working with styles and tables.

Comparing Word Web App and Word

Unless you have been living under a rock, you have probably used or heard of a program called Microsoft Office Word. Word is an aptly named word processing application. Word is a *thick client,* meaning that you run it from your local computer. You click Start and then All Programs and you browse to your office applications and you click Word to fire up the program. Word then runs on your computer. A web-based application, on the other hand, runs on a computer in a data center, and you access it over the Internet. If you use Hotmail for e-mail or browse a web page, then you are using a web application. You access a web application by using a web browswer, which is a program installed on your computer.

Although the Word Web App is still Microsoft Word, there are some differences between the two. The biggest difference is that Word runs on your local computer, and Word Web App runs in the cloud and is accessed by using your web browser.

When you fire up Word on your local computer and create a document, that document stays on your computer. When you click the Save button and save the document, you are prompted for the directory on your local computer in which to save the file. You may save the file to your My Documents folder or to your Desktop. In any case, your creation is a physical file located on your local computer. When working with the Word Web App, however, you do not have a local physical file. When you create a document and save it, your document lives out in the cloud. In the case of Office 365, your document lives within a SharePoint Online document library.

You don't have to be a subscriber to Office 365 to work with Word Web App. It is free with a Windows Live account.

Getting the Basics

You need to know some basic things about the Word Web App, such as how it differs from the traditional Word application that runs on your desktop or laptop. You also want to become familiar with the Word Web App interface and discover how you can easily work with documents right from your web browser.

Using the Word Web App interface

The Word Web App interface is almost identical to the regular Word interface, except that it runs within your web browser. The interface contains a Ribbon at the top of the screen, which contains such tabs as Home, Insert, and View.

The Home tab contains common functionality in groupings, such as Clipboard, Font, Paragraph, Styles, Spelling, and Office, as shown in Figure 11-1.

Going behind the scenes

The cloud is just a fancy way of describing the act of accessing software and computer resources over the Internet. For example, when you create a Word Web App document, it is not some mystical and magical fog that is conjured up from the mists of the Internet. To track down where the actual Word file lives requires a bit of detective work, but it is entirely possible.

Office 365 is nothing more than server software that Microsoft has installed on computers in their data centers around the world. For example, if you are on the West coast, then the physical data center that your Office 365 software is running in might be in the state of Washington. You access this server software over the Internet. Because you don't know, or even really care, where the actual data center is located, you can say it is running "in the cloud".

Now, to track down that physical file you created with Office Web App, you need to think about where you saved it. You saved it into a SharePoint document library. We know that SharePoint uses a database product called SQL Server to store all of its content and configuration information. So when you are saving something to SharePoint, you are actually saving it to an SQL Server database. That SQL Server database is running in the Microsoft data center in the state of Washington (or Hong Kong, or Germany — or wherever the closest Microsoft data center is located).

Opening your web browser, pointing it at SharePoint Online, and clicking on a Word Web App document to open or print it is actually very easy to accomplish. Behind the scenes, however, SharePoint Online (running in a Microsoft data center) is contacting the SQL Server program (also running in the Microsoft data center) and requesting the specific Word Web App document. SharePoint then sends that to your web browser, and you see it magically appear, as shown in the figure.

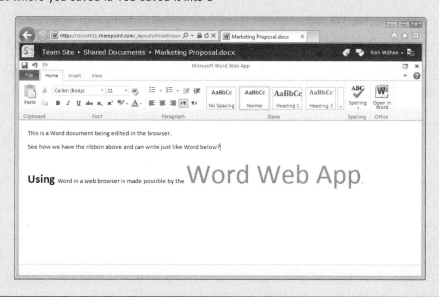

Figure 11-1:
The Home
tab on the
Office Web
App Ribbon.

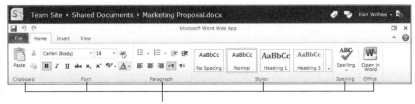

Common functionality groupings

You use the Insert tab to insert objects into your document, such as a table, a picture, clip art, or a link. The Insert tab is shown in Figure 11-2.

Figure 11-2:
The Insert
tab on the
Office Web
App Ribbon.

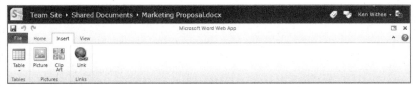

The View tab allows you to flip between an Editing View and Reading Mode. When in edit mode, you can work with the Home and Insert tabs to modify and develop your document. The View tab is shown in Figure 11-3.

Figure 11-3:
The View
tab on the
Office Web
App Ribbon.

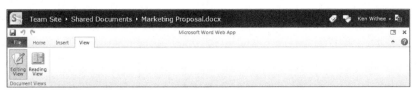

In addition to the standard tabs in the Ribbon, there are also specialized tabs that only show up when you are working with certain objects. For example, when you select a picture by clicking on it, you will see a new tab — Picture Tools, as shown in Figure 11-4. The Picture Tools tab contains functionality for working with a picture, such as adding alternate text or resizing the image.

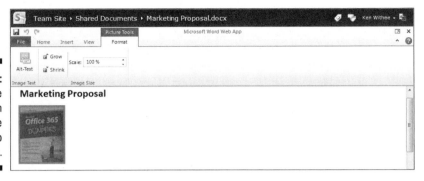

Figure 11-4:
The Picture
Tools tab on
the Office
Web App
Ribbon.

In addition to the Ribbon tabs, the interface also includes a File menu. The File menu allows you to save the document, or open it by using the traditional Word application located on your computer, or close the document and return to the document library that houses the document. The File menu is shown in Figure 11-5.

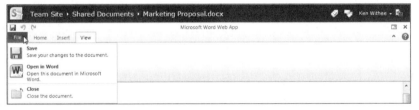

Figure 11-5:
The File
menu on
the Word
Web App
interface.

Working with documents

Creating a new Word document in a SharePoint document library is easy. You simply browse to the Documents tab on the Ribbon and then click the New Document button on the Ribbon, as shown in Figure 11-6.

The New Document button is used to create a new document. The type of document that is created depends on the default content type for the library. The Shared Documents library, which comes standard out of the box with SharePoint, uses the Word document as its default content type. If you, or your administrator, changed the default content type or created a document library based on a different content type, then clicking the New Document button creates whatever document type is set as the default content type. For example, if you set an Excel document as the default content type, then clicking New Document will create an Excel document.

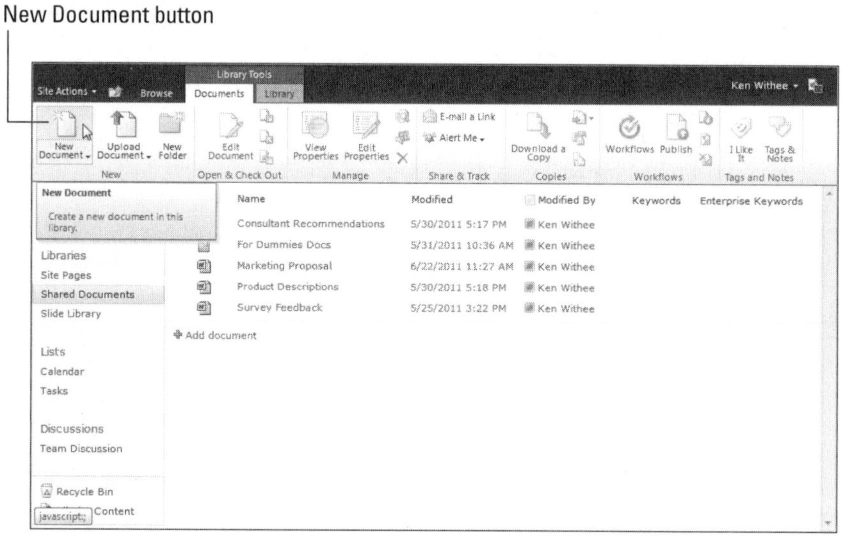

New Document button

Figure 11-6:
Creating
a new Word
document in
a SharePoint
document
library.

When you create a new document, SharePoint is smart enough to determine if you already have Microsoft Office Word installed locally on your computer. If you do have Word installed locally, then Word will open so that you can develop your document in the full-featured application. If you do not have Word installed, then the new Word document will open in the browser in edit mode so that you can develop your document by using the Word Web App.

After you have finished developing your application, you can save it. Doing this automatically saves it to the document library in which you created it. You can then click on the document to view it and then edit it further by using either the Word Web App or the local Word application running on your computer.

Editing and Reading Modes

The preceding section discussed working with Word documents in Editing Mode. There are times however when you simply want to read the document and not edit it. When you want to only read the document you can switch to Reading Mode, which looks very similar to a document that is printed on paper. A document in Reading Mode is shown in Figure 11-7.

Working with Advanced Functions

The Word Web App contains features beyond just adding and modifying text-based content. In particular, you can work with styles in order to standardize the look and feel of your document and tables to create rows and columns.

Styles

The styles let you format a document by selecting a predefined style rather than going through a manual process. For example, you may want your headings to be larger font and a different color. You can, of course, type the text and then highlight the text and make it bigger, and also change the color, but using this method is a lot of work for every heading. A style allows you to simply click the Heading style to make the change, as shown in Figure 11-8.

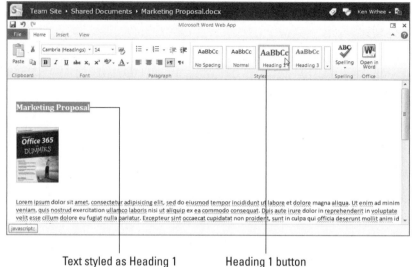

Figure 11-8:
Setting a
heading
style in
the Word
Web App.

Text styled as Heading 1   Heading 1 button

Tables

A table provides a mechanism for organizing content in your document. A table is divided into vertical columns and horizontal rows. You can insert a table with the Word Web App by following these steps:

1. **Click on the Insert tab.**

   The Insert tab displays the Ribbon that allows you to insert items into your document.

2. **Select the Table button.**

   When you select the Table button, you are presented with a grid that allows you to visually choose the number of rows and columns you want to include in your table, as shown in Figure 11-9.

3. **Highlight the number of rows and columns you desire for the table and then click the left mouse button.**

   The table is automatically inserted into the document.

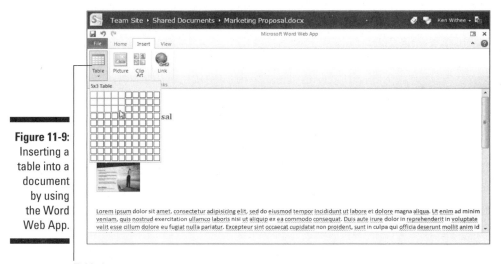

Figure 11-9:
Inserting a
table into a
document
by using
the Word
Web App.

Table button

After the table is created, you can add content to the cells of each column.
The table provides a lot of flexibility in the look and feel and layout of the
content in your Word document.

Chapter 12

Plunging into the Excel Web App

. . . .

In This Chapter

▶ Discovering how the Excel Web App differs from Excel

▶ Understanding some of the basic features of the Excel Web App

▶ Developing your understanding of Excel Web App functions and data manipulations

. . . .

> *The number one benefit of information technology is that it empowers*
> *people to do what they want to do. It lets people be creative. It lets people*
> *be productive. It lets people learn things they didn't think they could learn*
> *before, and so, in a sense, it is all about potential.*
>
> — Steve Ballmer

The Excel Web App is a new version of Excel that is part of the Office 365 offering. This new version of Excel runs as a web application in your web browser. Working with Excel as a web application has a number of benefits, including the simple fact that you don't need to have the full version of Excel installed on the computer you are using to edit your document. All you need is a web browser and access to your SharePoint site. You might be on a cruise or using a computer in a café or working from a shared computer at your organization. You can still work with your spreadsheets without having to have Excel installed on the computer you are using.

In this chapter, you explore some of the basic, as well as the more advanced, features of the Excel Web App and discover how it differs from the traditional version of Excel.

Comparing Excel Web App and Excel

Microsoft Office Excel is one of the most popular data analysis tools on the planet. By using Excel, you can enter numbers into a spreadsheet and use functions to manipulate them and perform analysis. In addition to analyzing numbers, Excel is often used for tracking and managing other data, such as customers, for example. In many organizations Excel has turned into a database-type application where all types of information is stored. Excel is what is known as a thick client in that it runs from your local computer. You click Start⇨All Programs and you browse to your office applications and you click Excel to fire up the program. Excel then runs on your computer. A web-based application, on the other hand, runs on a computer in a data center that you access over the Internet. If you use Hotmail for e-mail or browse a web page, then you are using a web application. The way you access a web application is by using a web browser, which is a program installed on your computer.

You will find that the Excel Web App is still Microsoft Excel but it does have some differences. For one thing, Excel runs on your computer, and Excel Web App runs out in the cloud and you access it by using your web browser.

When you create a document on your local computer with Excel, that document is stored locally on your computer. When you click the Save button to save a document, you are prompted for the directory on your local computer in which to save the file. You may save the file to your Desktop or any other folder on your computer. In any case, your creation is a physical file located on your local computer. When working with the Excel Web App, however, you do not have a local physical file. When you create a document and save it, your document lives on a computer in one of Microsoft's data centers. Because you don't know exactly which computer in which Microsoft data center, you can just say that the document lives out in the cloud. In the case of Office 365, your document lives within a SharePoint Online document library.

You don't have to be a subscriber to Office 365 to work with Excel Web App. You can use it for personal use for free with a Windows Live account.

Covering the Basics

Working with the Excel Web App is easy after you find your way around the interface. If you have used the traditional Excel application, then you can recognize that it is extremely similar and you won't have any trouble at all using the Excel Web App. If you've never used Excel, then you are in for a treat with the Excel Web App.

Using the Excel Web App interface

The Excel Web App interface is different from the traditional Excel application in that the web app runs within your web browser. The Ribbon at the top of the Excel Web App interface screen contains tabs, such as Home and Insert.

The Home tab contains common functionality in groupings, such as Clipboard, Font, Alignment, Number, Tables, Cells, Data, and Office, as shown in Figure 12-1.

Figure 12-1:
The Home tab on the Excel Web App Ribbon.

Table 12-1 describes the sections of the Home tab on the Excel Web App Ribbon.

Table 12-1	Features of the Home tab
Home Tab Section	*Description*
Clipboard	Allows you to cut, copy, and paste data between cells within the spreadsheet
Font	Allows you to adjust the font size and style
Alignment	Set the alignment of the data in the cells and allow text to wrap
Number	Change the formatting of numeric data
Tables	Sort and filter tables or access the table options
Cells	Insert or delete cells in the spreadsheet
Data	Find data in the spreadsheet or refresh any connections to external data
Office	Open the spreadsheet in Excel located on your local computer

The Insert tab allows you to insert a table or hyperlink into your Excel Web App document. A table allows you to manipulate data with functionality, such as sorting the data in ascending or descending order or filtering the data based on specific criteria. A hyperlink allows you to create clickable text that, when clicked, opens up a new website. For example, you can create a hyperlink with text that says "Learn More" that takes anyone viewing the Excel Web App document to a news article. The Insert tab is shown in Figure 12-2.

Figure 12-2:
The Insert tab on the Excel Web App ribbon.

In addition to the Ribbon tabs, the interface also includes a File menu. The File menu allows you to perform functionality, such as saving the document as a different name, opening the document in the traditional Excel application located on your computer, downloading a snapshot of the document, or downloading a copy of the document. The Excel Web App's File menu is shown in Figure 12-3.

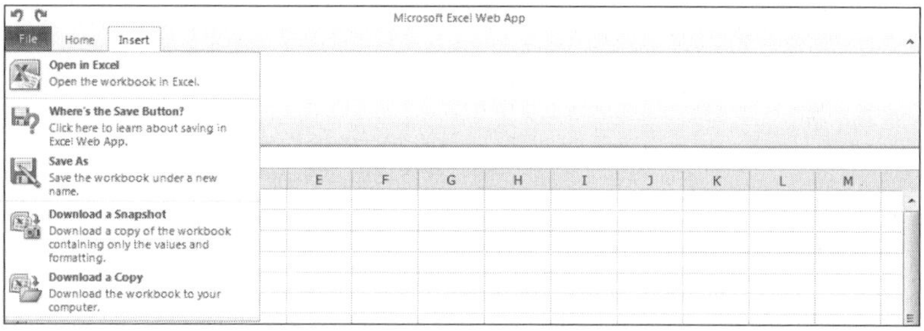

Figure 12-3:
The File menu on the Excel Web App interface.

Working with workbooks

Creating a new Excel document in a SharePoint document library is easy. On the Ribbon, click the Document tab and then click the New Document button, as shown in Figure 12-4.

Figure 12-4:
Creating a
new Excel
document in
SharePoint.

The New Document button is used to create a new document. The type of document that is created depends on the content type that is set as the default for the library. When you create a new document library, you can choose the type of content it will hold. If you choose Excel Spreadsheets as the type of document, then clicking the New Document button will create a new Excel document. If you choose Word Document, then clicking the New Document button will create a new Word document.

When you create a new document, SharePoint is smart enough to determine if you already have Microsoft Office Excel installed locally on your computer. If you do have Excel installed locally, then Excel will open up so that you can develop your document in the full-featured application. If you do not have Excel installed, then the new Excel document will open in the browser in Editing Mode so that you can develop your document by using the Excel Web App.

After you have finished developing your spreadsheet, you can save it, which will automatically save it to the document library in which you created it. You can then click on the document to view it and then edit it further by using either the Excel Web App or the local Excel application running on your computer.

Editing and Reading Modes

There are times when you do not need to edit a document. For example, you might want to just view the latest spreadsheet report or show a colleague a set of data. The Excel Web App contains two different modes. When you are editing the document you are using Editing Mode. When you want to read the document, you can simply click it in SharePoint to open it and view it. This reading view is called Reading Mode, which looks very similar to a document that is printed on paper. A document in Reading Mode is shown in Figure 12-5.

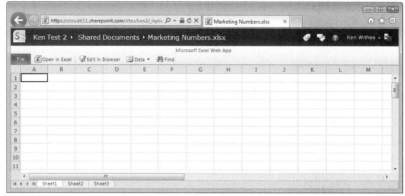

Figure 12-5:
An Excel
document
in Reading
Mode in
the Excel
Web App.

Using Advanced Features

In addition to the basic features that you will use in the Excel Web App, there are also some advanced features. In particular, you can work with formulas and functions, manipulate data, and even coauthor spreadsheets in real time in the cloud.

Adding functions

One of the primary reasons for the popularity of Excel as a data analysis tool is the seemingly endless supply of functions. A *function* is a bit of logic that performs some calculation or manipulates data in a certain way. For example, you may want a cell to display the addition of two other cells. You can use a simple plus (+) sign to accomplish this addition. Going farther, however, you might want a cell to display the current time. You can use a function, such as Now(), which would display the current time.

To enter a function in a cell, enter the equal (=) sign followed by the function. For example, to enter the Now() function, you type =Now(), as shown in Figure 12-6.

After you finish entering the function and press Enter, you will see the current time rather than the =Now() function in the cell. This simple yet powerful functionality is what lets users create very valuable and complex spreadsheets with minimal training.

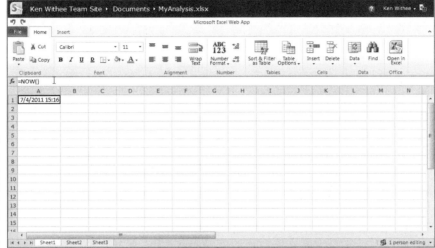

Figure 12-6:
Using
the Now()
function in
the Excel
Web App.

If you are following along, notice that as you begin to type the function, the Excel Web App automatically starts to show you all the functions and narrows in on the list of possible functions as you continue typing. This feature is useful when you cannot remember the exact name of the function but remember it starts with a specific letter.

An excellent list of the available Excel Web App functions listed by category is available on the Microsoft Office website at the following URL:

```
http://office.microsoft.com/en-us/excel-help/list-of-
        worksheet-functions-by-category-HP005204211.
        aspx
```

Manipulating data

The ability to manipulate data is a staple of Excel and continues in the Excel Web App. You can manipulate data by using functions or by creating your own formulas. Functions exist for manipulating numeric data and also text data. You can dynamically link the contents of a cell to other cells. For example, you might have a column for sales and a column for costs and then a third column that denotes profit by subtracting the costs column from the sales column. Using functions and mathematical equations, with nothing more than your web browser, you can quickly whip data into shape by using the Excel Web App.

Coauthoring workbooks in the cloud

One of the exciting new features found in the Excel Web App is the ability to coauthor spreadsheets with others in real time and at the same time. For example, imagine that you are in Seattle and your colleague is in Manila. You can edit the same document in real time by using the browser. When your colleague enters text or numeric data, you see it appear on your screen. Coauthoring allows for a much more productive experience because you are both editing the same document, which maintains a single version of the truth.

With a spreadsheet open in the Excel Web App, you can see the other users who are currently editing the document in the lower-right hand corner of the screen. For example, if two people are editing, you will see text that says "2 People Editing." If you click on this text, you will see the two users who are currently editing the spreadsheet, as shown in Figure 12-7.

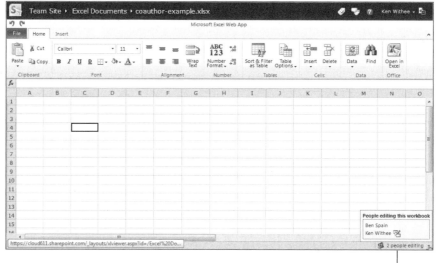

Figure 12-7:
Multiple people editing the same spreadsheet with the Excel Web App.

Multiple people editing

When one of the users makes change to the document, everyone who is currently viewing the document will see the changes take place in their view as well. This turns out to be an extremely useful feature because the new changes do not have to be e-mailed to other people in order for them to see the most recent version of the spreadsheet. The spreadsheet only exists in one place, so there is only one version of the truth for this spreadsheet.

Chapter 13

Powering Up the PowerPoint Web App

In This Chapter

▶ Understanding how PowerPoint has leveled the playing field for all

▶ Comparing the web app with its desktop cousin

▶ Applying basic PowerPoint Web App functions

> *"I don't believe in death by PowerPoint. PowerPoint is a powerful tool to support your story. I do believe in death by people who create PowerPoint. The software is not the problem. It's the person behind the keyboard. Think like an artist and your PowerPoint presentations will truly look like works of art."*
>
> — Carmine Gallo, Communications Coach

*W*hether you like or loathe PowerPoint, there is no denying that it is here to stay. It has leveled the playing field for anyone who understands his audience — including students, small-business professionals, and big-business executives. The new version of the software comes loaded with advanced features for animating text and graphics, video editing, and even broadcasting slide shows!

In Office 365, PowerPoint Web App is a component of the Office Web Apps services available in both the professional and small business plan (P plan) and the enterprise plan (E plan).

The web app combines a variety of web services to display high-fidelity presentations on a browser. This is a boon of some organizations that may have users without access to the desktop application.

In this chapter, you explore the basics of PowerPoint Web App, compare the user experience between the web app and it's desktop companion, and get started on using the web app interface.

After you become familiar with the basic functions, step up to the next level by applying advanced capabilities like the Broadcast Slide Show feature. We don't want you to compromise the quality of your presentations, so in this chapter, we include tips and tricks for taming bullets, lists, alignments, and graphics in PowerPoint Web App.

Going Over the Basics

Opening a file in the PowerPoint Web App initiates a series of processes and services in the backend to give you the best viewing experience for your presentation. Images, HTML, JavaScript, and Silverlight (if installed) all come together to render your document in high fidelity, giving you the familiar user interface you experience in the desktop application.

When you click on a PowerPoint file from your SharePoint Online document library, the PowerPoint Web App displays your presentation in Reading View. If the slide has animation or transition, you can see those effects in the Reading View. You can choose to open the presentation in your desktop PowerPoint application, edit the presentation right in the browser, or immediately start the slide show.

Comparing the PowerPoint Web App and PowerPoint 2010

The PowerPoint Web App is designed to be a companion to it's desktop cousin, PowerPoint 2010. It allows users to collaborate on files and make light edits to a presentation right on the browser regardless of the user's platform (Windows PC or Mac).

As long as the minimum system requirements are met and a supported browser is used, you can expect to perform most of the basic PowerPoint tasks on the web app that you do on the desktop version.

Due to technological constraints, and because by design PowerPoint Web App is a companion and not necessarily a replacement for the desktop version, there are features in the desktop application that are not available in the web app version as follows:

✔ **Macros:** Macro-enabled documents created in PowerPoint 2010 can be viewed in the web app but the macros will not run. Also, you can't edit a macro-enabled document in the web app.

✔ **Printing:** As of this book's writing, printing directly from the PowerPoint Web App in Office 365 is not enabled. If you are using Windows Live Sky Drive, however, you can print PowerPoint slides by using a .pdf reader.

✔ **Coauthoring:** You cannot coauthor in the web app through the browser as you would in the desktop application. For example, if you have two users working on the same file on their desktop applications, both users can see each other's changes but not in the web app.

✔ **Buttons and Commands:** The Ribbon in the web app has the same look and feel as the desktop application but with fewer buttons and options. In the Editing View, for example, only a limited number of fonts and formatting options are available. Fortunately, the fonts display in full what-you-see-is-what-you-get (WYSIWYG) glory, albeit with a very short lag.

Familiar right-click commands in the desktop application are nonexistent in the web app. It's funny, because the web app display is so similar to the desktop app that you might end up right-clicking the slides to change the slide layout when working on the web app, only to be reminded that feature is not there! The same thing goes for formatting text or graphics with your right mouse button.

✔ **Navigation:** In PowerPoint Web App, the Previous and Next slide buttons are displayed in the middle of the status bar. In the desktop application, they are displayed on the bottom right in the Reading View.

✔ **Smart Art:** Be aware that in the web app, options of Smart Art are limited. You do not get an array of graphics to choose from that are grouped by type as you do in the desktop version.

✔ **Design Templates:** You cannot apply a design template nor create one in the PowerPoint web app. Adding or inserting transitions, animations, tables, audio, video, and symbols are some features that are missing in the web app version. We believe that as Office 365 web apps continue to evolve, some or all of these features will become available in the future.

Using the PowerPoint Web App user interface

As a default, the PowerPoint Web App opens files in Reading View and runs animations and transitions that are embedded on the slide. Immediately after the file is loaded on the web app, you have access to commands that allow you to access the File menu, open the file in the PowerPoint desktop application, edit the file on the browser, or start a slide show (see Figure 13-1).

Figure 13-1:
PowerPoint
Web App
user
interface.

When you click the Edit in Browser command, you are taken to the Home tab on the Ribbon. You see some familiar editing buttons and icons that enable you to format text and paragraphs, navigate and manipulate slides, and access the cut, copy, and paste icons (see Figure 13-2). Editing the file in the rich desktop application is a one-click action from the Home tab with the Open in PowerPoint icon.

Thumbnails of your slides are displayed on the left. You can jump from one slide to another by clicking the thumbnail, change the order by dragging and dropping the thumbnails, and duplicate or hide slides by selecting them and clicking the appropriate icon on the Ribbon.

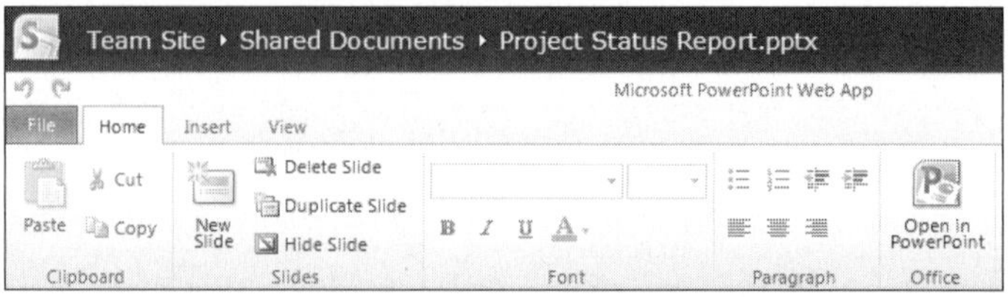

Figure 13-2:
PowerPoint
Web App
Home tab.

Inserting pictures, SmartArt graphics, and links are done in the Insert tab as you would in the desktop application. As shown in Figure 13-3, the web app user interface does not have as many buttons in the Insert tab as in the desktop application.

Figure 13-3: PowerPoint Web App Insert tab versus PowerPoint 2010 Insert tab.

The View tab in PowerPoint Web App displays only four buttons: Editing View, Reading View, Slide Show, and Notes. Clicking the Notes icon will toggle the display of your slide notes on and off. Figure 13-4 gives you an idea of the richness of the View tab in the desktop application versus the web app.

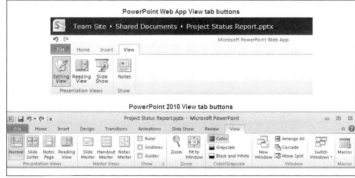

Figure 13-4: PowerPoint Web app View tab versus PowerPoint 2010 View tab.

Working with presentations

In the professional and small business subscription plan, you create a new presentation with the PowerPoint Web App as follows:

1. **Click the PowerPoint icon from the portal.**

2. **Enter a filename at the prompt.**

3. **Click OK.**

After you click OK, the web app will launch and you can start editing your presentation on the browser. Your file will be saved in the default team site document library called Documents.

In the mid-size businesses and enterprise plans (E plans), there are no web app icons on the portal. Creating a new presentation requires opening the PowerPoint 2010 desktop application. After creating the document, add it to your document library so that you and others can view and edit the presentation by using the PowerPoint Web App.

Alternatively, you can add the PowerPoint content type in your document library so that you can create presentations right from SharePoint Online.

The story behind the Reading View

Few people realize the thoughtful considerations that went behind the default Reading View in the PowerPoint Web App. Microsoft has gone to a lot of trouble to come up with the best experience for people who are accessing presentations online.

Let's say, for example, a colleague gave you a PowerPoint file of an earlier presentation you had missed. You probably would want to view the file in Normal view so you would see the speaker's notes. In doing that, however, you wouldn't see the transitions and animations embedded on the slide. If you viewed the file in Slide Show mode, you may not have context on the bullet points and images on the slides, which are noted in the speaker's notes.

PowerPoint Web App solves this problem by creating a Reading View (in addition to Editing and Slide Show Views) that displays slides with animation and transitions, as well as a control for showing or hiding the notes. You can easily navigate through the slides with the Previous and Next Slide buttons in the middle of the status bar. If you have the Silverlight plug-in installed, your presentation will automatically resize to fit the size of your window. Not only that, you are also presented with quick access to the Editing and the Slide Show Views on the Ribbon.

Note that in the Reading View, the Previous and Next buttons are displayed in the middle of the status bar. In the Slide Show view, you need to hover your mouse over the bottom-left corner to display the Previous and Next buttons.

The File menu in the Reading and Editing Views are a little bit different. In the former, one of the three commands in the File drop-down menu is the ability to view the presentation in Outline view. In the latter, the Outline View command is missing and is replaced with a Where's the Save Button? Command.

Content types, as well as instructions for adding them to your site collection, are discussed in detail in Chapter 8.

Editing presentations is as easy as clicking the Edit in Browser button from the Reading View when your document is loaded on the page.

There is no Save button in the PowerPoint web app — your file is saved automatically.

To close an open presentation, click File from the menu in the Editing View and then click Close.

Using Advanced Functions

Despite its reputation for "light editing only," PowerPoint Web App is not intended to hamper your creativity or stop you from producing the best-ever sales pitch. When you're on the run and need to spruce up your presentation with text formatting, SmartArt charts, or images, the web app does just fine. In addition, the new Broadcast Slide Show feature in Office 2010 uses PowerPoint Web App to run a live presentation to audiences anywhere on their browser and even on smartphones.

Broadcasting a slide show

With broadband Internet access becoming part of our daily lives, our ability to connect and collaborate efficiently with our colleagues has gotten a lot easier. The Office 2010 Broadcast Slide Show feature takes advantage of high-bandwidth networks to deliver almost full-fidelity slide shows for remote presenters and attendees.

In Office 365 where Office Web Apps is installed in a SharePoint environment, Broadcast Slide Show runs on the PowerPoint Web App technology. Being able to conduct ad hoc meetings and presentations with your colleagues, regardless of location, can mean savings for your business as you reduce the cost of travel, training, and conference services.

Step-by-step instructions on how to enable PowerPoint Broadcast Slide Shows by using Microsoft's PowerPoint Broadcast Services or your own company's private broadcasting service are discussed in Chapter 7. The process for broadcasting a slide show as outlined below, however, remains the same regardless of what service you use.

1. The presenter starts the broadcast from his PowerPoint 2010 desktop application.

2. The presenter is provided a URL that can be shared with others to connect to the slide show through the PowerPoint Web App.

3. The attendee follows the URL provided by the presenter through IM or e-mail.

4. The attendee sees the presentation on the browser in real time with transitions and animations synchronized with the presenter.

Adjusting alignments, bullets, and numbered lists

You find alignment, bullets, and numbering commands on the Home tab under the Paragraph group. Don't be alarmed when your bulleted or numbered list displays characters other than your template's styles. As soon as you click outside of the content placeholder, the default formatting you saw while editing the text is replaced with your template's style.

Two shortcut keys that may come in handy are the Tab and the Shift+ Tab keys. The Tab key indents your list to the right and the Shift+Tab key indents your list to the left.

Adding pictures and Smart Art graphics

To add pictures to your presentation from the PowerPoint Web App, click the picture icon in an empty placeholder on your slide. You are prompted to select a file from your hard drive. As soon as the picture is added to your slide, the Picture Tools Format tab displays, allowing you to further customize your picture.

You can also insert a picture through the Picture command on the Insert tab on the Ribbon.

To add a Smart Art graphic, click the Smart Art icon on an empty content placeholder and make your selection from the choices on the Ribbon. You can also add Smart Art graphics directly onto your slide through the Smart Art command on the Insert tab on the Ribbon.

Chapter 14

Figuring Out the OneNote Web App

In This Chapter

▶ Getting introduced to the OneNote technology

▶ Using OneNote Web App to drive productivity

▶ Searching and quickly finding information in OneNote

▶ Using tags to give your notes dimension

". . . The author of this article LOVES OneNote! His objectivity has been shattered by an application that can find sources he used a year ago in seconds, that records his voice notes on the same page as his written notes, and has made the 60 lbs. of notebooks threatening a home office shelf less necessary. Oh, yeah, it also catalogs his PAPER-BASED notebooks."

— Disclaimer in Brian Nelson's (writer and small
business owner, ArcticLlama, LLC)
blog about Microsoft OneNote

*M*icrosoft OneNote 2010 is a digital notebook perfect for gathering and storing all your notes, scribbles, e-mails, digital handwriting, audio and video recordings, research materials, links, and other types of digital information. When you use OneNote, you get the benefit of powerful search capabilities so you can quickly find the information you need from a single location. In addition, OneNote allows you to share your notebooks with others for easy and effective collaboration.

OneNote Web App is Microsoft OneNote's cloud cousin that comes bundled with Office Web Apps in Office 365. Like Word, Excel, and PowerPoint, the OneNote Web App allows you to create, view, and edit notebooks from a web browser.

In this chapter, you find out about the basics of Microsoft OneNote software. To set the right expectations, a comparison between the desktop application and the web app version of OneNote is covered in this chapter.

Instructions for tagging your notes, managing pages and sections, and restoring the previous version of a notebook are covered under the "Using Advanced Features" section of this chapter.

Exploring Basic Functions

With the release of the OneNote Web App, OneNote 2010 functionality and user experience are now extended to the Web, making it easy for users to collaborate anytime, anywhere.

Beyond than just browser-based editing, OneNote Web App enhances collaboration because it allows you to share your notebook online and lets others contribute to it without worrying about what version of OneNote they are using. This and much more is a good reason for you to start using this technology for your business or organization.

Introduction to Microsoft OneNote

Microsoft OneNote is a beefed-up word processing program. You can enter text and graphics to gather, organize, search, and share literally anything you can think of — meeting notes, ideas, references, instructions, brainstorms, and so on. Unlike word processors, however, OneNote lets you input free-form sketches, add unbound text, insert screen captures, and record audio and video directly into any section of the application's page.

Information in OneNote is stored as a page that becomes a part of a section belonging to a notebook, as shown in see Figure 14-1. A notebook can be like a binder you use to keep track of your personal activities with tabs for home remodeling, finances, and events. In the home remodeling tab, you would have pages with a link to your house plan, contact information, drawings and sketches, photos of lighting and fixtures.

Because you can have multiple notebooks in OneNote, in essence, OneNote is all you need to be efficient and productive at home, at school, and at work.

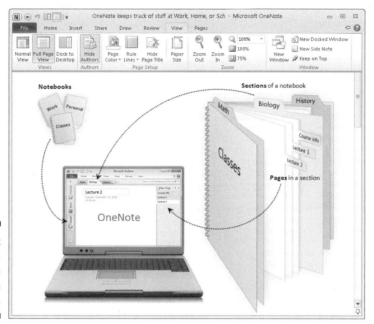

Figure 14-1:
How infor-
mation in
OneNote is
organized.

A great example of how to use OneNote at work is for getting new employees up to speed. With a new employee handbook in OneNote, you can have
a living document that contains critical information to help speed up a new
employee's onboarding time. Figure 14-2 illustrates how in a notebook you can
have several sections (Welcome, Culture, Structure, for example) and under
each section, you can have several pages (see Table of Contents, General
Information, Message from the CEO on the right). Notice how neatly the CEO's
message is integrated with his photo and an audio version of the message. If a
new CEO were to join the company, updating the page is easy and eliminates
the need (and the waste) of printing new employee handbooks.

One of our favorite features in OneNote is the search capability. Using the
search box, you can quickly find content based on keywords, jump to a page
based on text on within the pictures, and even find your handwritten notes!

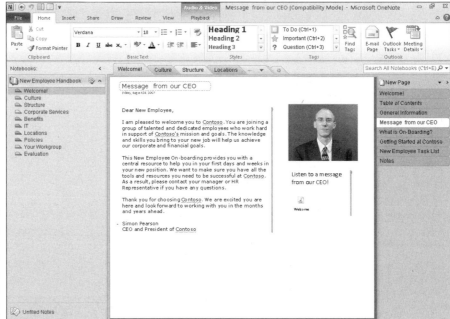

Figure 14-2:
Create
the new
employee
handbook in
OneNote.

Comparing OneNote Web App and OneNote 2010

OneNote Web App is the online companion of the rich desktop OneNote application. Both versions share a similar user interface, making it easy for users to quickly get started using the web app with little or no learning curve. Because OneNote Web App is browser based, most users with light editing and collaborating needs can get by without the desktop version. You can create and edit OneNote documents with the web app regardless of your platform (PC or Mac) or your browser (Internet Explorer, Safari, or Firefox). Documents are displayed on the web app in high fidelity, providing users with the same clarity and formatting as in the desktop application. Coauthoring in the web app is a snap because users can see each other's entries in real time.

When using the OneNote Web, App be mindful of the following differences between the web app and the desktop version:

  ✔ **Audio and Video Capabilities:** Because it is meant as a companion — not a replacement — OneNote Web App has limitations. For example, opening a page with audio or video in the web app displays a message in the notification bar warning you that the page contains items that cannot be displayed. You can still view and edit the page, but you cannot play the audio or video. The audio and video icons on the page are replaced with the text [File] in gray highlight.

✔ **Shapes, Images, and Tables:** You can't insert shapes on pages in the web app, but you can insert tables, pictures, clip art, and hyperlinks. Your handwritten notes or digital ink from the desktop OneNote application are displayed as an unknown object in the web app.

✔ **Protection:** Password-protected sections are not displayed in the web app. You are prompted, however, to open the notebook in the desktop application so that you can enter the password and view the sections.

✔ **Search** functionality is not available in the web app, although you can use your browser's "find" function (CTRL + F) to find keywords on the page that is currently open.

✔ **Text Editing:** Basic text editing in the web app is pretty good. You can change fonts, apply formatting, and select styles. Unfortunately, the handy Format Painter feature is not available in the web app.

Despite its limitations, OneNote Web App still wins hands-down compared to the competition in terms of boosting productivity in an organization. The mere fact that it allows users to access their notebooks from the cloud, share them, collaborate with others in real time, view version histories, find recent edits, see who made the edits, and sync with SharePoint online is not bad for a free app.

If you do have the OneNote 2010 client, you may be pleased to know that you have at your fingertips access to the following new features:

✔ Multilevel subpages that can be collapsed

✔ Dock to desktop command from the View menu, which is handy when you're trying to grab links and contents from external sources like the web or other applications

✔ Send content from the web pages to a section or page in OneNote complete with links!

✔ Ability to link to other notes — wiki anyone?

✔ Auto link notes to web pages and documents

✔ Quick access to the style sheet for formatting headings

✔ Ability to insert math functions

✔ Ability to quickly create tasks in Outlook from OneNote

Using the OneNote Web App interface

OneNote Web App's browser-based experience is a pared-down version of the OneNote 2010 user interface. By using a combination of HTML and JavaScript, the app renders a OneNote notebook in the browser that is ready for the user to edit and manipulate. Accessing more commands and features from the rich desktop application is as easy as clicking the Open in OneNote icon on the Home tab or choosing it from the drop-down menu on the File tab.

You find four tabs on the Ribbon in the web app: File, Home, Insert, and View (see Figure 14-3). Unlike the rest of the tabs, the File tab displays three drop-down menus to choose from: Open in One Note, Where's the Save Button?, and Close. There is no Save button in the web app — your notebook is automatically saved.

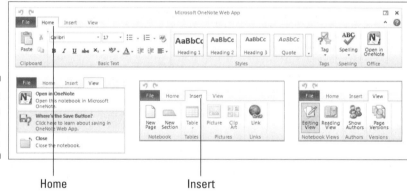

Figure 14-3: OneNote Web App Ribbon tabs.

Home

Insert

Sections in the web app are displayed on the left navigation pane similar to the desktop application. Pages within the sections, however, are displayed right below the section in the web app, unlike the desktop app where pages are displayed on the right navigation pane. Clicking the section in the web app hides or unhides the pages below the section. Clicking a password-protected section displays an error message with a prompt to open the section in the desktop application.

Working with notebooks

If OneNote is one of the content types available in your document library, creating a new notebook is easy. To do so, follow these steps:

1. **From the Library Tools on the Ribbon, click the Documents tab⇨New Document and then select OneNote content type (see Figure 14-4).**

   The default OneNote template starts unpacking and you are prompted to enter a name for your new notebook.

2. **Enter a name and click Create.**

   Your new notebook opens in OneNote 2010 with a new section and a new untitled page under the section.

Back at your document library in SharePoint Online, your new notebook is listed as one of the items in the library. When you click on the item, OneNote Web App displays your notebook with the default new section and an untitled page below the section.

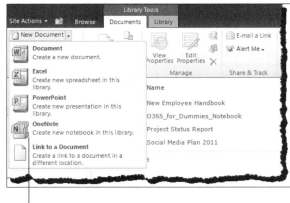

Figure 14-4: Creating a new notebook from a document library.

OneNote content type

If OneNote is not one of the content types listed in your document library, you first need to create your notebook in the desktop application and then upload the file into your document library. Chapter 8 provides an overview of content types and instructions on how to add content types to your document library.

OneNote Web App opens a notebook in Edit mode by default. You can immediately make changes to your notebook and as you type, your changes are saved automatically. If another user opens the same notebook in either the web app or the desktop application, simultaneous coauthoring automatically begins. Changes made by each of the authors will be synchronized in near real time.

To close the notebook, click File from the menu and then select Close.

The Editing and Reading Views

In the Editing View, clicking the View tab presents the user with more options for interacting with the online notebook. Within this tab, you can switch from the Editing View to the Reading View. Clicking the Show Authors icon displays the notes on the current page with a bracket on the right, indicating the author of the content. Clicking the Page Versions icon displays all the page's versions with a time stamp and the author's name right below the page name. You can toggle between displaying and hiding the page versions by clicking the Page Versions icon to turn it on or off.

In the Reading View, the web app displays four commands on the toolbar: File, Open in OneNote, Edit in Browser, and Show Authors. Because there are no changes to be saved in the Reading View, clicking the File command only brings up two options: Open in OneNote and Close.

Using Advanced Features

Just because OneNote Web App is a pared-down version of its desktop counterpart doesn't mean that you can't get fancy with it. There is no shortage of creative ways to give your notebooks the wow factor. Although you're having fun being creative, save some time and get things done faster by using the shortcuts available in the web app.

Tagging and proofing your notes

You can use a variety of tags to give your notes another dimension, as shown in Figure 14-5.

Use the following keyboard shortcut keys to easily assign tags to your notes.

- Ctrl + 1 tags your note with To Do
- Ctrl + 2 tags your note as Important
- Ctrl + 3 tags your note with a Question
- Ctrl + 4 tags your note with Remember for later
- Ctrl + 5 tags your note with Definition
- Ctrl + 6 tags your note with Highlight
- Ctrl + 7 tags with note as a Contact

✔ Ctrl + 8 tags your note as an Address

✔ Ctrl + 9 tags your note as a Phone number

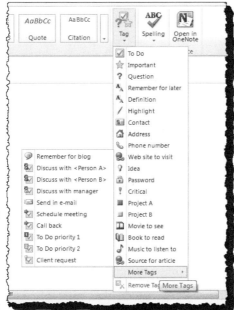

Figure 14-5:
Tags
available
in OneNote
Web App.

Similar to Microsoft Word, OneNote Web App automatically checks your spelling as you type. A wavy red underline displays beneath misspelled words and typical Auto Correct actions are applied, including correcting misspellings and converting characters to symbols. If you click the down arrow below the Spelling icon on the Home tab, you have the option to choose the dictionary for the proofing language by selecting Set Proofing Language.

Managing pages and sections

To add a new page in a section, you can use the following three ways:

✔ Click the New Page icon in the left navigation pane to the right of the section name (see Figure 14-6).

✔ Right-click the section name and select New Page.

✔ Go to the Insert tab and then select the New Page icon.

The last two options for adding a new page is also the procedure for adding a new section.

Figure 14-6:
Adding a
new page
with the
New Page
icon.

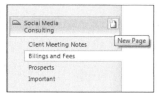

Right-click a section name to rename or delete the section. Right-clicking a page name brings up a window that allows you to delete the page, promote or demote pages if you have subpages within the section, show versions of the page, and copy a link to the page.

Viewing and restoring page versions

Sometimes coauthoring notebooks with other users can create undesirable results. For example, say a co-worker overwrote your carefully worded instructions in your onboarding notebook for new employees. Not to worry. A page version is saved every time someone edits a shared notebook. OneNote Web App allows you to view, restore, or delete previous versions of the page. To do this, follow these steps:

1. **Go to the View tab and click the Page Versions icon.**

   You see a list of all the page versions listed under the page name on the left pane with a date stamp and the author's name.

2. **Click any of the versions to view it.**

3. **After you determine the right version to restore, right-click the versions to display the option to hide, restore, or delete it.**

   When you click on a previous version, you see a notification bar at the top of the page indicating that the version is read-only.

Inserting pictures, tables, and hyperlinks

A picture is worth a thousand words, so why not add pictures to your notes? If you're more of a data person, use tables to organize information in columns and rows. Need to share a link but don't want to display gobbledygook? No worries, the Link command is here to save the day.

Popping in pictures

You can insert pictures from a file in your hard drive or add ClipArt from Office.com.

You can access the Picture icon from the Insert tab of the web app. When you select a picture in your page, the Picture Tools Format tab appears, providing you with options to scale or resize your picture or to enter an alternative text to represent your picture if, for some reason, it can't be viewed.

Creating tables

To insert a table, go to the Insert tab and click the Table icon. Hover your mouse over the grid and select the number of columns and rows you want to add. The Table Tools Layout tab appears, giving you additional options to manipulate your table like table, column, row, and cell selection; deleting tables, columns, and rows; adding rows above or below the selection or adding columns to the left or right of the selection; hiding table borders; and aligning the text within the cells left, right, or center.

Adding links

You can insert a link by using two methods:

- Go to the Insert tab and click the Links icon. A window appears, prompting you to enter the URL and the text to display for the URL.
- Use the keyboard shortcut by pressing Crl + K to open the same pop-up window.

Part V

Instant Messaging and Online Meetings

The 5th Wave   By Rich Tennant

"I hate when you bring 'Office' with you on camping trips."

In this part . . .

This part walks you through the wonderful world of instant communication and ad-hoc meetings. Making everything possible is an Office 365 component known as Lync Online. The Lync product is a new spin on a very useful product. In the past, Live Meeting was known to provide instant online meetings but now Live Meeting, and a whole lot more, has been rolled into a new product called Lync. You can walk through the Lync product and discover how presence information throughout the Office 365 applications can keep you in instant communication with the key members of your organization. You take a look at how Lync is integrated with such products as SharePoint Online and Exchange Online. Finally, you get some hands on experience with the power of being connected in a very dispersed and disparate world.

Chapter 15

Getting Empowered by Lync Online

In This Chapter

▶ Understanding how Lync can make an impact in your organization

▶ Finding out about new ways to converse with your team members

▶ Integrating Lync with your familiar Office applications

▶ Running effective meetings by using Lync technology

> *"...I've come to a conclusion: Lync is rapidly emerging as Microsoft's next killer platform for channel partners... Assuming Lync maintains its current sales trajectories, it will become Microsoft's next $1 billion application business. That fact alone warrants your attention."*
>
> — Joe Panettieri, Executive VP and Co-founder, Nine Lives Media Inc.

*T*rue to Microsoft's vision to transform communication and collaboration with software, Lync is a combination of the words *link* and *sync*. Lync is a unifying system that empowers businesses and organizations to reach a new level in their quest for an integrated, effective, and efficient means of communicating, collaborating, and connecting.

In this chapter, you discover the benefits of using this next-generation cloud communication service from Microsoft. You find out a new meaning of the word *presence* as it applies to Office 365 technologies. As you become familiar with the application, take your organization to the next level of collaboration by integrating Lync technology with Exchange Online and SharePoint Online.

We include a list of best practices for a successful Lync meeting in this chapter, so check it out impress your colleagues with your efficiency and effectiveness in your next online meeting!

Benefitting from Lync Online

Lync Online is available in both theprofessional and small business (P) and enterprise (E) plans in Office 365. The features include instant messaging (IM), audio, and video calls, presence, online meetings, online presentations, and the ability to connect with Windows Live Messenger contacts and other external users running Lync. The technology is integrated throughout the Office 2010 applications, as well as SharePoint Online, which means that you can quickly view your co-worker's presence status and initiate a conversation without leaving the Office application or SharePoint site. What this means for your organization is access to an intuitive interface guaranteed to keep your team connected by using the latest and up-to-date software subscription service.

To use Lync Online, end users need to install the desktop client, Microsoft Lync 2010. The desktop client is available as a free download from the Microsoft Office 365 portal.

External users who do not have an Office 365 account can still attend online meetings by using Lync Web App, a browser-based version of Lync 2010. It come with limited features and requires the latest version of Microsoft Silverlight installed. If Silverlight is not installed, the user will be prompted for installation.

For Windows users, all in-meeting features are available in Lync Web App except for computer audio/video capabilities and the ability to upload Microsoft PowerPoint presentations. It does not support features outside of the meeting experience, such as presence, contacts, IM, and telephony features.

If an external user needs the full-feature set of an in-meeting experience, such as audio/video capabilities and uploading PowerPoint presentations, have the user download and install the free Lync 2010 Attendee client. As with Lync Web App, Lync 2010 Attendee client does not support features outside of the meeting experience.

Connecting you, your team, and your work

Stay current with what's happening in your organization with one of the many features Lync has to offer. If you like the real-time connectedness found in social media applications, you may be pleased to know that status updates, IMs, content sharing, and groups are now part of the daily work environment through Lync.

One of the core principles for effective collaboration is knowing when others are available to communicate. If you are a member of a geographically distributed team, you probably have experienced the frustration of trying to repeatedly reach a co-worker in a different time zone by phone only to realize that he can't take your call because he's sound asleep.

Be frustrated no more. The next sections can help get you more connected to your co-workers so that you can do great work together.

Letting people know your presence status

Foster collaboration in your organization by giving your co-workers an at-a-glance status of your whereabouts and availability. Share what you're up to by entering text in the Personal Note section, as shown in Figure 15-1. You can enter text and hyperlinks in this section and your entries are displayed in the Activity Feeds, which provide real-time status of shared information within your organization.

Figure 15-1: Personal Note, Presence Status, and Location.

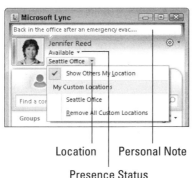

Location | Personal Note

Presence Status

Lync automatically displays your presence status based on your activity or Outlook calendar.

You can also manually update your status by selecting one of the following options from the Presence Status drop-down menu:

- ✔ Available (green): Online and can be contacted
- ✔ Busy (red): In a call or a meeting
- ✔ Do Not Disturb (maroon with a white bar in the middle): Filter conversation alerts only from Workgroup contacts

✔ Be Right Back (yellow): Stepping away from computer for a few moments

✔ Off Work (yellow): Not at work, can't be contacted

✔ Appear Away (yellow): Displays when computer is idle

✔ Out of Office (light gray with an asterisk at the bottom): On vacation or at work but not in the office

✔ Offline (light gray): Not signed in to Lync 2010

Your location displays information based on the network to which you are connected. Make your location meaningful by giving it a more descriptive name (Home, Office, or Work). You can create a custom location simply by typing into the Location bar and pressing Enter.

Starting a conversation

The contact card is a great way to initiate a conversation with a co-worker or your team members. In addition to your personal note, presence, and location, it also displays your organization information like your title and phone numbers.

To view the contact card, hover over a person's picture and click the chevron to see more options. After it is expanded, you can initiate an e-mail, an IM, a phone call, or start a video call.

If your contact is not listed, type your contact's name in the search box and select the appropriate contact from the search results.

A quick way to start a conversation if you don't need all the information from the contact card is to simply double-click your contact's listing. Doing this opens a new window with — by default — your mouse's cursor inside the IM box ready for you to type in your message.

If you don't have access to Lync 2010, double-click your colleague's name under the Contact List in Outlook Web App to start a conversation (see Figure 15-2). After you enter text in the message box and press Enter, your colleague will be notified that you are trying to start a conversation.

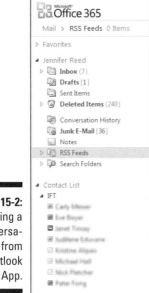

Managing contacts and conversations

Lync helps you manage your contacts by populating the Frequent Contacts group with contacts based on recent conversations. You can manually add your favorite contact to this group by typing the person's name in the search box, right-clicking the person's name, and then selecting Pin to Frequent Contacts.

One of the four areas of notification in Lync, shown in Figure 15-3, is the Conversations area. This area shows your past and present conversations with a contact. You can view any of the conversations without leaving Lync.

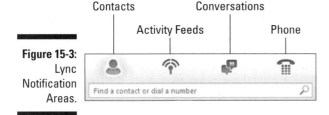

Lync Integration with Outlook and SharePoint Online

Lync seamlessly integrates with Outlook and SharePoint Online so that you can view your contact's presence and easily start a conversation from within Outlook or SharePoint Online. If you hover over the contact's name or presence in an open e-mail, the contact card will pop up, allowing you to start a conversation. This feature is called *click-to-communicate*.

In SharePoint Online, Lync embeds the same presence indicator for users in a SharePoint site. If you have a task list in SharePoint, you can set it up so that the Assignees are displayed with the user's presence status. You can also add a web part that displays members of the site with their presence status. You can initiate an IM session by clicking the presence status of the user.

Conferencing and Collaborating with Lync

Conducting an effective online meeting regardless of the participants' locations is simple even for those who are not technically inclined. Scheduling online meetings and delivering presentations during the meeting do not necessitate a steep learning curve.

To schedule an online meeting, follow these steps:

1. **On the Home tab in Outlook, Click New Items⇨Online Meeting.**

   A new window pops up with your untitled meeting, complete with links and instructions for the participants attending your meeting.

2. **Complete the meeting information and then click the Send button.**

Alternatively, you can start an online meeting by going to the Calendar view, double-clicking the time you want to have the meeting, and then clicking Online Meeting in the toolbar.

If you plan to have any of the attendees deliver presentations or share any content during meetings, assign them presenter privileges for the meeting. By default, meeting organizers and assigned presenters are the only ones who can share content.

To customize the presenter options, do the following.

1. **Create or open an existing online meeting in Outlook.**

2. **On the Ribbon, click Meeting Options (see Figure 15-4).**

Figure 15-4:
Customizing
Lync
Meeting
Options.

3. **In the Online Meeting Options window, choose the appropriate access level to specify who gets directly into the meeting without waiting in the lobby under the Access group.**

4. **Choose an option for the presenters to specify who can share content and admit people to the meeting under the Presenters group.**

   If you select People I choose, click Manage Presenters to add Attendees to the Presenters list. Click OK after you add all the presenters.

5. **Click OK on the Online Meeting Options window.**

6. **Click the Send button to update the meeting.**

You can also promote and demote attendees to be presenters during the meeting. Right-click the attendee name from the People pane in your meeting and then click Make Presenter.

With presenter access, you can share your desktop, share one or more programs in your computers, deliver a presentation, conduct a poll, white board, and send files during the meeting. To start sharing content, click the Share drop-down menu and select your sharing option. A bar appears at the top of the screen with glow bars around the screen to indicate that you are now sharing content.

While sharing, you can give or take control back of your sharing session. Click the Give Control icon on the sharing bar at the top of the screen and then select the name of the person you want to give control. Note that this person can use his mouse and keyboard to control your shared content. To take back control, click Take Back Control on the Give Control menu.

Before you share your desktop, make sure that you close applications with confidential or personal information you don't want others to see.

Using voice and video features

Lync supports calls from computer to computer, computer to telephone, telephone to computer, computer to audio conference, and video calls and conferencing.

Making a call

To make a call, click Call on the person's contact card. The contact's work number is the default number dialed, but you can click the Call menu to select other numbers to call. You can manually enter a phone number to call by entering a phone number in the dial pad, which you can access from the Phone icon.

Answering a call

To answer a Lync call, click the notification icon (green phone) from the window that pops on your screen. The Conversation window appears and the call is started. You can direct the call to another number or decline the call by clicking on the appropriate link from the notification window.

Using best practices for a successful Lync meeting

Using Lync to conduct meetings, especially for participants who are distributed globally, can result in great savings for your organization. It reduces carbon footprint and is, therefore, good for the environment, and it gives your participants flexibility. You can attend productive meetings at all hours in your pajamas without losing credibility or compromising your professionalism.

Technology, however, can only do so much. Lync alone is not enough to ensure a successful meeting. Here are some best practices we've compiled from experience that you may want to consider.

- ✔ Wired networks provide for a better meeting experience than wireless connections. Audio quality is not optimal in wireless connections, so if you are speaking a lot, plan to be hard wired. Virtual Private Network (VPN) connections also affect audio quality negatively.

- ✔ Mute your audio unless you are speaking. Hearing a participant typing or a dog barking in the background is not cool.

✔ When you first join the meeting via Lync, your audio is automatically muted. This is not true when you join by phone. If you don't want your team members to hear you ordering Starbucks coffee during the meeting, you may want to use your phone's feature to mute the call.

✔ Have alternative means for connection in case you get disconnected. Have the dial-in number handy in case you get dropped off from the Lync conference.

✔ If you have multiple people in the same room, try to have only one computer logged in to the meeting to prevent audio feedback.

✔ If you are a presenter, load content prior to the meeting. Sometimes loading content can take time and you don't want to waste your participants' time by having them wait while the content is loaded.

✔ In the interest of respecting the participant's time, set up and test your audio devices before others arrive.

✔ The best screen display for sharing content is 1024 x 768 pixels.

Understanding the Lync Web App Join Experience

The Lync web app is a browser-based alternative for joining Lync online meetings. For it to work, the browser must have Silverlight enabled. Silverlight is a cross-browser (Internet Explorer, Safari, Chrome, and so on.), cross-platform (Mac, Windows, and Linux) plug-in that enhances user experience and the delivery of applications on the Internet.

Attending a meeting by using the web app is similar to attending the meeting by using the desktop client. The advantage of using the web app, however, is that the participants do not need to install additional software to attend and view online meeting presentations. When using the web app, you will not be able to use the Present a PowerPoint feature of Lync. In addition, voice and video capability is not yet available for the web app, so participants must connect to the audio portion of the meeting by using a dial-in number.

To join a Lync online meeting by using the web app, follow these steps:

1. **Open the Online Meeting invitation (see Figure 15-5).**

2. **Click the Join online meeting link or copy and paste the meeting URL into a browser.**

3. **Complete the onscreen information, such as your e-mail address, and click Join Meeting.**

4. **Enter your office or cellphone number on Phone Details and click Call Me.**

   The Online Meeting calls you and connects you to the conference.

Figure 15-5:
Lync
Web App
invitation.

Chapter 16

Your Presence Unlimited

In This Chapter

▶ Driving productivity

▶ Understanding how the Lync features work

▶ Working with the Presence Indicator

"Our team is more collaborative, and it's easier to stay in touch with presence. You can talk and solve problems in real time."

— Fabio Baglioni, MS Systems Engineer, Telecom Italia

*I*n today's frenetic and "always on" world, the only way to get ahead in the game is to stay connected with the right people who have the information you need when you need it. It used to be true that you also had to be at the right place at the right time; but not anymore. Unified Communications (UC) through Microsoft Lync changes all that.

If you do an Internet search for *unified communications*, be prepared to see a bunch of discussions about whose definition for UC is right. For this book's purpose, we offer a simple definition.

If it helps you create a seamless connection with people you need to be connected to inside or outside your organization in a way that increases collaboration and productivity, it is unified communications.

As you explore the practical application of the features available in Lync in this chapter, you will realize how Microsoft continues its tradition of building its brand around the magic of software with the rollout of Lync. And with that magic, your business undergoes a transformation for the better.

Understanding Why Presence Drives Productivity

When you are on the go, and especially if you work with a global team, timing isn't always perfect. But just because it isn't perfect doesn't mean that you have to miss out on business opportunities. Presence in Lync allows you to immediately connect with your co-workers to get the information you need whether face to face from your office, in the meeting room, or across the globe.

Exploring the Lync user interface

The Lync application is designed to be a beautiful and social experience for the users. The high-quality treatment of pictures enables you to have a sense of actually seeing the face of the person you are communicating with — a fundamental element of social interaction. The pictures displayed in Lync are picked up from your profile photo in the SharePoint Online My Site feature.

To the left of your picture, you find a vertical bar that shows the color of your presence state or status (see Figure 16-1). Your presence is automatically updated by the system. Based on your Outlook calendar appointments, your presence displays "In a meeting" if your calendar is blocked as busy, "Available" if your calendar is open, and "In a call" if you pick up your Lync phone to make a call.

Having the system automatically update your presence is important so that people you work with will be confident of your presence state. If presence state was manually updated and people forget to update their presence, then the confidence goes down and so will productivity.

Figure 16-1:
Lync
Presence
State.

Location, location, location

Another important feature of the Lync user interface is the Location feature (see Figure 16-2). This feature's social value is akin to Foursquare's location-based social networking and Facebook's check-in feature, which allow people to use global positioning systems (GPS) to let friends know where they are.

In Lync, you can enter your location manually or have the system automatically detect your location through wireless access points or the network to which you are connected.

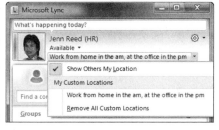

Figure 16-2:
Lync's
Location
feature.

Beyond just location-based social interaction, Location was built to support enhanced emergency services or E911 capabilities. The idea behind Lync is to ultimately replace the enterprise Private Branch Exchange (PBX) system. Having a feature that not only knows how to reach me, but also knows where I am in an emergency is real estate worth its gold in the compact Lync user interface.

Is my contact present? Looking for contacts in Lync

The Contact View allows you to immediately know your co-workers' presence. If you don't see the person for whom you're looking, enter a name in the search box to search for contacts from your organization's Active Directory, your Outlook contacts, and contacts from other organizations that are federated with your organization. (Microsoft has over 2,000 companies they federate with today.)

When you hover over a contact's listing, the contact card appears with more information to help you decide a course of action. For example, if your contact's status says "Looking forward to my vacation in 3 days...," you'll probably want to reach out to her sooner rather than later.

Monitor the presence of your team members by adding them to your contact list. You can give your contacts a group name and get creative in sorting and displaying the information. The only caveat is that you can't add more than 250 contacts to your Lync contacts list.

Working with ambient Activity Feed

Lync's tagline is about connecting people in new ways. The activity feeds feature (see Figure 16-3) achieves this end and is important so that workers can have an ambient sense of who's doing what, where, and when. Lync does a good job of rendering an enterprise version of Facebook's newsfeed, but better than Facebook, though, is the automatic updates a contact's feed will display if he changes office location or titles.

Figure 16-3:
Lync Activity
Feeds.

As if that weren't enough, Microsoft didn't stop there. You know how we all like the redial button on our phones? Lync's Activity Feeds is the mother of all redials. In the feed, you can see a conversation history of all your phone or video calls, instant messages, and conferences. With one click, you can pick an activity — no matter how old — and resurrect it. Doing this helps provide context to communications, especially if you pick up a conversation that is over a few days old and may have been forgotten.

Using the Soft Phone feature

If your Office 365 Enterprise subscription comes with the enterprise voice capability, your Lync user interface will display a phone icon along with the Contacts, Activity Feeds, and Conversations icons. With Lync's Soft Phone feature, shown in Figure 16-4, you can make and receive calls within the software. If you have voicemail, the phone icon will display a number to indicate how may voicemails you have. Within this feature, you can easily see who called and listen to the message they left. And because messages are stored in the Office 365 Exchange Online service, you can view the same message in Outlook and read the transcription of that message.

Figure 16-4:
Lync's Soft Phone feature.

Having your devices at your fingertips

Lync wouldn't be Lync if it didn't give you options. With that in mind, you can easily switch from any devices hooked up to your computer with one click (see Figure 16-5). Not only that, but you can check the audio device settings and even check call quality from within this little icon on the bottom-left corner of the Lync user interface. The rich telephony capability lets you switch the call to your cellphone or desk phone, forward your calls, set the ringer to ring both on your desk phone and on your computer, and a whole lot more!

Switch devices

Figure 16-5:
Switching
devices.

Presence Indicator in Office Applications

Lync embeds presence with both Office 2010 and Office 2007 applications. With this integration, you have access to the Click-to-Communicate feature that allows you to click on the presence and instantly initiate communication through Lync.

Click-to-Communicate through Lync from Outlook

Figure 16-6 shows the Click-to-Communicate buttons for Lync within Outlook. The IM icon gives you the option to Reply with IM or Reply to All with IM. The More button allows you to call the sender of the e-mail or call all the recipients of the e-mail in a conference — all within the Lync application.

To create an online meeting based on an e-mail, simply select the e-mail and then click the meeting icon. When a reminder pops up for an online meeting, you can simply click on the Join Online button to immediately join the meeting through Lync.

Shows presence status

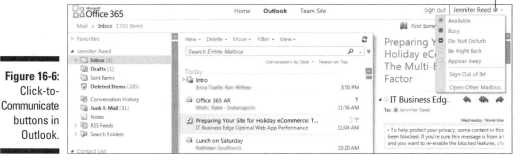

Figure 16-6:
Click-to-
Communicate
buttons in
Outlook.

Viewing presence status with Exchange Online and Outlook Web App

Lync is fully integrated with Exchange Online. Status updates based on Exchange calendar information, as well as out-of-office messages are also displayed in Outlook Web App, as shown in Figure 16-7).

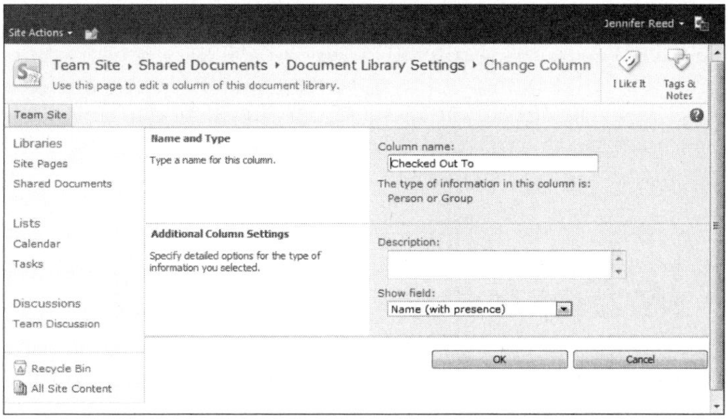

Figure 16-7:
Presence
in Outlook
Web App.

Locating presence in Word, Excel, and PowerPoint

When you collaborate on documents with your team members, it's super helpful to see your collaborator's presence without leaving the application you are currently using.

In either Word, Excel, or PowerPoint, you can view the presence of your document's authors and contributors and start a conversation as follows:

1. **Click File on the menu to go to the Backstage.**

2. **On the right pane within the Info navigation on the left, check out the Related People section.**

   There you see the name of the document's author and who modified it last.

3. **As with Outlook, click on the presence indicator to initiate communication with the contact.**

The Save & Send button in the Backstage view gives you the option to send the file by using the Instant Message (IM) feature in Lync.

Presence is also shown alongside names of contributors who are collaborating on the same document at the same time. For example, if co-workers Jane and Jill are editing the same document, Jane can see the sections Jill is working on indicated by Jill's name and her presence. If Jill locks a paragraph for editing and her presence indicates she is away, Jane can quickly IM Jill to ask her to unlock the paragraph. Without this feature, Jane may have to wait for minutes or hours and even days to be able to edit the locked paragraph.

Presence Indicator in SharePoint Lists and Libraries

There is an undeniable truth about working in this day and age: No one exists in a vacuum. We are all in a symbiotic relationship with interdependencies and personal connections. Lync's integration into SharePoint allows us to leverage those relationships and connections to work better together.

Presence is by default displayed with the user's name when you view SharePoint site permissions. By default, a presence is shown alongside a user's name when the Created by or Modified by columns are displayed in a SharePoint list or library. As with Outlook applications, clicking the presence indicator opens the contact card and gives you the option to send an e-mail, start an IM session, make a voice or video call, or share screen and white board.

Part VI
Preparing to Move

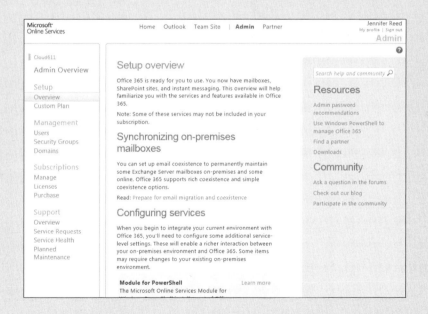

In this part . . .

This part takes you through the adoption process for moving into the Microsoft cloud. You get an overview of the requirements for Office 365. Because Office 365 is made up of a number of different components, you will explore requirements such as hardware, software, web browsers, and operating systems. You then find out what it takes to plan and implement Office 365 including data migration planning and rolling out users after the implementation is in place. Finally, you get an overview of what it takes to manage the Office 365 infrastructure. Luckily, Microsoft has created some very intuitive and user-friendly web interfaces that let administrators manage the enterprise software that makes up Office 365 without the headache.

Chapter 17

Meeting Office 365 Requirements

• •

In This Chapter

▶ Understanding the attraction the cloud offers

▶ Determining the pros and cons of the cloud

▶ Defining the requirements for Office 365

▶ Exploring the requirements for the components of Office 365

• •

> *Computing is not about computers any more. It is about living.*
>
> — Nicholas Negroponte

Moving from a nice and cozy on-site data center (or storage closet) to the cloud is a big change. You won't be able to walk through the server room and see all the computers with the lights flashing, disks whizzing, and screens glowing. You have a connection to the Internet, and the software and data live *out there* somewhere. To access your software, you begin by using it. You won't need to go through a lengthy installation and deployment process. It can take some time to get used to, but the change can be well worth the effort.

This chapter covers some of the pros and cons of moving to the cloud, as well as the specific requirements of the Microsoft Office 365 offering.

Cloud Attraction

One of the biggest pain points in the corporate world is the interaction between business users and tech people. The business users couldn't care less about technology and just want the ability to do their job easier and more efficiently. The tech folks want to provide the best solution possible for the business users but get bogged down with time-intensive technical tasks. This concept is illustrated in Figure 17-1.

Figure 17-1:
When infra-structure is on premise, IT spends time keeping the lights blinking green, and the business users spend time pester-ing the IT team for help.

The cloud attempts to alleviate this tension by offloading the infrastructure to someone else — Microsoft in the case of Office 365. This frees up the tech people and lets them spend time optimizing the software for their business users instead of keeping the lights blinking green. Business users are happy because they get a better solution, and IT people are happy because their valuable time is not wasted searching the Internet for instructions on installing and configuring the latest software patch to fix a particular problem. This new paradigm is illustrated in Figure 17-2.

Figure 17-2:
Using the cloud lets someone else handle the infra-structure, and lets the IT focus on the needs of the business users.

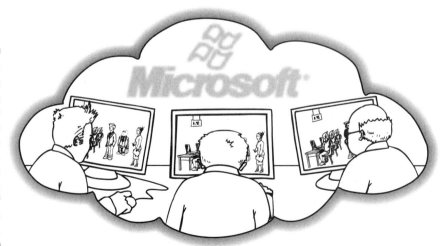

Offloading the work it takes to manage and maintain infrastructure allows you to repurpose resources to more valuable tasks, such as providing solutions that use software, including SharePoint to help sales.

Looking at the Pros and Cons of the Cloud

As with any decision in life, there are generally pros and cons; moving to the cloud is no exception. Depending on whom you are talking with, the cloud is either the greatest thing since the invention of the wheel or a devilish ploy by big companies to wrestle away control of your data. The truth is, many people find that the benefits of the cloud greatly outweigh the detriments.

Some of the benefits of moving to the Microsoft cloud include the following:

- ✔ Outsourcing the hassle of installing, managing, patching, and upgrading extremely complex software systems.

- ✔ Having predictable and known costs associated with adoption.

- ✔ Keeping the lights blinking green and the software up-to-date and secure falls on Microsoft and is backed by service guarantee.

- ✔ Reducing cost in not only immediate monetary value but also in efficiency and resource reallocation benefits.

- ✔ Backing up and securing your data. After all, Microsoft may not be perfect, but its teams of engineers are extremely specialized and are experts at hosting the software that their colleagues have developed.

- ✔ Using the software over the Internet — simply sign up and you're ready to go. Without the cloud, a SharePoint deployment could take months.

Some of the cons that come along with adopting a cloud solution in general include the following:

- ✔ Relying on network and bandwidth. If your Internet provider goes down, then you haven't any access to your enterprise software and data. Microsoft does not control how you access the Internet and, therefore, cannot account for any failures.

- ✔ Having data controlled by someone other than your employees. Your data is hosted in Microsoft's data center. That can be both a benefit and a detriment. If you feel uncomfortable with your data *out there* somewhere, then you can either research the Microsoft data centers further or keep your data and applications locally in your own controlled data center. In addition, when you sign up for enterprise licensing of Office 365, you also gain licensing rights to On Premise deployments. This capability makes it possible to store extremely sensitive data or user portals on site. For example, you may want your executive, accounting, and human resources portals on site but the rest of your SharePoint implementation in the cloud. Microsoft lets you mix and match this way to fit your comfort level.

Microsoft has invested billions of dollars in its state-of-the-art data centers and has gone to great lengths to calm the concern of not knowing where your data is located. For a great video on the Microsoft data centers, check out the video on YouTube by the MSGFSTeam titled "Microsoft GFS Datacenter Tour." You can find this video by searching for "MSGFSTeam" on YouTube and then looking for the specific video.

Overall Office 365 Requirements

Although by definition a cloud offering is available to anyone with an Internet connection, there are a few other requirements that must be observed should you choose to use Office 365. In particular, you must be located in a supported country and must have supported software and a high-speed Internet connection.

Geographic requirements

Microsoft has released Office 365 to a specific set of initial countries and will roll it out to the rest of the world in the future. Table 17-1 outlines the supported countries and the data center location that serves each country.

Table 17-1   Supported Countries and Data Center Locations

United States Data Center	Singapore Data Center	Ireland Data Center
Canada	Australia	Austria
Costa Rica	Hong Kong	Belgium
Columbia	India	Cyprus
Mexico	Japan	Czech Republic
Peru	Malaysia	Denmark
Puerto Rico	New Zealand	Finland
Trinidad and Tobago	Singapore	France
United States		Germany

United States Data Center	Singapore Data Center	Ireland Data Center
		Greece
		Hungary
		Ireland
		Israel
		Italy
		Luxembourg
		Netherlands
		Norway
		Poland
		Portugal
		Romania
		Spain
		Sweden
		Switzerland
		United Kingdom

Software requirements

To get the most out of Office 365, it is best to use Windows 7 with Office 2010 and the latest Internet Explorer browser. Doing this gives you the fully integrated experience. Office 365 does, however, support various software configurations, as shown Table 17-2.

Table 17-2	Office 365 Supported Software	
Operating Systems	**Web Browsers**	**Office Clients**
Windows XP SP3	Internet Explorer 7 +	Office 2007 SP2
Windows Vista SP2	Firefox 3 +	Office 2010
Windows 7	Safari 4 +	Office 2008 for Mac
Mac OS X 10.5 (Leopard)	Chrome 3 +	Office 2011 for Mac
Mac OS X 10.6 (Snow Leopard)		Lync 2010
Windows Server 2003		
Windows Server 2008		

A key feature of Office 365 provides the ability for your business's Active Directory instance to sync with your Office 365 account. To achieve this integration, however, your Active Directory domain must be a single forest.

Internet access requirements

Because the Office 365 software lives in a Microsoft data center and is accessed over the Internet, having high-speed Internet access available on a regular basis is important. For some of the components of Office 365, such as the Outlook Web App, high-speed Internet access is not required, but as a general rule, you want to make sure that your users have a pleasant experience and that equals a high-speed Internet connection when dealing with the cloud.

Understanding bandwidth

It definitely takes some time to get your mind wrapped around bandwidth. What exactly is bandwidth anyway? Trying to understand bandwidth can be like trying to understand warp speed in Star Trek. Nobody really understood what it was, but we knew that it made the Enterprise ship go very fast. Punch it, Scotty! Because bandwidth is such a fuzzy topic, it is best to use an analogy in order to understand it.

In a nutshell, bandwidth is the amount of data that can pass over a network at any given time. The best analogy for this is water moving through a hose or pipe. You can think of your data as a pool full of water. If you have a lot of it, such as those massive PDF documents, or 300-page PowerPoint presentations, then you have a lot of water. Say the amount of an Olympic-size swimming pool. If you have just a little, such as a two-page Notepad document, then you just have a small cereal bowl-size of water.

Now, to get that water from Point A to Point B, you need to pipe it through plumbing. If you have a massive 3-foot diameter pipe, then your water will move very quickly. If you have a garden hose, your water will move very slowly. This concept is illustrated in the figure.

The rate at which you can move water through the plumbing and data through the network is called bandwidth. The 3-foot diameter pipe provides high bandwidth and the garden hose provides a small amount of bandwidth. The trick with bandwidth is to remember that the least common denominator always wins. For example, in the water analogy, you might be moving that swimming pool full of water across town, but if the pump siphoning the water out of the pool is only a small hose that attaches to a 3-foot diameter pipe, then guess what — the water will only move as fast as the small hose can move it. The 3-foot pipe will just trickle the water along as it comes out of the small hose. On the other hand if you have a 3-foot pump to go along with that 3-foot hose, then the water will fly through the pipe at a rapid rate.

It is the same with data over the network. If you have a very slow wireless router in your house, then it doesn't matter how fast the Internet speed is coming in and out of your house.

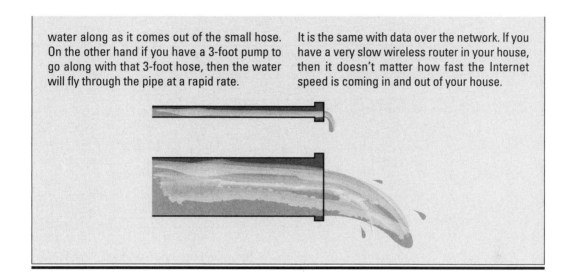

Because Office 365 can be accessed from any computer anywhere in the world with an Internet connection, you have no control over the network connectivity. The good news, however, is that the types of things your users will do from on the road are check e-mail, edit documents in the browser, or download a quick document from the SharePoint site — tasks that work fine with slower connection speeds (with the exception of downloading documents). Most users, however, understand that the speed of their Internet connection directly relates to the speed a document will download and will not blame the Office 365 service for a slow download.

Figuring Out Browser Requirements

There are many points of contact with Office 365, and depending on which computer you are using to access the cloud services, you will want to make sure that your web browser is supported. Table 17-3 summarizes the browser requirements for the Office Web Apps, Outlook Web App, and SharePoint Online.

Table 17-3	Office 365 Supported Browsers	
Office Web Apps	*Outlook Web App*	*SharePoint Online*
Internet Explorer 7 + (on Windows)	Internet Explorer 7 + (on Windows)	Internet Explorer 7 + (32-bit)
Firefox 3.5 + (on Windows, Mac, or Linux)	Firefox 3.0.1 + (on Windows, Mac, or Linux)	Internet Explorer 7 + (64-bit) [with some limitations]
Safari 4 + (on Mac)	Chrome 3.0.195.27 + (on Windows)	Firefox 3.6 + [with some limitations]
	Safari 3.1 + (on Mac)	Safari 4.04 + [with some limitations]

A light version of Outlook Web App exists if you happen to find yourself using or borrowing a computer that does not meet the minimum requirements for the full-featured experience. The light version also loads much faster and is useful if you are temporarily using a very slow Internet connection. Even though the light version is not as feature rich as the full version, it accomplishes the basic tasks of e-mail very well.

For a detailed list of the limitations per browser when working with SharePoint, check out the Microsoft TechNet article at the following URL:

`http://technet.microsoft.com/en-us/library/cc263526.aspx`

Lync Requirements

As we cover in Part V, Lync is a powerful communication platform that is used for online meetings and instant communication. Lync installs as a client on your computer and has its own requirements for installation. Table 17-4 outlines the Lync installation requirements.

Table 17-4	Lync Installation Requirements		
Operating System	*Processors*	*Memory*	*Browser*
Windows 7	Intel Pentium 4 +	2 gigabytes (Windows 7 or Windows Vista)	Internet Explorer 7 +
Windows Vista	AMD Athlon 64 +	1 gigabyte (Windows XP)	Mozilla Firefox 3.0.1 +
Windows XP with SP3 or later			
Windows Server 2008 with SP2 or later			
Windows Server 2003 with SP2 or later			

If you are using an authenticated HTTP proxy with Exchange Online, then you will need to use Internet Explorer 8 or higher. In addition, for video, the processor requirement is at least a dual core 1.9 GHz, quad core 2.0 GHz processor, or the latest version of VGA or HD.

In addition to installation requirements, Lync uses a high amount of bandwidth for communication using voice, video, and screen sharing. For these reasons, Microsoft recommends a fairly robust computer setup with at least a 128 megabyte graphics card and a microphone, speakers, and webcam. For more specific and up-to-date requirements check out the Lync requirements page at the following URL:

```
http://technet.microsoft.com/en-us/library/gg412781.aspx
```

Chapter 18

Planning for Your Office 365 Implementation

. . . .

In This Chapter

▶ Gaining an understanding of the Office 365 plans

▶ Understanding the Office 365 deployment process

▶ Planning and preparing to deploy

▶ Determining how best to work with an implementation partner

. . . .

A journey of a thousand miles begins with a single step.

— Lao Tzu

Reading this book is the first step of preparing for your Office 365 journey. Throughout the book, we explain how Office 365 can benefit your organization. Now that you are up to speed on the product, you can plan your implementation.

In this chapter, you find information for planning your Office 365 implementation. You walk through preparing and then planning for deploying Office 365, including such tasks as choosing a plan, cataloging your internal resources, and finding a partner.

Choosing an Office 365 Plan

The advantage to a product, such as Office 365, living in the cloud is that it is available for organizations of all sizes and shapes. The disadvantage, however, is that all those organizations have different needs. Microsoft decided to break the Office 365 product down into three primary plans to suit the needs of all organizations. These plans are:

- ✔ Professionals or small business: Designed for organizations from 1 to 50 people
- ✔ Large and mid-size customers: Designed for organizations with 50+ people all the way up to tens of thousands of people
- ✔ Educational institutions: Designed specifically for educational organizations

The professionals or small business plan is very simple and is only $6 per month. The large and mid-size customer plan, however, is broken down into a number of options, with some options designed for kiosk workers or those who are not sitting at a desk regularly. The educational plan is paid on a per-case basis, and we recommend that you contact Microsoft for details that relate to your particular institution.

The products and features associated with each plan are outlined in Table 18-1. Note that the plan for professionals and small business is denoted as P1 and the plan types for enterprise customers are denoted E1 through E4. The enterprise plan also includes a kiosk worker type, which is denoted as K1 through K3.

Table 18-1   **Office 365 plans and features**

Feature	P1	E1	E2	E3	E4	K1	K2
SharePoint Online (limited)	X	X	X			X	X
SharePoint Online (advanced)				X	X		
Exchange Online	X	X	X	X	X	X	X
Advanced Exchange Archiving, unlimited e-mail storage, and voicemail with Exchange.				X	X		
Lync Online	X	X	X	X	X		
License Rights for On Premise SharePoint, Exchange, and Lync		X	X	X	X		
Office Web Apps (View Only)	X					X	
Office Web Apps (Edit Capability)	X		X	X	X		X
Office Professional Plus				X	X		
Fully integrated voice capabilities with Lync On Premise					X		

Unfortunately, Microsoft does not provide a full matrix chart with a full list of clearly defined features in a matrix format across each Office 365 plan. The details of each feature are outlined in what Microsoft calls the Service Descriptions. These documents are Word documents for each component of Office 365 and can be downloaded by searching the Microsoft download center for Office 365 Service Descriptions. The Microsoft download center can be found at the following URL:

```
http://www.microsoft.com/download
```

When choosing a plan, keep in mind that you cannot move a P plan to an E plan at a future date. After you choose either a P plan or an E plan, you are stuck in that plan structure.

Laying the Groundwork

You should keep in mind that the size and complexity of your organization, as well as the Office 365 plan you choose, will directly affect your implementation. If you are a one-person consultant or small business using the professional and small business plan, then your implementation will be very straightforward. If your organization contains thousands of employees with offices around the world, your implementation will be a bit more in depth and will require extensive planning.

Regardless of your organization's size and the plan you choose, your implementation follows three primary steps — plan, prepare, and migrate, as outlined in this section and illustrated in Figure 18-1. The migration phase is covered in Chapter 19.

Although it seems that the planning phase should precede the preparation phase, this is not so. The best implementation processes follow an iterative cycle in that you continually plan, prepare, and migrate. You need to start somewhere, however, and you always start with a plan. When you get your plan in order, you then move onto preparing to migrate. As you are preparing, you realize some additional things that you didn't include in your plan. As a result, you continually update your plan. Perhaps a better representation of the process is shown in Figure 18-2, even though this might not sit well with organizations that have extensive gating requirements for every project undertaken.

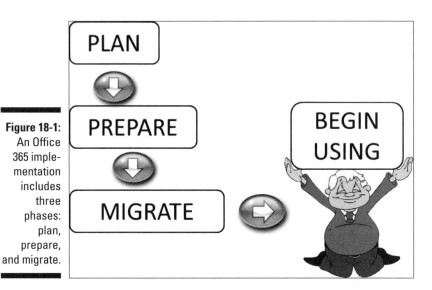

Figure 18-1:
An Office 365 imple-mentation includes three phases: plan, prepare, and migrate.

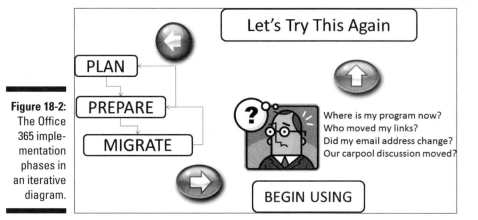

Figure 18-2:
The Office 365 imple-mentation phases in an iterative diagram.

Planning phase

The planning phase of an Office 365 implementation greatly depends on many factors, including whether you are using the professional and small business plan or the enterprise plan. Regardless of which plan you are using, you want to get a handle on the resources and roles that you need for the imple-mentation as well as the following tasks:

✔ Meeting synchronization
✔ Issue tracking

✔ Strategies around e-mail, such as mailbox size and e-mailed integration with SharePoint

✔ Account provisioning and licensing

✔ Internet bandwidth consideration

✔ Software and hardware inventories

✔ Administrator and end-user training

✔ Communication planning

Getting a handle on resources you will need

The in-house, human-based resources that you need for an Enterprise implementation are outlined in Table 18-2. Note that if you are implementing the professional/small business plan, then a single person or hired contractor might playall these roles with a negligible amount of work required for each role. If you are a large organization implementing the enterprise plan, then you may contract out these roles to a partner or have a team of in-house staff assigned to specific roles.

Table 18-2	Human Based Resources
Resource	*Description*
Project Manager	The Project Manager is responsible for making sure that each resource is on the same page as the Office 365 implementation proceeds.
Office 365 Administrator	Responsibilities include managing the Office 365 interface with such technical tasks domains, security groups, users, and licenses.
SharePoint Administrator	Responsible for administering the SharePoint Online platform, including creating sites, installing solutions, and activating features.
Exchange Administrator	Responsible for maintaining the settings for user mailboxes and e-mail, including the settings required for connectivity with Outlook.
Lync Administrator	The Lync Administrator is responsible for all configuration with the Lync program.
Network Administrator	Responsible for maintaining the Internet connection for the organization. Because Office 365 is in the cloud and accessed over the Internet, the connection is critical.
Trainer	Takes on the role of learning how the software works and then teaching others the best practices as they relate to your organization.

The enterprise plan includes a number of additional roles that can be used to create a very granular distribution of duties. These include a global administrator, billing administrator, user management administrator, service administrator, password administrator, and finally, the users themselves. In addition, SharePoint administrators can control the SharePoint Online environment to the site and even individual lists and library level. For example, you may have an accounting department that has very sensitive data. The SharePoint administrator for that accounting site can add or remove user rights for different parts of the site. All this SharePoint administration is done within SharePoint and is not part of the Office 365 administrative interface.

Synchronization meetings

With any Enterprise software adoption, maintaining open lines of communication is important. If everyone is on the same page, then it is easier to navigate issues as they arise rather than at the end of the project. Pulling a page from SCRUM methodology, it is a good idea to have daily stand-ups where the teams stands in a circle and quickly announces what they are working on and what obstacles are blocking them from continuing with their tasks.

The software development methodology known as SCRUM is a process for completing complicated software development cycles. The term comes from the Australian sport of rugby where the entire team moves down the field as one unit rather than as individual players. If you are not familiar with SCRUM, then we highly recommend you check out the Scrum Alliance website at www.scrumalliance.org.

Issue tracking

Tracking issues as they arise is critical, and you need a process in place. SharePoint is ideal at issue tracking, so you may want to use a pilot implementation of Office 365 that includes SharePoint Online to track your issues for your Office 365 implementation. Isn't that tactic a mind bender?

E-mail strategies

E-mail plays a very important role in nearly every organization. When moving to Office 365, you will be moving your e-mail system. E-mail can be widely spread and integrated into many different nooks and crannies of your infrastructure. You want to make sure that you do a thorough audit to find out which systems and applications are using e-mail, and which you want to move to Office 365. In addition, the size of users e-mail boxes should be understood and the amount of e-mail that will be migrated to Exchange Online (which is the e-mail portion of Office 365). In particular, take note of how you are using SharePoint and how SharePoint is using e-mail. If you are new to SharePoint, then you are in for a treat because you gain an understanding of how the product integrates with e-mail. For more on SharePoint, check out Part III or check out *SharePoint 2010 Development For Dummies* by Ken Withee (Wiley).

Account provisioning and licensing

The good news is that Office 365 is very flexible in licensing, user provisioning, and administration. With that said, however, you want to plan out the number of users and the licensing requirements you need for your organization. You may choose to adopt Office 365 all at once or as a phased approach by moving a single group over to Office 365 as a pilot. In either case, you need to understand your licensing requirements so that you can plan resources and costs accordingly.

Internet bandwidth consideration

Because Office 365 lives in the cloud and is accessed over the Internet, your connection must be top-notch. Your network administrator or IT consultant can use a number of different network bandwidth testing tools so that you have firsthand reports on how much bandwidth you are currently using in your organization and how moving to the cloud will affect the users.

Software and Hardware inventories

Undertaking an audit of your current software and hardware resources is important. Fortunately, Microsoft has a tool available for just such a task. It is called the Microsoft Assessment and Planning (MAP) toolkit, and it can be downloaded by searching for it in the Microsoft Download Center located at:

```
www.microsoft.com/download
```

After you have a handle on the software and hardware in your organization, you need to reference the requirements for Office 365 to determine if you need to make changes. Refer to Chapter 17 for Office 365 software and hardware requirements.

Administrator and end-user training

As with any new system, training is a required element. Office 365 has been designed with intuitive user interfaces for both administration and end users, but without a training plan, you are rolling the dice. A popular and successful approach to training when it comes to intuitive designs is called train the trainer. The idea being that you invest in formal training for a power user and then that user trains the rest of the company. This strategy is very powerful even for large organizations because the training scales exponentially. As people are trained, they then train other people.

Communication planning

The best communication is clear, transparent, and all-inclusive. Everyone in the organization has ideas and an opinion. By garnering as many thoughts and as much brainpower (crowd sourcing) as possible, the organization will accomplish two clear objectives.

The first is that you will shed light on problems, issues, and risks early and often and can adjust early in the process rather than down the road when it is too late. The second big win an organization achieves involves ownership and engagement. In order for a project to be successful, you need for the users to be engaged and take ownership of the solution.

Microsoft has taken great effort to make the adoption of Office 365 as painless as possible but, in the end, it will still be a change. It can be argued that it is a change for the better in moving to Office 365 and taking advantage of all the cloud has to offer, but any change at all involves discomfort, apprehension, and stress. Having a good communication plan keeps everyone in the loop and feeling a part of the process. When you effect change at a grassroots level and let the wave of adoption swell up from great user experiences, then the organization as a whole wins.

Migration needs

One of the biggest aspects of moving to Office 365 will be migration of content, including mailboxes and other content. The ideal situation is that your organization has been living under a rock and has no document management system in place or custom portal functionality. In this scenario, you simply start using SharePoint in all of its glory and bathe in the efficiency and productivity gains of a modern portal environment.

The chances are, however, that you already have a number of systems in place. These systems might be SharePoint, or they might be a custom developed solution. In any case, you need to plan to migrate the content and functionality of these systems into Office 365. The good news is that Office 365 is definitely a product worth spending the time, effort, and resources in adopting.

Preparing phase

After you have a good handle on what you plan to do, you need to prepare to do it. Keep in mind that because every organization is different, you should only use these steps as a guide. If you are a small organization, then moving to Office 365 might be as easy as a walk in the park. If you are part of a thousand-person multinational organization with offices around the world, then the process will be much more involved.

As you begin preparing, you will inevitably realize some deficiencies in your plan. Think of these steps as iterative. When you know more about what you should include in your plan, include it. Go back and update your plan. As you walk through the preparation phase, you will know more than you did during the planning phase. This is why an iterative process is so very important. You don't know what you don't know, and to think that you could plan everything without being all-knowing is a ridiculous thought.

DNS

The Domain Naming System (DNS) is a standard used to let computers communicate over the Internet. For example, Microsoft manages the domain microsoft.com. All the Microsoft computers that are accessed over the Internet are part of this domain, and each is assigned a specific number, known as an Internet Protocol (IP) address. When you send an e-mail to someone at Microsoft, your computer asks the microsoft.com DNS server what computer handles e-mail.

When you move to Office 365, you must make changes in DNS so that network traffic understands where it should be routed. In essence, what happens is that when the DNS is changed, anyone sending you an e-mail will have that e-mail routed to your Office 365 implementation rather than to the current location.

Mailboxes

As you just discovered in thepreceding section on DNS, there are specific computers responsible for hosting your e-mail. If you keep your e-mail on your local computer, then you won't have any e-mail data to migrate. However, if you leave your e-mail on the server, thenall that data will need to be migrated to the Office 365 mailboxes. This migration can be one of the most technically difficult parts of moving e-mail systems, but with guidance from a partner, it can be pain free.

Portals

A web portal, also known as an Intranet site, can be as simple as a static web page, or as complex as a fully integrated solution. SharePoint provides a tremendous amount of functionality, and it has seen massive adoption in the last decade. Office 365 includes SharePoint Online, which is nothing more than SharePoint hosted by Microsoft. During the migration phase of an implementation, you need to decide which content you want to move to SharePoint and which you can leave where it is currently located. In addition, you need to decide which functionality you want to integrate into your portal and which systems are better left in place.

Logins and Licensing

If you are a part of a very large organization, then your IT team probably manages your users with a Microsoft technology called Active Directory. For large organizations, you can sync this on-site management of users with the Office 365 users, which results in a single login and simplified access to the cloud environment. If you are part of a small organization, then you might manageall your users in Office 365 directly. In either case, you need to come up with a list of the people who need to have access to Office 365 and the associated licensing.

Training

Even the best software is useless unless people know about it and know how to use it. Microsoft has created a wealth of documentation and user training that can be had for little or no cost. In addition, any partner you decide to work with will have training plans available and can conduct training for Office 365.

Support

After users start adopting Office 365, they are bound to have questions. You need to have a support system in place in order to accommodate even the simplest questions. The support system should include power users as a first point of content and then a formal support system that escalates all the way up to Microsoft supporting Office 365.

Office 365 Online Documentation

This chapter alone is not intended as a complete guide for implementing Office 365. Microsoft has released an inclusive guide designed for just such a task, which is wrapped up in 181 beautiful pages of PDF. The Microsoft implementation guide is called the *Microsoft Office 365 Deployment Guide;* Search the Microsoft Download Center for the title. The Microsoft Download Center can be accessed at the following URL:

```
www.microsoft.com/download
```

In addition to the deployment guide, a wealth of training, information, and documentation is available on the Office 365 website located at:

```
www.microsoft.com/office365
```

Choosing a Partner

Throughout the chapter, we cover planning and preparing for an Office 365 implementation. As noted, the process is not linear but is iterative. For example, you do not plan and then stop planning and move into preparing, and then stop preparing and move into migration. Instead, it is an iterative process in that you know what you know at the time and you will know more later on down the road. Luckily, if you use a partner, that partner will have been through this iterative cycle many times with other customers and can make the process much easier than undertaking the process on your own.

Microsoft provides the ability to find a partner on their Office 365 product page. Simply click the Support tab and then choose Find a Partner from the menu, as shown in Figure 18-3.

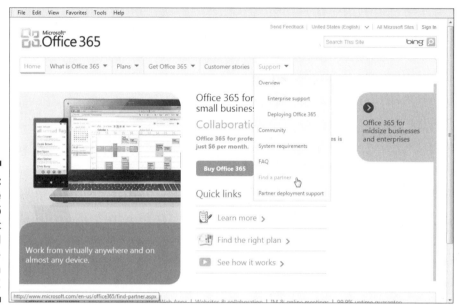

Figure 18-3: Using the Office 365 product page to find an implementation partner.

The Find a Partner link takes you to the Office 365 Marketplace. The Office 365 Marketplace lets you search by the top Office 365 Microsoft partners, recommended deployment partners, or by searching for a partner name directly in the search menu. The results use Microsoft Bing to show you the geographic location of each partner, as well as ratings and reviews.

Reading the reviews and doing your homework can pay huge dividends when it comes time to implementing Office 365. An experienced partner can make the process seem like a dream, whereas an inexperienced partner can taint your view of the Office 365 product forever.

Chapter 19

Implementing Office 365

• •

In This Chapter

▶ Discovering how to deliver training and support

▶ Understanding how to migrate to Office 365

▶ Getting your head around the tasks required with migrating

• •

> *A desire to be observed, considered, esteemed, praised, beloved, and admired by his fellows is one of the earliest as well as the keenest dispositions discovered in the heart of man.*
>
> — John Adams

*I*n Chapter 18, we detail how to prepare and plan for an Office 365 implementation. In this chapter, you get to throw the switch and make the move to the Microsoft cloud.

Office 365 is designed for nearly every type of organization — ranging from a one-person shop to a multinational enterprise. Because of this massively different audience, every implementation is different, both in complexity and in time. This chapter covers the general process and gives you some pointers on where to go for more information. If you are a small organization, then some of the steps in this chapter may be overkill. If you are a very large enterprise, then you will surely want to work with a partner, such as an IT services firm specializing in Office 365, that can guide you through the process.

This chapter provides a high-level overview of the steps required to implement Office 365, including preparing users through training, activating licensing, providing a support mechanism, and migrating data and custom portal functionality.

Getting Users Ready for Office 365

Microsoft Office 365 is easy to use and has very intuitive interfaces. However, that doesn't mean that you can just turn it on and tell everyone to "go wild." Although you may be familiar with the Microsoft Office products, understanding how these same products integrate and the value that results from that integration is critical in increasing productivity and boosting efficiency. To get users ready for the plunge, you need to start with training and follow up with a support system so that everyone knows where to go when they need help.

Training

We recommend using a simple formula known as the tell, show, do method. Here's what you do:

1. Tell people how Office 365 works.

2. Show everyone how it works with a live demo.

3. Let people get their hands dirty and do it on their own.

This strategy works great for all types of technology training.

The Office 365 product is made up of a basket of products. These products include Office Professional Plus, SharePoint Online, Exchange Online, and Lync Online. The different plans that make up Office 365 include various permutations of product features. For example, in order to get Office Professional Plus with your plan, you need to purchase Enterprise plan E3 or E4. For more information about the features that make up each plan, refer to Chapter 18.

Attempting training for such a broad product as Office 365 can be challenging. For example, providing training on just the Office Professional Plus piece can consume a great deal of effort because the product is made up of a number of applications, including Word, Excel, PowerPoint, Outlook, OneNote, Publisher, Access, InfoPath, SharePoint Workspace, and Lync. Rather than focus on training for each of these components, a better strategy might be to focus on how they integrate with SharePoint Online, Exchange Online, and Lync Online.

Microsoft has a number of partners that provide training for Office 365. You can search the Office 365 Marketplace for the word 'training' to find a list of training companies. Access the Office 365 Marketplace by using the following URL in your browser:

```
http://office365.pinpoint.microsoft.com
```

Support

Even the most experienced and seasoned mountain climbers have a support system, and your organization shouldn't be any different. Planning a support system doesn't mean spending a lot of money. A support system can be as simple as a go-to power user on the team or as complex as a full-fledged call center. Depending on the size of your organization, your support system can take many different forms. A good strategy, however, is to take a tiered approach by starting with communal support through some of the collaborative features of Office 365, such as SharePoint and Lync. Besides, isn't it poetic to use Office 365 to support Office 365? You can find out more by checking out Part III (SharePoint) and Part V (Lync).

The community can provide base-level support and work together to figure out the technology. When the community cannot help, then you can call in the big guns by requesting support from your partner or even from Microsoft itself.

By creating a vibrant community that collaborates and supports each other, your organization will have a much better Office 365 experience. The cultural changes that come about from an integrated and connected workforce can add a tremendous return on investment to the organization. With Office 365, you have the tools, but every employee must use them to make the transition effective.

When you need to enter a service request with Microsoft, you can do so right from within the Office 365 administrator portal, as shown in Figure 19-1.

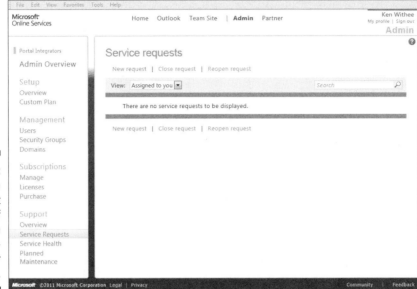

Figure 19-1:
The Service
Request
section of
the Office
365 admin-
istrator
interface.

Migrating to Office 365

The nice thing about Office 365 is that it lives in the cloud and is very flexible. You can migrate small trial runs of data to a trial Office 365 subscription and figure out what might go wrong when you migrate the entire organization. In fact, we highly recommend that you sign up for an Office 365 trial right now. The trial is absolutely free, and you can be up and exploring the product in a matter of minutes.

In the past, it was difficult to gain access to enterprise software, such as SharePoint, because it took an astute tech person to set up the environment. The tech person had to find hardware capable of running the software and then install the operating system, all supporting software, and finally SharePoint. Even if everything went as planned, the process took at least a half day and possibly a lot longer. With Office 365, you, as a business user, can go straight to the Office 365 website, sign up for a trial, and explore SharePoint in a matter of minutes!

Activating licensing

The process for assigning and activating licensing varies slightly, depending on whether you are using the P plans or the E plans. To add licensing, you need to add users to the plan by clicking on the Users tab, as shown in Figure 19-2.

Figure 19-2:
The Users tab in the Office 365 'E' plan administrator interface.

You begin the process of adding a user by selecting the New⇨User button from the Ribbon of the Users screen. As you walk through the wizard, you are asked to enter information, such as the users first and last name and administrative rights the user should be assigned. In addition, you have the opportunity to assign specific licensing to the user, as shown in Figure 19-3.

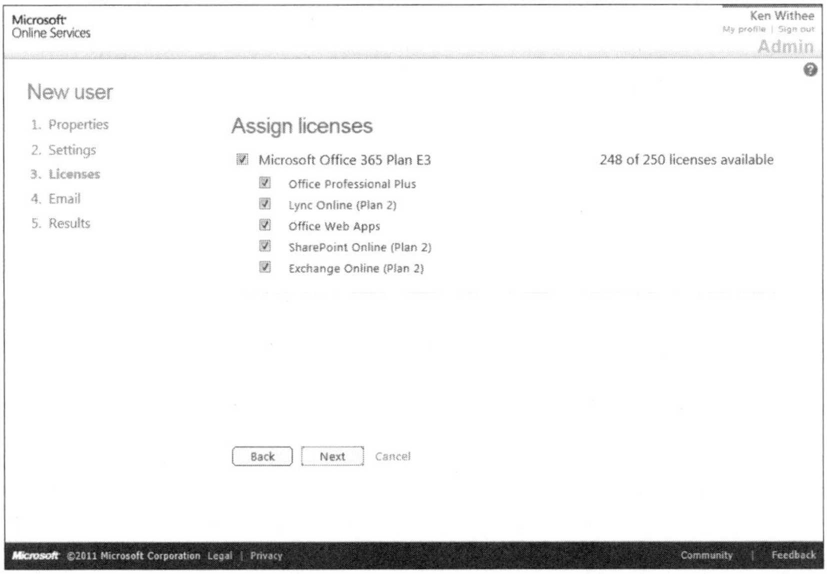

Microsoft
Online Services

Ken Withee
My profile | Sign out
Admin

New user

1. Properties
2. Settings
3. Licenses
4. Email
5. Results

Assign licenses

☑ Microsoft Office 365 Plan E3   248 of 250 licenses available
  ☑ Office Professional Plus
  ☑ Lync Online (Plan 2)
  ☑ Office Web Apps
  ☑ SharePoint Online (Plan 2)
  ☑ Exchange Online (Plan 2)

[Back] [Next] Cancel

Microsoft ©2011 Microsoft Corporation Legal | Privacy   Community | Feedback

Figure 19-3:
Assigning
Office 365
licensing to
a new user.

Migrating mailbox data (Exchange)

One of the most visible aspects of an Office 365 implementation is the migration of e-mail data into the Exchange Online system. To begin a migration, you use the E-Mail Migration page. You can access this page by clicking the Manage link under the Exchange Online section on the main Office 365 management page and then clicking the E-Mail Migration button, as shown in Figure 19-4.

To begin a new migration, click the New tab to begin walking through the Migration wizard, as shown in Figure 19-5. The Migration wizard will let you migrate your Exchange settings. If you are migrating from Exchange 2007 or later, the wizard will use Autodiscover to autodetect settings. If you are migrating from Exchange 2003 or IMAP, then you need to enter the settings manually. After completion of a migration, user e-mail will be available in the Office 365 system.

A number of other tools and partners are available to assist in e-mail migration. Find these resources in the Office 365 Marketplace located at the following URL:

```
http://office365.pinpoint.microsoft.com
```

E-mail Migration button

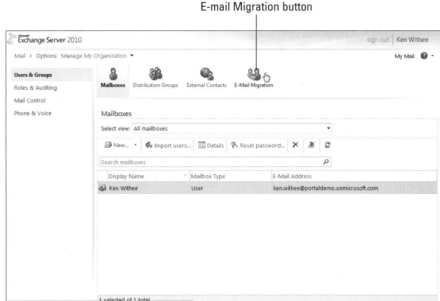

Figure 19-4:
Accessing
the E-Mail
Migration
button
on the
Exchange
Online
Management
page.

New button

Figure 19-5:
Beginning a
new e-mail
migration in
Office 365.

Migrating portal content and functionality (SharePoint)

The SharePoint platform has become the most successful product in Microsoft's history. As SharePoint experts, we have spent countless hours working with clients in every industry on SharePoint projects. SharePoint is a platform and as a result, it tends to get complicated, which often leads to an organization employing the help of consultants. Much of the complexity of SharePoint lies in the infrastructure of the platform. A SharePoint implementation requires a number of different engineers all working in unison to make the platform available to users. The good news with Office 365 is that Microsoft takes over this complexity of building and maintaining the platform, and you, as a user, can focus on just using the product.

Migrating to SharePoint Online (which is part of Office 365) requires you to migrate any content or custom functionality that you may currently be using in your portal environment. As you begin to delve farther into SharePoint, you find that one of the major attractions is the ability to consolidate the functionality of multiple disparate systems into the SharePoint platform. This consolidation creates a one-stop shop for business tasks as compared to logging into multiple systems that rarely communicate with each other.

Migrating content to SharePoint Online

Migrating content to SharePoint can be as easy as uploading the documents you have saved on your local computer or as complex as moving massive amounts of digital content from one Enterprise Content Management (ECM) system to another. If you are a small or medium organization, then you can gain familiarity with content management in SharePoint and in particular with document libraries. SharePoint document libraries are covered in Chapter 6.

Migrating custom functionality to SharePoint Online

One of the best things about SharePoint is that it is a platform and not a specific tool. As a result, you can build just about any business functionality you need to run your business right into your SharePoint implementation.

With so much power at your disposal in SharePoint, you need to think about what you have developed. If you are one of the rare few who has never used SharePoint, then you can simply start using SharePoint Online. If, however, you have already used SharePoint either on premise or through another hosting provider and are moving into SharePoint Online, then you will need to move your custom functionality into your new portal. Migrating functionality that you have developed can be a challenge. One of the best ways to tackle this challenge, however, is to carefully document your current environment and then determine if it is better to try to migrate the functionality or re-create it in the new environment.

If the functionality you have developed is a simple list or library, then you can go into the List Settings page and save the list as a template with content. This creates a physical file that you download to your computer and then upload to SharePoint Online. After you install the template into SharePoint Online, you can then re-create the list or library by using the template. The result is that your list or library is transported into SharePoint Online with only a few clicks of a mouse.

For more advanced functionality, you can either redevelop it in the new environment or hire a consultant to undertake the project under your guidance.

Throwing the switch

After you have migrated both e-mail and portal data, you are ready to throw the switch and direct all traffic to the new Office 365 environment. Throwing the switch is accomplished by updating your Domain Name System (DNS) records in your domain registrar. The results of this simple procedure are enormous. After you update DNS, every user of your current system is directed to the Office 365 system.

A DNS record is a translator from human readable computer names to computer readable computer names. For example, if you type `www.microsoft.com` into your web browser, the Microsoft web page appears. How does this happen? Your computer sees `microsoft.com` and knows it is a text entry. Computers talk to other computers by using numbers known as Internet Protocol (IP) addresses. Your computer needs to find out the IP address of the computer running the `microsoft.com` website. It does this by querying a DNS server. The DNS server looks up the text-based address (known as a domain name) and sends back the IP address. Your computer can now use the IP address to contact the Microsoft computer.

When you update the DNS records for the e-mail, for example, you are telling the DNS lookup system that when someone wants to send you an e-mail, their computer should use the IP address of Office 365 rather than the one you were using before. In essence, after you update DNS you have thrown the switch and are using Office 365rather than the old system.

Configuring mobile phones

The cloud offers the advantage of being fully connected at all times to your important data and communications. There is no better way to access your Office 365 environment on the go than with your mobile phone. If you are using one of the new Microsoft Windows Phone 7 phones, then you can connect with your SharePoint and office documents as well. If you are not using a Microsoft phone, you can still access your e-mail and calendars from your device; however, the experience is not seamlessly integrated.

You can find more information about setting up your mobile phone with Office 365 by navigating to the following URL:

```
http://help.outlook.com
```

On Outlook support page, you can find the relevant setup information by clicking on the Mobile Phones link. The Mobile Phones help page is shown in Figure 19-6.

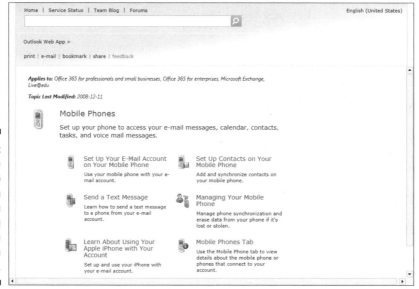

Figure 19-6:
The Mobile Phones help page with information for setting up a mobile phone with Office 365.

Chapter 20

Managing Office 365

In This Chapter

▶ Finding your way around the Office 365 management pages

▶ Managing Exchange Online

▶ Managing SharePoint Online

We think in generalities, but we live in detail.

— Alfred North Whitehead

A s you find out throughout the book, the Office 365 product is actually a suite of products consisting of SharePoint Online for portals, Exchange Online for e-mails, Lync Online for instant and ad hoc communication, and Office Professional Plus for productivity. When it comes time to manage these components, Microsoft has created a web-based interface that is intuitive and easy to use.

In this chapter, you explore the management interfaces for Office 365. You can gain an understanding of the general Office 365 management pages and then move into exploring the specific management pages for each of the individual services.

Going Over Office 365 Management

The folks at Microsoft have taken a great deal of time and put a tremendous amount of resources into developing the management interface for Office 365. Microsoft developers designed this interface for everyday users with the idea being that it doesn't take an IT expert in order to manage the Office 365 product. The main Office 365 management interface is actually a website you navigate to with your favorite web browser.

A web interface for managing an online product is nothing new. If you have ever used Facebook or LinkedIn, then you are familiar with using your web browser to manage an online product. The Office 365 management interface is no different; it is just the interface designed by Microsoft to manage their business cloud product.

The Office 365 management page can be accessed by navigating to the following URL in your web browser:

```
http://portal.microsoftonline.com
```

You sign in by using the credentials you used to sign up for the Office 365 product. After you have signed in, the Office 365 management website appears, as shown in Figure 20-1.

The management interface discussed in this chapter focuses on the medium/enterprise plan. If you are using the professional/ small business plan, you will have fewer management options. A sample plan is shown in Figure 20-2.

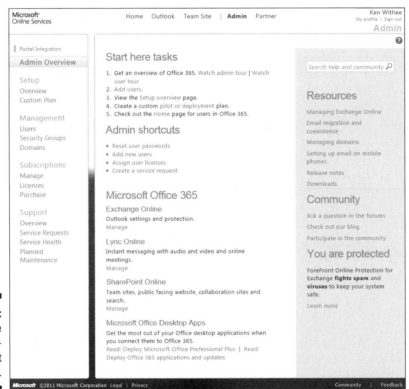

Figure 20-1: The Office 365 management website.

The management website includes sections down the left-hand navigation for Setup, Management, Subscriptions, and Support. In addition, you can click a link at the top of the page that lets you quickly navigate to your e-mail by using the Outlook Web Application (OWA) and a link to take you to your company portal (SharePoint Online).

Table 20-1 outlines the functionality of the left-hand navigational groups and links.

Table 20-1	Office 365 Administration Links	
Group	*Link*	*Description*
Setup	Overview	The overview page provides information on setting up the Office 365 environment. This includes such information as synchronizing on-premise mailboxes and configuring services.
Setup	Custom Plan	The Custom Plan link takes you to a wizard that guides you through the steps to adopting Office 365. You answer questions about your specific scenario. The result is a plan put together for you that guides you through the steps to migrating to Office 365.
Management	Users	The Users page allows you to create, edit, and delete Office 365 users.
Management	Security Groups	Using the Security Groups page, you can create e-mail distribution and security groups in which you can add Office 365 users.
Management	Domains	The Domains page allows you to add your own domain to Office 365. For example, if your company already owns portalint.com, then you can point that domain to your Office 365 account by using this page.
Subscriptions	Manage	Using the Manage page, you can handle the billing and subscriptions for your Office 365 implementation.
Subscriptions	Licenses	The Licenses page shows you the number of licenses available and the number of licenses assigned or expired in your environment.

(continued)

Table 20-1 *(continued)*

Group	Link	Description
Subscriptions	Purchase	You can use the Purchase page to buy additional Office 365 plans and licensing.
Support	Overview	The Overview page provides information regarding community forums, common issues documentation, delegation for administrators, service request overview, and diagnostic tools.
Support	Service Requests	A Service Request is a support incident with Microsoft. Using this page, you can open and monitor service requests.
Support	Service Health	The Service Health page shows a dashboard of the health of your Office 365 services. Each service is outlined per day with icons for normal service, service degradation, service interruption, additional information, and service restored.
Support	Planned Maintenance	The Planned Maintenance page provides an overview of maintenance that is both scheduled for the future and that has been completed in the past.

The center of the administration screen contains a list of tasks you should perform right away. These are titled "Start here tasks" and include items such as watching overview videos, adding users, and creating a deployment plan. In addition, there are shortcut links to administrative tasks such as assigning licenses, resetting user passwords, and creating a service support request.

The final part of the main administrative page includes links to the management pages for each of the Office 365 components, including Exchange Online, Lync Online, SharePoint Online, and Office Professional Plus. We explore these management pages later in the chapter.

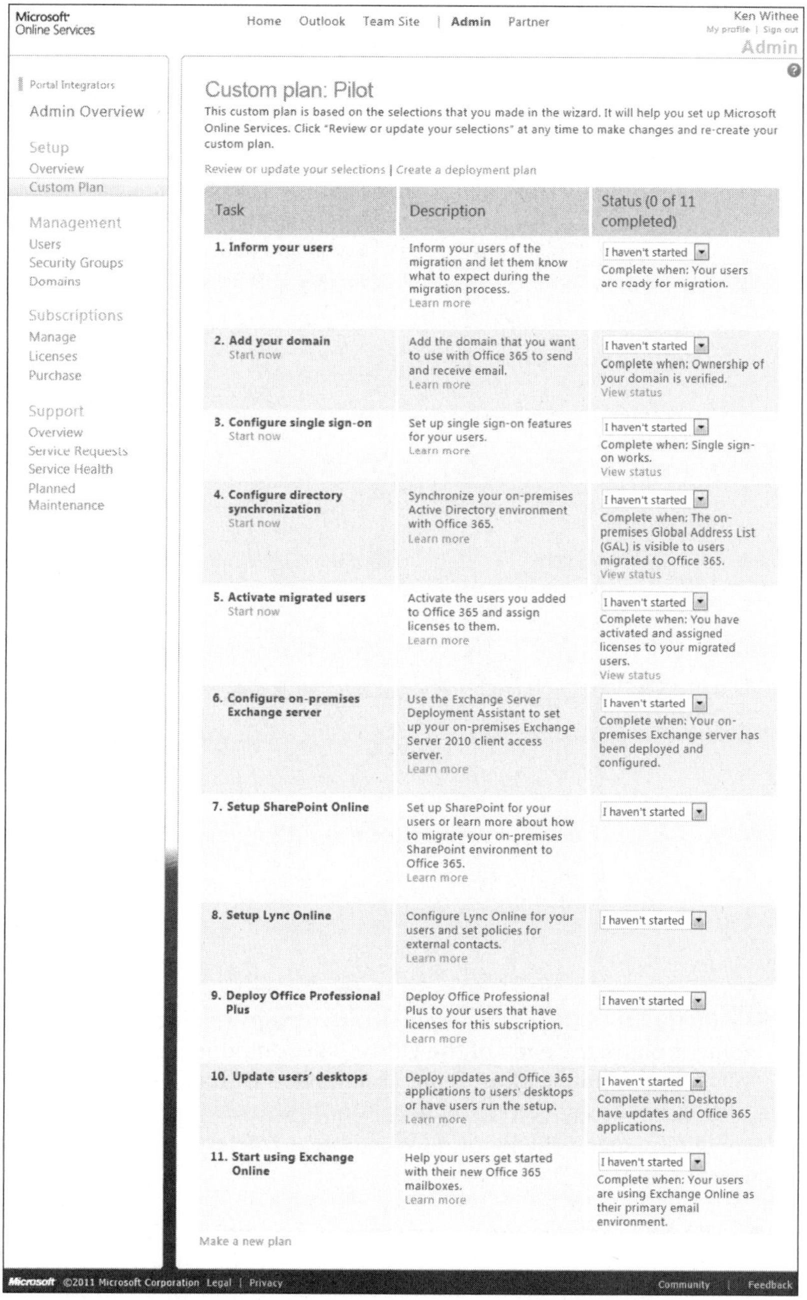

Figure 20-2:
A sample Office 365 plan created by using the Custom Plan wizard.

Managing Exchange Online

The management section for Exchange Online can be accessed by clicking on the Admin Overview link in the upper-left corner on the main Office 365 administration page and then clicking the Manage link under the Exchange Online section, as shown in Figure 20-3.

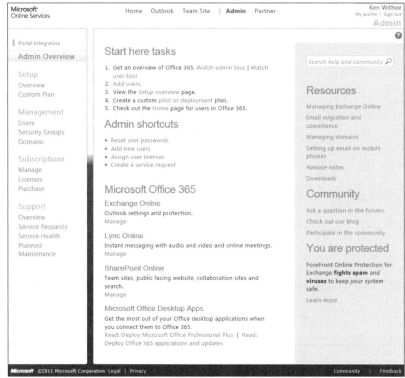

Figure 20-3: Accessing the Exchange Online management pages from the Office 365 main page.

Depending on your level of access, you can choose to manage the entire organization, yourself, or another user. You select which you want to manage by using the drop-down menu at the top left of the screen, as shown in Figure 20-4.

The Exchange Online management pages contain a tremendous number of configuration settings that could only fully be covered with a dedicated book on the topic. The following sections provide an overview to managing Exchange Online for yourself or your organization.

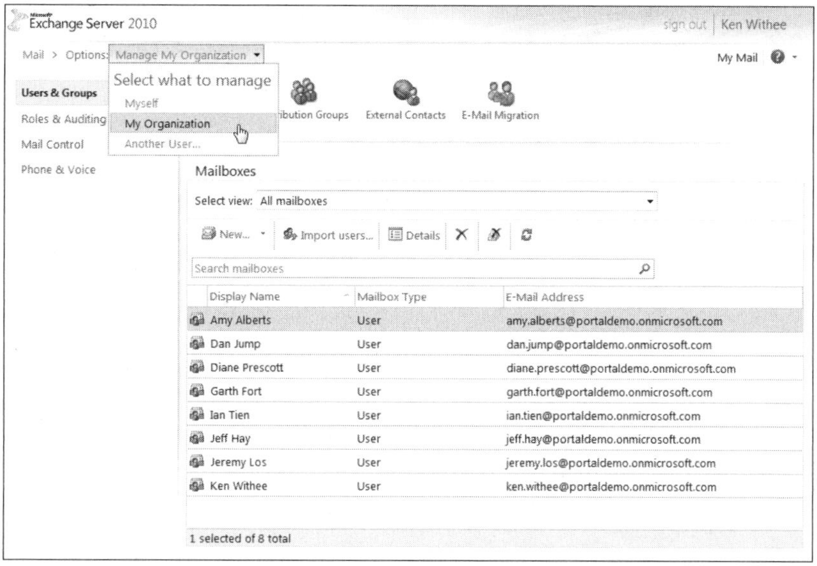

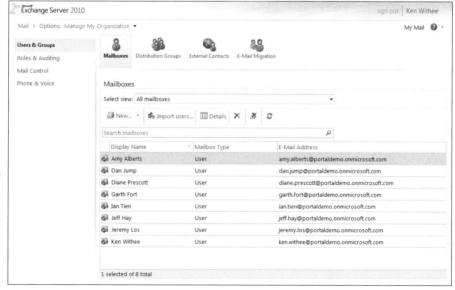

Figure 20-4: Selecting to manage Exchange Online for yourself, your organization, or someone else, depending on your level of access.

Managing your organization

The management pages for managing the organization include sections for managing users and groups, roles and auditing, mail control, and phone and voice, as shown in Figure 20-5.

Figure 20-5: The management page for the organization.

Users & Groups

The Users & Groups section provides configuration options for managing users and groups. Buttons across the top of the page let you switch between managing user mailboxes, e-mail distribution groups, contacts that are external to your organization, and a wizard for migrating e-mail into the Exchange Online environment.

Roles & Auditing

The Roles & Auditing section provides the ability to manage user roles and administrative roles. You switch between the management screens by using the buttons at the top of the page. In addition, there is a button for auditing that provides a number of reports, such as determining the users that access a mailbox that is not owned by them, running a litigation hold report to determine the mailboxes that have a hold, and searching for administrative changes to roles and groups.

Mail Control

The Mail Control page provides the ability to create rules, configure domains, journaling, and reports of e-mail delivery.

Rules let you control the flow of e-mail within your organization. For example, if an e-mail is sent to a mailbox such as info@portalint.com, then you can have a rule that forwards the e-mail to everyone within the support team.

You can also configure domains and journaling. Configuring domains allows you to accept e-mail for specific domains, such as portalint.com. Configuring Journaling lets you record e-mail communications in support of e-mail retention or archiving policies. This functionality is critical for highly regulated industries, such as banking.

Finally, you can use delivery reports to search for specifics on e-mail communication, such as messages with certain keywords or from a specific person.

Phone & Voice

The Phone & Voice page enables you to configure unified messaging that connects your phone system with the rest of the Office 365 services. Using the Phone & Voice page, you can connect Exchange Online to your phone system that includes mobile phones and office phones. The end result is that your physical telephone system becomes an integrated extension of the Office 365 product.

Managing yourself or someone else

You also have the ability to manage personal settings by selecting to either manage yourself or manage another user's mailbox from the drop-down menu at the top of the Exchange Online management screen. By using the personal management screen, you can set settings for your mailbox, such as your account information, your e-mail groups, your phone settings, and the e-mail you want to block or allow into your mailbox.

In addition, you can connect external accounts so that you can view e-mail from other systems and organize your e-mail by creating rules for auto replies, retention policies, and delivery reports. You can accomplish the configuration on the personal settings pages, as shown in Figure 20-6.

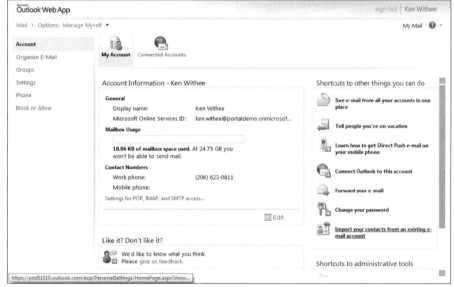

Figure 20-6: Managing your personal mailbox in Office 365.

Managing Lync Online

You can manage Lync Online by clicking the Manage link under the Lync Online section of the Office 365 management screen. Refer to Figure 20-3 to view the link.

When on the Lync Online management screen, you can configure domain federation, public Instant Messaging (IM) settings, and user information.

Domain federation

Domain federation lets you control the domains that your organization can connect with using Lync Online. You can allow preferred domains or domains outside of your corporate network so that partners can connect with employees and block other domains to avoid unwanted distractions.

Public instant messaging

With Lync Online, you can enable or disable public instant messaging. This functionality lets you control whether you let users chat with the general public or whether you want to restrict messaging to only users on the corporate network or preferred domains. If you choose to allow communication with the general public, your users can add contacts from the Windows Live, AOL, Yahoo, and Google chat programs.

User information

The user information screen of Lync Online allows you to configure options and external access for individual users. In particular, you can enable or disable file transfers, audio and video, domain federation, and public Instant Messaging (IM) connectivity, as shown in Figure 20-7.

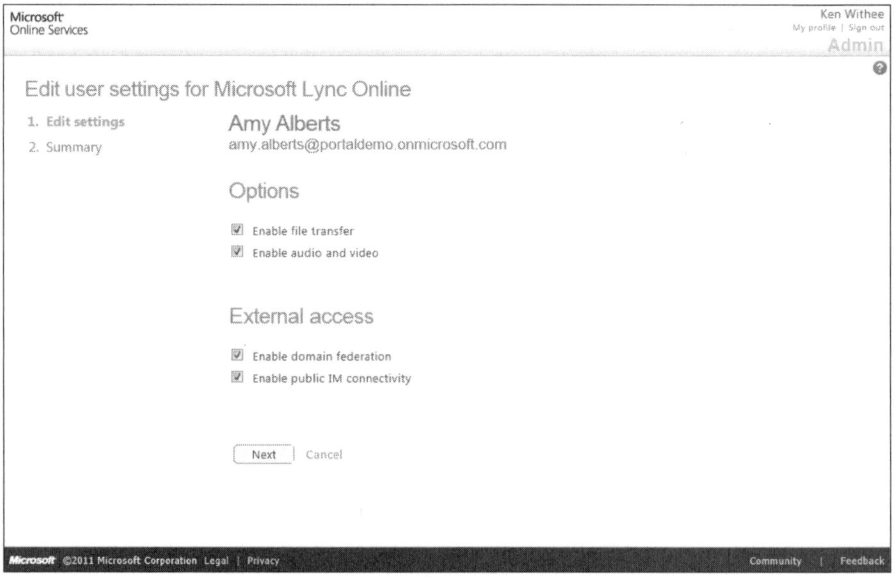

Figure 20-7: Configuring individual user information in Lync Online.

Managing SharePoint

The SharePoint Online management screen is also called the SharePoint Administration Center. You can access this screen by clicking the Manage link under the SharePoint Online section of the Office 365 management screen. Refer to Figure 20-3 to view the link.

The SharePoint Administration Center provides the ability to manage site collections, configure InfoPath Form Services, manage user profiles, and manage the SharePoint Term Store.

The SharePoint Administration Center is unique to the enterprise versions of the Office 365 product. If you are using the professional/small business plan, then you have a single site collection.

Managing site collections

A SharePoint site collection is a logical collection of SharePoint websites. A site collection isolates SharePoint components, such as user permissions, navigational components, and content types. You may want a site collection for sensitive areas of the organization, such as Accounting or Human Resources and then a separate site collection for the general company portal.

The site collection management screen lets you create and configure site collections. In particular, you can perform tasks, such as assigning site collection administrators, allocating resources, and setting resource, and domain information.

InfoPath Form Services

InfoPath is a component of Microsoft Office that provides the ability to create interactive forms without needing to write programming code. The component of SharePoint responsible for integrating InfoPath forms with SharePoint is called InfoPath Form Services.

The InfoPath Form Services configuration screen provides the ability to allow users to enable InfoPath forms in the web browser, render forms based on InfoPath templates, and specify which user agents will receive forms in a searchable format known as eXtensible Markup Language or XML. Some of the options include sending the XML data to Google, MSN Search, or Yahoo.

User Profiles

The user profile page provides the ability to manage SharePoint Online components that relate to user profiles, such as the ability to manage people, the organization, and the configuration settings for the personal SharePoint site functionality known as My Site, as shown in Figure 20-8.

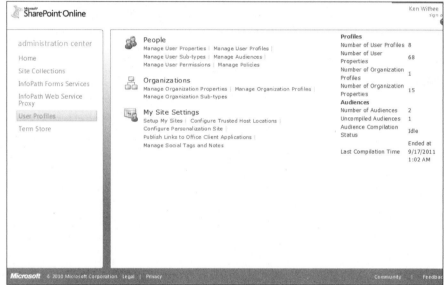

Figure 20-8:
The User Profiles configuration page for SharePoint Online.

People

The People section lets you manage user properties and user profiles. You can create new profiles and edit existing profiles. In addition, you can manage audiences, user permissions, and policies.

An audience is a grouping of users that match specific criteria. For example, you might create a policy for everyone with the department property of their profile set to Executive. You could then target specific SharePoint functionality for only this audience. A policy provides specific functionality for users, such as the ability to add colleagues to their profiles themselves.

Organizations

The Organizations section of the User Profiles screen lets you manage the properties and profiles of the organization. For example, one of the properties of the organization might be the company logo, and another property might be the physical address or web address. By using this screen, you can create new properties or edit existing properties. The profiles section lets you manage a separate profile for different departments within the organization.

An easy way to think of properties and profiles throughout SharePoint is that properties define the fields used in the profiles. For example, a property might be First Name, and the profile would use this property but would associate Ken Withee with the property in the profile.

My Site Settings

A SharePoint My Site is a personal site for every single user. A My Site allows users to create their own SharePoint space without worrying about having the right administrative access to a shared site. The My Site section provides the ability to set up and configure the My Site functionality for SharePoint Online.

SharePoint Term Store

The Term Store is a global directory of common terms that might be used in your organization. The idea behind the Term Store is that you want to create consistency in the way data is entered and managed throughout your SharePoint environment. For example, you might have a Human Resources Department. You don't want people to enter data, such as 'HR', 'HR Dept.', 'Human Resources Dept.', and 'Human Resources Department'. These are all actually the same thing, but because people enter names in different ways, it becomes difficult to maintain consistency. Using the Term Store, you can enter the term as 'Human Resources Department' and know that every place throughout SharePoint that uses this field will enter it in a consistent way when referring to that specific department.

The SharePoint Online Term Store page is shown in Figure 20-9.

In addition to the configuration information discussed in this section regarding Office 365, you also have full access to configuring the site collection within SharePoint. SharePoint development and configuration is beyond the scope of this book but to find out more, you might start with both *SharePoint 2010 For Dummies* (Wiley) for configuration and *SharePoint 2010 Development For Dummies* (Wiley) for development efforts.

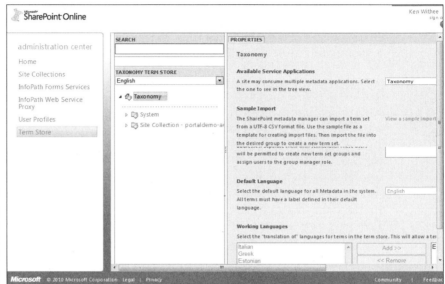

Figure 20-9:
The
SharePoint
Online Term
Store page.

Part VII
The Part of Tens

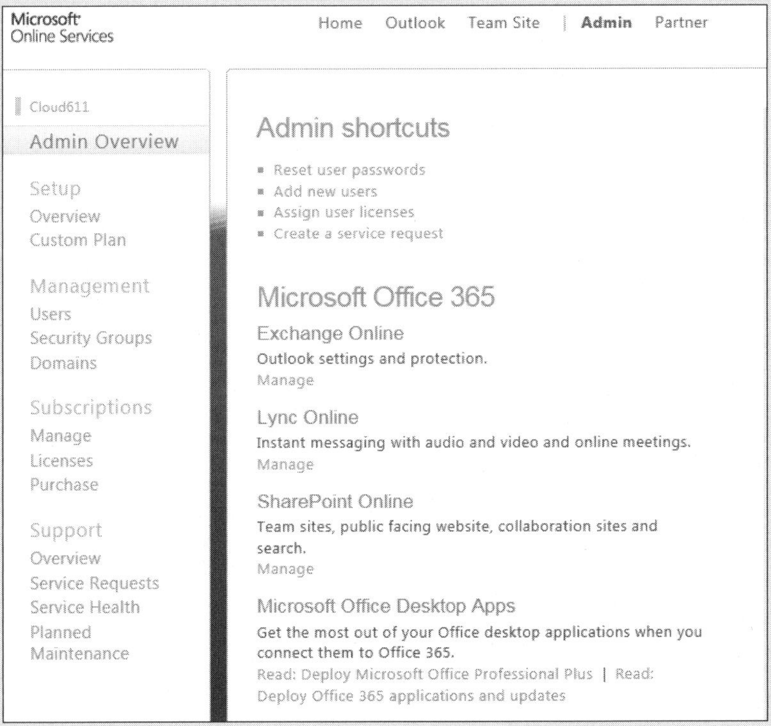

In this part . . .

This part walks you through some of the ten most important aspects of Office 365. You uncover ten signs that it
might be a good time to move to the cloud followed by ten
value propositions that are worth exploring if you are considering Office 365. Finally, you nail down ten tips for
increasing efficiency and boosting productivity with the
components of Office 365 including Exchange Online,
SharePoint Online, Lync Online, and Office Professional Plus.

Chapter 21

Ten Signs It's Time for You to Move to the Cloud

In This Chapter

▶ Deciding what's best for your organization with the tools available in the cloud

▶ Protecting your company's data and avoid business disruptions with off-premise solutions

▶ Empowering team members to be a part of the cloud strategy

▶ Leading your organization into the future

> *"A power surge nearly destroyed our in-house e-mail server. Had we not recovered it, a great deal of historical knowledge and valuable information would have been lost forever, not to mention the lost productivity for days or weeks. Now we have a secure, redundant, cloud e-mail system we can access anywhere, anytime, with a consistent interface, and it's made our business stronger."*
>
> — Kevin Hart, Partner and Founder, Hart-Boillot
> (10-employee communications agency)

Microsoft has already made it easy for your business with the release of Office 365 and its portfolio of cloud products. Whatever cloud investments you make now will work for you in the future. And even if you're not a Microsoft fan, your options for cloud technology are not wanting, considering the array of companies (Google, Amazon, AppNexus, and GoGrid) offering cloud services.

Still looking for a crystal ball? Abandon the search and instead use the following ten signs to know when it's time for you to move to the cloud.

You've Experienced a Document-Versioning Nightmare

Cloud and collaboration is a match made in heaven. Using collaboration tools hosted in the cloud allows you and your colleagues to simultaneously make edits to a document online. If you use SharePoint Online, you can turn on versioning control, so if you ever need to restore an older version of a document, all it takes is a few mouse clicks. You can also set your document library up in such a way that only one person at a time can edit the document without blocking others from viewing a read-only copy of the file.

Compare that to the nightmare of coauthoring documents over e-mail. You can easily get lost in the sea of document versions as each author individually e-mails you back his edits. On top of that, you have to deal with folks like me who will continue to make improvements to the final, final, final copy down to the wire.

If you desire the peace of mind of having colleagues across the hall or across the globe contribute to a document without you having to consolidate all their edits instead of having document versioning nightmares, then there's no doubt you need to move to the cloud.

Your Job Includes Maintaining Your IT Infrastructure

Enterprise-size companies spend a lot of money buying, installing, configuring, maintaining, and upgrading their IT infrastructure. In addition, there are soft costs associated with justifying these IT infrastructure purchases such as

- Writing the business case
- "Selling" the proposal to management
- Sending out the Requests for Proposal (RFP) to potential vendors
- Reviewing and vetting the bids received
- Selecting and contracting with the selected vendors

If you are running a small business, don't make the mistake of thinking that because you don't do all the tasks that most large companies do, your IT infrastructure cost is negligible. You may not house a roomful of servers with technicians, but the time you spend running to Costco to buy hardware and software, installing the programs, calling tech support because your computer crashed due to incompatibility issues, and running back to Costco to return the software all adds up to not just hard and soft costs but also productivity loss.

Cloud computing eases the burden of maintaining and reduces the cost of owning IT infrastructure. Instead of spending money on hardware, maintenance, and headcount, you pay a fixed monthly fee that can scale up or down based on your organization's needs.

If you are a small-business person or a professional selling your services, cloud computing means that you can now focus on your core offerings and forget about doubling up as the IT guy.

So the next time you have to sit down to think about justifying an IT purchase, take that as a sign that it's time for you to move to the cloud.

A Malfunctioning In-House Server Nearly Obliterated Your Data

Cloud computing allows you to let the cloud services provider be the caretaker of your data. Regardless of whether your data is highly confidential or low priority, your data is stored, backed up, replicated, and protected in redundant remote data centers accessible anywhere there's an Internet connection. Microsoft alone has invested billions of dollars in data centers across the globe to handle the demand for Internet-based e-mail and business software applications. As industry standard dictates, cloud providers have limited liability proportionate to the damages resulting from data loss due to service issues. Microsoft prides itself with a 99 percent financially based Service Level Agreement (SLA), so you no longer have to bear the risks solely on your own.

So don't wait until it happens again — move to the cloud now before a malfunctioning server threatens your business.

You Think That "On Demand" Can Apply To Your Business

Most of us have enjoyed the benefits of "On Demand" movies and TV shows from our cable companies. The model is simple. You sign up for a service and you get access to movies and TV shows at your leisure.

Translate that model to your company's computing needs and factor in the challenging economic environment we're in and what you have is a formula for cutting cost, as well as increasing efficiency and flexibility for your business.

"On Demand" cloud computing means that you only pay for the capacity that you need at any given period. If you need high computing resources only 10 days of the month, that's all you pay for: 10 days. You don't have to own the infrastructure with capacity good for 30 days when you only need it for 10. It's like paying for metered services just like you do for electricity and water.

So when "On Demand" hits you as something more than just cable TV, take that as a sign that it's time for you to move to the cloud.

Popping Packaging Bubbles No Longer Excites You

When you opt not to use cloud-based applications, you are basically committing yourself to hours of downtime installing new software or software updates. Many people have done a variation of popping packaging bubbles out of boredom while giving up a whole afternoon (maybe even a day) in front of the computer, configuring or troubleshooting software.

As a business owner, you also have the additional burden of ensuring that all your software installations are safe and legal. The last thing you want is to have law enforcement knocking on your door for software piracy or noncompliance.

Software licensing is much more simplified in cloud computing and adherence is a lot easier. The pay-per-use pricing model means no high capital investment for software and corresponding hardware with protracted return on investment. To top it all, you can be assured that everyone in your organization is using the latest version of the software, so there is no question of tracking and managing who's got what version of the application.

From the perspective of software vendors, cloud computing affords them the ability to roll out new features and updates as often as needed rather than the traditional one and a half to two years' time frame for new version and enhancement releases. As a customer, you won't need to wait for a long time to see a software vendor's response to your feedback and suggestions.

You've Made Your Workplace Green but Feel You Can Do More

From recycling to composting to carpooling to driving hybrid cars, you've put in your share of effort to encourage a green workplace. Yet you still feel a yearning in your heart to do more. Listen to your heart because you're right; you can do more.

Logic dictates that shifting to the cloud will reduce IT carbon emissions footprint through data center efficiencies. Cloud companies such as Google and Yahoo are building new data centers by using renewable hydroelectric and wind resources. Microsoft's $2.3 billion investment in cloud infrastructure was built from the ground up to be environmentally sustainable.

To bring the "cloud is green" message home, think of your company's reduced energy consumption if you get rid of unneeded hardware. You also eliminate the need for packaging peanuts and bubble wraps if you don't have to buy packaged software!

So the next time you feel bad about having to print color copies of your presentation or graphics, use the cloud instead to share your content. You can feel good about yourself and help the environment too!

Opportunity Knocked While You're on Vacation

We all want a work/life balance and would rather not do business while on vacation. But ifopportunity knocks in the form of a potential investor when you're on vacation and strolling on the beach, do you really want to close that door?

Although it may be true that success is in large part due to luck, it's also true that the harder you work, the luckier you get. With cloud computing, you don't have to work harder, just smarter!

For example, say that you're vacationing in a remote village in Asia, when to your surprise, you meet someone interested in investing in your start-up company. You intentionally left your laptop at home, so you begin to panic at the thought of a lost opportunity. Then you remember that all your demos and presentations are hosted online at your SharePoint site through your Office 365 subscription. You relax and walk over with your potential investor to the nearest Internet café and conduct an impromptu presentation. The pitch works, and you now have a new partner!

If you have ever lost such an opportunity, it's time for you to move to the cloud!

You Covet Enterprise-Class Web Conferencing

Web conferencing is not new to the Enterprise, considering that the technology has proven to be a real timesaver and cost reducer. Most of us probably have seen movies of high-powered board meetings with good-looking CEOs and senior management hooked up by live video conferencing to their operations folks in multiple locations across the globe. As a small-business owner or a professional, you've probably secretly coveted the sophistication of the people and the meeting by virtue of the technology they used.

Well, covet no more. The very same technology the big guns are using is now available to non-enterprise companies at an affordable cost through the cloud. You don't need to invest in expensive equipment or hire an IT staff to conduct effective, high quality, high-definition web conferencing. Between giants, such as IBM, Microsoft, Cisco, and lesser-known providers, such as SightSpeed, Inc., Fuse Meeting, and onNovia Technologies, you have lots of options.

The advent of Unified Communications (UC) to seamlessly connect people within and outside organizations has changed the landscape for web conferencing. Nowadays, you can start out with an instant messaging (IM or chat) session with a co-worker, add voice to the session, invite more people to the conversation, convert the session into a web conference, share screen, whiteboard, conduct a poll, and for good measure, record the web conference. The Microsoft Lync web conferencing solution allows for high-definition video capability, using off-the-shelf webcams with a resolution display that adjusts to the waxing and waning of your Internet connection.

So put on a suit and a tie (pajama bottoms OK), turn your webcam on, and start using a cloud-based web conferencing solution to wow yourself and your customers. There is no better time to join the cloud bandwagon than now.

Your IT Department Needs a Morale Boost

If you've grown your business big enough to have an IT department, then you've probably heard the following common complaints in one form or another from the "business" against IT.

As a business owner, you have the opportunity to bring business and IT together with cloud computing. The way to do this is to allow the business to make cloud-based technology decisions to serve the organization's needs. Outsourcing technology needs to cloud providers empowers the sales manager to select his team's CRM tool, authorizes the developer to decide where he wants his computer capacity to come from, and affords a payroll manager the freedom to choose a technology solution that fits her team's learning curve. IT on the other hand, transitions from the bad guy to the business's friendly tech jungle guide, the advisor to help choose the right solution, an advocate in negotiating with cloud providers, and the gatekeeper to help ensure alignment with the overall company IT strategy.

So, if you are ready to have your business and IT departments work and strategize arm in arm to transcend their bitter struggle, look to the cloud to get you there.

You Are Ready to Take On Gartner Research 2012 Predictions

Cloud computing is the future and there's no way around it. Unless you possess some kind of special skill to manage and maintain or have a special affection for 1990s technology, your choice is actually limited to two: Move to the cloud now or wait until later.

If you still can't make up your mind between the two choices, consider the following 2012 predictions from Gartner Research.

✔ By 2012, 20 percent of businesses will own no IT assets.

✔ By 2012, India-centric IT services companies will represent 20 percent of the leading cloud aggregators in the market (through cloud service offerings).

- By 2012, Facebook will become the hub for social network integration and Web socialization.

- In 2012, 60 percent of a new PC's total life greenhouse gas emissions will have occurred before the user first turns the machine on.

Are you ready to lead your organization to the future? If you are, then that is an unmistakable sign that you are ready for the cloud!

Chapter 22

Ten Office 365 Value Propositions

In This Chapter

▶ Discovering how Office 365 can increase efficiency

▶ Understanding the value of moving to the cloud

▶ Understanding the value created by the integrated products in Office 365

▶ Finding out how the Microsoft cloud provides value through centralized data

> *An individual poor person is an isolated island by himself and herself. IT can end that isolation overnight.*
>
> — Professor Muhammad Yunus

*I*f you are relatively new to enterprise software, such as SharePoint, then moving to the Microsoft cloud is a straightforward decision. After all, you don't have an IT team in place and there is no chance of disrupting employees because they aren't currently using enterprise class software. In this situation, there is nothing but upside. If, on the other hand, you are a very technologically mature organization, then moving to the cloud can be a scary proposition. Anytime there is change at the enterprise level, there is a chance for things to go wrong. Even if the cloud takes the risk of the technology causing problems, such as installation or patching, there is still the risk of user adoption, confusion, and push back for the new way of doing things.

In this chapter, you explore ten value propositions for Office 365. Although change can be scary, the cloud has a lot to offer regardless of the size of your organization. In particular, you explore some of the value that results from freeing up your technical folks and letting them focus on solving real-world business problems by using technology instead of keeping the lights blinking green. You also explore some of the productivity gains that come with moving to the cloud, such as the ability to connect anywhere you have Internet connectivity and the value added by using an integrated suite of products.

Offloaded Responsibility

You have probably heard the expression that "it takes an army" to do something. When it comes to Information Technology, this saying rings true. When you start thinking about all the people and resources responsible for enterprise class software, the results can be mind-boggling. You need networking people, operating system administrators, e-mail administrators, server administrators, domain administrators, DNS people, web developers, programmers, provisioning experts, backup engineers, infrastructure, maintenance, patches, backup generators, and the list goes on and on. It is no wonder that it used to take a very large company to adopt software, such as SharePoint.

The cloud is changing the paradigm behind enterprise class software by offloading the responsibility for the infrastructure to someone else. In the case of Office 365, that someone else is none other than Microsoft. Microsoft has invested heavily in building out data centers, installing computers, operating systems, backup systems, and maintenance plans. Microsoft takes care of it all. When you use Office 365, you simply sign up and start using the products over the Internet. The result is that you don't have to worry about the heavy lifting. You are free to focus on using the software instead of worrying about keeping the software running.

Reduced Infrastructure

The infrastructure required to run software grows exponentially as the organization adopts enterprise applications. Even a relatively modest set of servers needs a redundant power supply, multiple Internet connections, a backup plan, and a secure and fireproof location in which to reside. As an organization grows, the amount of infrastructure required grows quickly until an entire team is dedicated to keeping the servers running 24 hours a day.

The costs involved in purchasing, managing, and maintaining the infrastructure involved for enterprise class software can be downright daunting. When you move to Office 365, you are removing the need for onsite infrastructure. That is all taken care of by Microsoft. Without the need for all the servers and software required to run the software, you can focus on the more important issues affecting your business. In a nutshell, you are removing the burden of having on-site infrastructure but still achieve the competitive advantage that comes with using software, such as SharePoint, Lync, Office, and Exchange.

Predictable Costs

If you talk to a chief financial officer, accountant, or project manager and ask them the type of project they prefer, they will tell you the one that comes in on budget. Unfortunately, in the technology industry, a predictable budget can be a difficult goal to achieve. Technology, by its very nature, has a lot of uncertainty and gray areas. An analogy people like to use for custom software or a difficult implementation has to do with painting. Great technologists are often more artist than engineer. As a result, you might get an absolutely phenomenal product, or you might get a complete disaster that is five or ten times over budget and completely unusable.

The result of uncertainty is difficulty in planning and conflict. A CFO or Project Manager would rather have an accurate figure than a low figure that could triple. When you move to the cloud, you are taking all the uncertainty out of the cost of the infrastructure and implementation. With Office 365, Microsoft has already undertaken all the risky implementation projects that come along with enterprise software. That is not to say that Microsoft teams did not come in over budget or that Microsoft did not spend three or four times what they thought it would take to get Office 365 up and running. But that doesn't matter to you. You know exactly how much Office 365 will cost you, and you won't have to worry about overruns. Microsoft won't tell you that it is actually going to cost four times more per month because the software is complicated. In fact, Microsoft has a service guarantee so that if the software is not up and running per the agreement, then they are on the hook for it.

Reduced Complexity

You would think that after being a SharePoint consultant for years and years and years, that Ken would know absolutely every possible thing you could or couldn't do with SharePoint. The secret that Ken will tell you that no other consultant will tell you is that consultants and experts still learn something new every single day. Now to think that is only one single product, SharePoint. The Office 365 product includes Exchange, Lync, Office, and also SharePoint. There are probably a few souls out there who are absolute experts on all these technologies, but the fact is that to maintain such enterprise software, you need a fairly significant team.

Microsoft has made managing software systems easier by introducing products, such as Small Business Server, but the fact is that managing software is still a complicated endeavor. With Office 365, you remove that complexity by using a simple web interface to manage the various products. Need to create a new SharePoint site collection? You do it from within the Office 365 interface. Need to create retention rules for e-mail? Again, the Office 365 management screens for Exchange are where you will find it. Microsoft engineers perform all the difficult responsibilities that go into keeping the lights blinking green on the servers. You just use the software in a way that best suits your business needs.

Anywhere Access

Office 365 lives in Microsoft's data centers and is accessed over the Internet. For this reason, you have connectivity to your enterprise software by using your desktop computer in your office, your laptop, or your mobile phone. In addition, all you need is an Internet connection rather than a special connection to your corporate network.

Having access to the software you use every day from anywhere provides a tremendous value and efficiency increase. When you have access, you can take advantage of unintended downtime. For example, you might be stuck waiting for someone and instead of just daydreaming away the time you could pull out your phone and respond to e-mails. You will no longer feel that nagging urge that you need to get back to your desk to check e-mail and respond to the people that need your input. After all, they might be waiting for you to respond so that they can do their job. In this way, you are not only maintaining your own efficiency during your downtime, but you are unblocking the people that require your input in order to maintain their efficiency and do their jobs.

Synchronized Data

A real inefficiency booster is having different versions of documents scattered all over the place. You might have one version of a document at work and another version on your home computer and yet another version on your laptop. Documents have a bad habit of multiplying as well. When you send a document to people in an e-mail, they save it to their computer and then make changes. Very quickly, there are multiple documents, and it becomes nearly impossible to determine which version contains the needed information.

With Office 365 and SharePoint Online, you have a centralized home for all documents. You can access those documents from multiple computers (or even your mobile phone) and by multiple people. Regardless of how many people or devices are accessing the document, only a single version of the document exists on SharePoint. Because SharePoint is in the cloud and accessed over the Internet, you only need an Internet connection or cell reception in order to access your enterprise data.

In addition to documents, Office 365 lets you synchronize all your e-mail, calendar, and contacts onto multiple devices. If you use Outlook at home and at the office, you don't have to worry about being on the wrong computer when trying to find a contact at work. You don't have to worry about missing an appointment because all the computers you use synchronize with Exchange Online. The result is that your appointments, e-mail, and contacts live in the cloud and are synchronized with your e-mail program.

You can sync your smartphone with Exchange Online as well so that you are never far from your appointments, contacts, and e-mail. This feature is one of the most valuable.

Integrated Software

As we cover throughout the book, the Office 365 product is actually a suite of products that is hosted in the Microsoft data centers and accessed over the Internet. Microsoft has gone to great lengths to integrate the software as seamlessly as possible, which results in an increase in efficiency for users. For example, you might be performing a search for a document in your SharePoint portal. When you find the document, you can see the author and view his or her presence information based on the color of the icon next to their name in SharePoint. You can click the presence icon to launch Lync for instant chat or Outlook to send an e-mail.

Office 365 even integrates with your phone system so you can even call the author directly from the SharePoint environment. The integration between SharePoint, Exchange, Lync, and Office makes performing daily tasks as easy as possible. The end result is that the technology gets out of the way and lets you and those you work with do your jobs without fighting with technology.

Mobile Access to Enterprise Data

In the distant past (perhaps a few years ago in technology time), you most likely had to be at your desk in order to access your enterprise data. If you had an important Word document or needed a PowerPoint, then you had to go into your office and copy it to a Flash drive or use a connection, such as Virtual Private Network (VPN) in order to connect remotely.

Being tied to your desk in this manner created a lot of frustration and inefficiency. Companies, such as Go To My PC, flourished by providing remote access to the computer in your office from a remote computer. And then, all of a sudden, smartphones appeared. Everyone quickly become accustomed to having a small computer with them in their pocket at all times. Need some information from the Internet? Need to check movie times? Need to browse a website or catch up on the latest news? All you need to do is pull out your smart phone.

The only problem was that the corporate environment did not move as quickly as the consumer market, so a gap emerged. Yes, you had the Internet in your pocket, but you still couldn't connect to your corporate network or access your enterprise data. With Office 365, you can finally access your data from anywhere by using your smartphone. Microsoft is taking anywhere access a step farther by integrating the new Windows Phone 7 with Office 365 with negligible configuration.

Now, for the first time, you can click a button on your phone and instantly browse your enterprise data in SharePoint, respond to corporate e-mail, see your calendars, book appointments, and pretty much do almost everything you would do at your desk. Only now you can do it from anywhere you have cellphone reception. You can access SharePoint by clicking the Office button on your Windows Phone.

You don't need a Windows Phone in order to integrate with Office 365. Windows Phone provides the richest integration, but you can integrate with your enterprise e-mail, calendar, and contacts from just about any smartphone device.

Increased IT Efficiency

Routine tasks have a way of creating snags that take hours or days to resolve. A small technical glitch has a way of cascading into an all-out war between the IT team and the software demons. What ends up happening is that the tech people spend all their time down in the weeds keeping the lights blinking green. The business folks become frustrated because they are not receiving the support they deserve, so the whole business and the culture suffer.

When you move to the cloud, you free up your IT resources to focus on working with your business users to solve problems that benefit the organization. Your business users receive the support they need, and the IT people receive the recognition they deserve.

Self-Service Enterprise Software

The most exciting aspect of Office 365 for many organizations is the inclusion of SharePoint Online in the mix. SharePoint provides a self-serve portal environment that can be developed to solve real-world business problems. The main premise behind SharePoint development is that you do not have to be a programmer to develop solutions on the SharePoint platform.

SharePoint development is covered in Chapter 9, but if you really want to go deep into what is possible, check out *SharePoint 2010 Development For Dummies* (Wiley), which is dedicated entirely to the topic.

Chapter 23

Ten Tips for Increasing Productivity and Efficiency with Office 365

In This Chapter

▶ Unlimiting your productivity with Microsoft's three-screen strategy

▶ Applying Lync's powerful features to work smarter, not harder

▶ Enjoying the Backstage view

> *"The first rule of any technology used in a business is that automation applied to an efficient operation will magnify the efficiency. The second is that automation applied to an inefficient operation will magnify the inefficiency."*
>
> — Bill Gates, former CEO and current Chairman of the Board, Microsoft

*O*ffice 365 as a cloud technology affords any organization the benefits of a sophisticated data center without the hassle and the cost of maintaining one. For as low as $6 per month per user, storing files in the cloud that are backed up in redundant servers relieves businesses from the burden of constantly backing up and archiving critical business data.

In this chapter, you find "ready-to-apply" tips and tricks for increasing productivity and efficiency in your organization or your practice. Think of this chapter as your shortcut to knowing how you can, as Bill Gates puts it, "magnify the efficiency" gains from a much-streamlined operation through the use of Office 365.

Leveraging the Service Health Dashboard to Save Time

A quick look at the user-friendly admin portal page gives you an idea of how easily you can manage your organization's subscription plan, users, security groups, domains, Exchange Online, Lync Online, SharePoint Online, and the Microsoft Office Professional Plus desktop apps.

If you are the designated admin for your organization, the links below the Support group on the left navigation of the admin portal give you quick access to your service requests, the current service health status of the Office 365 service, and planned maintenance schedule.

Check the Service Health status dashboard when you experience system issues such as signin, audio or video quality, and connectivity, to verify if your issue is isolated or a known issue currently being investigated. The Service health dashboard displays the last seven days' performance indicated by icons to denote normal service availability, service degradation, service interruption, normal service is restored, and additional information. Having insight as to what service is up or down will probably save you a phone call if you know that someone else has already made the call and the Office 365 support folks are working to resolve it.

Don't Lose Sleep over Confidential Data in Your Lost Phone

Office 365 helps you live a happy, healthy life by making it so that you don't have to lose sleep worrying about confidential data in the phone you just lost at a time when business is closed and none of your IT guys are returning your calls. You can easily wipe data from your wireless device and even delete the device from your account to prevent a security and/or privacy breach.

Quickly wipe data or delete your device for your Exchange Online account by taking these steps:

1. **Log onto the Office 365 portal at** `http://portal.microsoft.com`.
2. **On the Home tab, Click the Inbox link under the Outlook group.**
3. **Under Options on the top-right corner, select See All Options.**
4. **Click Phone on the left navigation.**

5. **From the Mobile Phones tab, select the device from the list of mobile phone devices synchronized with your Exchange account.**

6. **Click the Wipe Device or Delete (represented by an X) icons.**

Sharing the Workload to Manage SharePoint Online External Users

Cloud technology is undoubtedly going to reform how businesses will be using IT — if they even have an in-house IT department. If your company does have an in-house IT department, unburden your IT staff from tactical stuff so they can focus on strategic activities by redistributing typical IT tasks to the end users. If you don't have IT, no worries. You don't need to spend money on an IT consultant to do simple tasks, such as allowing team site owners to invite external users to collaborate on SharePoint Online.

With your admin privileges, you can set the stage to minimize hand-holding by allowing external access to SharePoint Online from the administration center. To do so, follow these steps:

1. **Log on to the Office 365 portal at** `http://portal.microsoft.com`.

2. **Under the Admin tab, click the Manage link under SharePoint Online to take you to the administration center.**

3. **Click the Manage site collections link.**

4. **On the right pane, select the site collection you want to make available to the external user.**

5. **From the radio buttons that pop up, click Allow and then click the Save button.**

After you do this, team site owners are now able to configure their own team sites to invite external users by going to Site Actions, Share Site, and then entering the e-mail addresses in the Share your SharePoint Site dialog box.

Chatting in Outlook Web App

You know how efficient working can be when you're in your office and have access to your Office desktop applications. From Outlook, you can easily instant message your co-workers, make a call, send an e-mail, and simply enjoy the bells and whistles of the rich functionality of desktop apps. But what if you're not in your office and you're using someone else's computer?

What if you need to quickly update a co-worker via IM on the status of a project you both are working on, and he's not answering his phone? Worse, you know he's online because his presence is showing green in Outlook Web App! Does that mean you have to give up productivity and efficiency because you don't have access to your desktop app? The answer is no.

If your co-worker is already in your Contacts list, starting a chat session by using Outlook Web App is simple. You can either double-click his name from your contact list or from an e-mail to open a chat window. Type your message in the bottom window and click Send. A chat window pops up in your co-worker's computer with your message allowing him to respond. When you're done, close the window by clicking the X button on the top-right corner.

To add a coworker to your Contact list, do the following:

1. **Click Add contact under Contacts List on the left navigation in Outlook Web App.**

2. **From the Address Book web page dialog box, double-click the user you want to add.**

   The user's name should appear in the box to the right of the Add command. If you work for a large organization, you can conduct a search for a user in the search box.

   Back at the Outlook Web App interface, you see the users you added to your Contact List.

3. **Your co-worker will receive your invitation and can either accept or decline it.**

   After the invitation is accepted, his name will become active and will appear in your Contact List.

In Outlook Web App, you will see two items on the left navigation that look the same: the Contact List and the Contacts folder. Don't confuse the two, especially because you may see the same contact on either one of them. You use the Contact List for chatting not only with your co-workers but also with Lync 2010 users in other companies, if domain federation is activated in Office 365.

The Contacts folder on the other hand, is where you store information about people and groups.

Publishing Your Calendar

One cool feature of the Outlook Web App is that the calendar is just as robust as the desktop application. You can apply colors to your appointments for an at-a-glance review of your day, week, or month, send a meeting request, set up alerts and notification, and a whole lot more.

To share your calendar from the Outlook Web App, click the Calendar icon from the left navigation, click Share, and then select Publish This Calendar to the Internet. There's a host of options you can choose from when sharing your calendar, so choose them wisely, knowing that whether you choose Restricted (won't appear in searches) or Public (can be searched) under Access level, your calendar is now shared on the Internet.

Doing Something With Content in the Backstage View

We typically think of chaos and confusion when we think of the backstage for most events to the extent where someone actually created a page on Facebook called "What Happens Backstage, Stays Backstage." In Office Professional Plus, the Backstage view is neither chaotic nor confusing.

In Word, Excel, and PowerPoint, the Backstage view is your efficiency one-stop shop. When you click File from the menu of the document you're working on, and then click Save & Send, you will be presented with a host of options for sharing your document. Here you can send your file as an e-mail attachment, save it to the Web through the Windows Live SkyDrive, save it to a SharePoint site (your most recent locations will automatically be listed), send via Instant Message in Lync, share your desktop window with colleagues by using Lync, and even publish your Word document as a blog!

There are many more features in the Backstage view you should check out, but in summary, think of it as the place where you *do something with* the content you created in a way that's as simple and intuitive as the "what you see is what you get"(WYSIWYG) feature of the Microsoft Office Ribbon.

Leveraging Microsoft's Three-Screen Strategy to Drive Productivity

Microsoft's three-screen cloud strategy aims to enable workers to "create, communicate, and collaborate across PCs, phones, and browsers." With access anywhere to e-mail, calendar, contacts, documents, and basically anything, it's easier than ever for people to work together and stay in sync, regardless of their physical location. You can create and edit documents online by using most browsers and see right before your eyes changes made by members of your team. Things get done quicker and faster as distributed teams brainstorm, create, annotate, publish, and even broadcast a PowerPoint presentation to any audience with a access to an Internet connection, a browser, and a smartphone. Whether on your desktop app or using the online version, you can group your e-mails in a Conversation view so you can respond to the latest thread of an e-mail discussion. You can "mute" the din of your inbox by using the Clean Up and Ignore features of the desktop version of Outlook 2010.

With Office 365, coming up with good excuses for not being productive has become extremely difficult.

Taking Your Files Offline and Resyncing Them

Regardless of how connected you are, you'll inevitably run into a situation where you don't have Internet access. Just because you are without access doesn't mean that your efficiency has to go down. To maintain efficiency, leverage the power of SharePoint workspace to take your documents offline, knowing that as soon as you have an Internet connection, changes you made to your files will be synced back online. With SharePoint Workspace, you have access to a robust search functionality and the ability to drag and drop files from one folder to another just as youdo with files in your hard drive. For instructions on using and setting up SharePoint Workspace, please refer to Chapter 7.

Administering Data Security Is No Longer an Onerous Technical Task

E-mail security and endpoint integrity challenges are two of the many small-business pain points that Office 365 solves. In the past, small businesses had to struggle with protecting incoming and outgoing emails from viruses, scams, phishing, and so on. With Office 365, small businesses can now have enterprise-class protection, using Forefront Online Protection for Exchange (FOPE). As a subscriber, you can be confident that the latest antivirus signatures are always up-to-date and compliant with the Microsoft Trustworthy Computing Initiative.

As your users access data through the Internet to and from Microsoft's redundant global data centers, you can relax, knowing that your data is safe and secure. The Office 365 built-in, tight 128-bit SSL/TSL encryption will render intercepted transmission unreadable if it occurs. After you no longer need to worry about backups and disaster recovery, you'll be able to focus more on growing your business.

And best of all? This service costs $6 to $27 per month, per user.

Glossary

Blog: A blog is a web log or online journal. A blog provides a forum for people to write communications that can be viewed across the entire organization or Internet. After a blog entry is posted, the content can be commented on and discussed on the blog entry page. Blogs are prevalent throughout modern society, and SharePoint provides the ability to get a blog up and running in a manner of minutes.

Cloud: A very broad marketing term and buzzword that refers to accessing software over the Internet.

Discussion Board: A discussion board allows for online discussion throughout the organization. A discussion board provides a forum for people to post questions and replies that can be viewed throughout the organization.

Excel Services: Excel Services is a feature of SharePoint that allows Excel documents to be surfaced through a SharePoint site and thus through a web browser.

Exchange: Exchange is Microsoft's e-mail server designed to handle the heavy lifting of managing and routing e-mails. In addition, Exchange handles functionality, such as contacts, calendars, and tasks. Users generally use an e-mail client, such as Outlook to connect to Exchange.

Exchange Online: Exchange Online is the term for Microsoft's cloud version of Exchange. The Online portion refers to the fact that you access your Exchange instance over the Internet while you are online. Microsoft installs Exchange on servers running in its data centers, and you connect to it and use it over the Internet.

Extranet: An extranet is a computer network that is accessible by people outside your organization's network but is not accessible by the public at large.

InfoPath: An application designed to create nifty and useful forms that are used to collect data from people.

Intranet: An intranet is a computer network that is private and only meant for your organization.

JavaScript: JavaScript is a scripting language that is designed for the web. You can use JavaScript to interact with a web page programmatically. Because JavaScript is run from the client web browser, you can create a rich interactive experience without the web browser having to communicate with the server, resulting in the page flickering and reloading with each interaction.

Lync: Lync is a communications system designed to provide instant communication and ad hoc meetings. Lync lets you conduct online meetings by sharing your screen or presentations online with multiple users simultaneously, while communicating via voice, chat, and surveys. Lync is integrated with the other products in Office 365 in order to provide instant ability to communicate regardless of what software you are using.

Lync Online: Lync Online is the term for Microsoft's cloud version of Lync. The Online portion refers to the fact that you access your Lync instance over the Internet while you are online. Microsoft installs Lync on servers running in its data centers and you connect to it and use it over the Internet.

Masterpage: A masterpage is a template that is responsible for the layout of the components that are found on every content page. For example, you wouldn't want to have to add navigational components to every single new page you create. If you did, and ever needed to make a change, you must change every single page. Using a masterpage, you would only create the navigational components once and then all the other pages would reference this masterpage for the common components.

Microsoft Business Intelligence: Business Intelligence means many different things to many different people. The definition of Business Intelligence involves using computer software to get a handle on the mountains of data that flow from modern business. The data is turned into information that is used to run a business in an intelligent fashion. Microsoft Business Intelligence refers to the Microsoft tools and technologies that fall into the Business Intelligence space.

Microsoft .NET: The Microsoft .NET technology consists of programming languages and libraries designed to increase developer productivity and compatibility across Microsoft client and server computers.

Office 365: The Microsoft product that contains SharePoint, Exchange, and Lync; all applications are installed and managed in Microsoft's data centers and accessed over the Internet (or in the cloud).

Office Professional Plus: Office Professional Plus is the nearly ubiquitous productivity suite used by information workers around the world. The Office product contains the following applications: Word, Excel, PowerPoint, Outlook with Business Contact Manager, OneNote, Publisher, Access, InfoPath, SharePoint Workspace, and Lync.

Outlook with Business Contact Manager: An application used for e-mail, contacts, and calendaring, including scheduling meetings, meeting rooms, and other resources.

PowerShell: PowerShell is a shell interface similar to DOS. Products, such as SharePoint have PowerShell instructions, called cmdlets, which let you build scripts to interact with the product. For example, you might develop a series of PowerShell cmdlets that increases the specific configuration information of your SharePoint site.

Report: A report is nothing more than information describing the status of some topic. A report can be developed by using a number of technologies, such as Report Builder, Dashboard Designer, Excel, or even SharePoint web parts.

SharePoint: SharePoint is a term used to describe a technology from Microsoft. SharePoint is comprised of two primary products. The first is a free version that comes with the Windows Server Operating System, and the second is a product that is purchased called Microsoft Office SharePoint Server (MOSS). SharePoint has become the leader in communication, collaboration, and content management. SharePoint continues to evolve as functionality is folded into the product and additional features are developed. SharePoint 2010 is the most current release of the SharePoint product.

SharePoint Designer: SharePoint designer is a software application that is used for SharePoint development. The content contained in a SharePoint application lives in a SQL Server database. SharePoint Designer provides a window into the SharePoint database that allows for customization and development.

SharePoint Document Library: A Document Library is a mechanism to store content within SharePoint. A Document Library provides functionality for content management including check in and check out, versioning, security, and workflow.

SharePoint List: A SharePoint List is simply a list of data. Much like you have a grocery list, a SharePoint List stores data in columns and rows.

SharePoint My Sites: The My Sites functionality of SharePoint offers every user their own SharePoint site.

SharePoint Online: SharePoint Online is the term for Microsoft's cloud version of SharePoint. You access your SharePoint instance over the Internet while you are online. Microsoft installs SharePoint on servers running in its data centers and you connect to it and use it over the Internet.

SharePoint Site: A SharePoint Site is nothing more than a website. SharePoint is a web site management system that provides a rich assortment of functionality that can be easily integrated into the SharePoint websites.

SharePoint Site Collection: A SharePoint site collection is a top-level site that contains other subsites. The difference between a site collection and a site is that a site collection contains separate security and is isolated from other site collections. A site, on the other hand, is contained by a top-level site collection and shares security and other aspects with other sites within the same site collection.

SharePoint Workflow: A SharePoint workflow is a set of tasks and actions that can be associated with a list, library, or site. For example, you might have a workflow to request feedback on new documents. When a new document is submitted to a library, the workflow might send an e-mail to a list of people for feedback. When each person has finished his task of reviewing the document, the workflow might send an e-mail back to the original author. SharePoint workflows are developed by using the Dashboard Designer.

SharePoint Workspace: SharePoint is great, but what happens when you aren't connected to the Internet and need to access and work with your website? SharePoint Workspace allows you to take SharePoint sites offline.

Silverlight: Silverlight is a technology designed to provide a rich user experience from within the web browser. The Web, in general, was not designed to provide the same rich user experience that an application running on your local computer provides. With a web application, the server is serving up pages that are viewed by the client computer by using a web browser. Each time the user interacts with the application, the web browser needs to send a message back to the server. This causes the web page to refresh and flicker. Silverlight runs on the web browser of the client computer and allows a rich interaction with the web application without the continual post-back of information to the server.

Visio Services: Visio Services provides SharePoint with the ability to render Visio diagrams through the web browser. Visio Services diagrams can be embedded right inside a SharePoint page. Visio Services is also used to provide a diagram of SharePoint workflow in real time.

Visual Studio: Visual Studio is a software application that is designed for development of Microsoft technologies. Visual Studio is called an Integrated Development Environment (IDE) because many development features are integrated into the application, such as the ability to run and test code, color-coded keywords, and IntelliSense. IntelliSense allows developers the ability to type the beginning of a keyword and have the editor show a list of available words. The list of words narrows down as the developer continues to type additional letters of the word. This aids the developer in finding the correct key- word without having to type the entire word.

Web App: A web app is a software application that is accessed over the Web, using a web browser. For example, if you have used Facebook or LinkedIn, then you have used a web app. The Office 365 product includes a number of different web apps. In fact, even the administrative interface you use to configure Office 365 is a web app because you access it by using your web browser. In addition, web apps are available for Outlook, Word, Excel, PowerPoint, and OneNote.

Web Part: A web part is a component of a web page that can be added, removed, or edited right from the browser. A web part is contained in a web part zone. A web part can be dragged and dropped between web part zones, using only the browser.

Wiki: A Wiki is a specialized website that allows community members the ability to update the content of the website on the fly. A Wiki is not specific to SharePoint; however, SharePoint provides Wiki functionality as a feature.

Word: Microsoft Office Word is used for word processing, such as creating and editing documents.

Index

• Numerics •

2012 predictions, 283–284

• A •

academic plans, 21–22
Access 2010 integration, 115–119
  Publish to Access Services feature, 118–119
Access application, 28
Access databases, 115–116
  contents, 116
  fields and records, 116
  objects, 116
Access Services, 100–101
Access tables, exporting to SharePoint
    lists, 116–118
Active Directory, 234
activity feeds, 35–36, 222–223
administration links
  Custom Plan, 263
  Domains, 263
  Licenses, 263
  Manage, 263
  Management group, 263
  Overview, 263–264
  Planned Maintenance, 264
  Purchase, 264
  Security Groups, 263
  Service Health, 264
  Service Requests, 264
  Setup group, 263
  Subscriptions group, 263–264
  Support group, 264
  Users, 263
administrator responsibilities, 243
Amazon
  EC2 (Elastic Compute Cloud), 12
  Mechanical Turk, 12
Announcements list, 145
AOL accounts, accessing, 56
Apps portfolio, 53
Asset Library, 147

• B •

Backstage View, 104–106, 297
bandwidth requirements, 234–235, 245
Blank Site template, 142
Blog template, 142
blogs
  creating with SharePoint Online, 71–72
  defined, 66, 299
Broadcast Slide Show feature, 193–194
browser
  requirements, 235–236
  using as development tool, 140–141
business
  interaction with IT department, 283
  mid-size plans, 19–20
Business Intelligence
  defined, 300
  search functionality, 99

• C •

calendar
  adding events to, 76
  sharing, 296–297
Calendar list, 145
Charitable Contributions Web Database
    template, 142
Circulations list, 145
cloud computing, 229–230
  advantages, 11
  collaboration, 278
  concept of, 10–11
  defined, 299
  deployment models, 10–11
  explained, 171
  future, 14
  IaaS (Infrastructure as a Service), 13–14
  importance, 14–15
  "On Demand," 279–280
  private cloud, 17
  pros and cons, 231–232

cloud computing *(continued)*
  public versus private, 10–11
  SaaS (Software as a Service), 13
  Salesforce.com, 10, 12
  service models, 13
  status of, 12–14
  on vacations, 281–282
"cloud is green" message, emphasizing, 281
Cloud Power, 15
cloud productivity, achieving, 17–18.
    See also productivity
cloud products
  SQL Azure database component, 16
  Windows Azure, 16
collaboration, 52–54, 278
Column Editor, 158
Comcast accounts, accessing, 56
conference room setup, 58–59. *See also*
    web conferencing
confidential data, protecting in
    phone, 294–295
contact cards, viewing, 212
Contacts list
  adding coworkers to, 296
  versus Contacts folder, 296
  described, 145
Contacts Web Database template, 142
Content Query Web Part, 86
Content Type
  Editor, 158
  using in Document Set, 96
Conversation View, 54–55
conversations
  grouping in inbox, 30–31
  managing in Lync Online, 212–213
costs, predictability of, 287
Ctrl key, using with notes, 202–203
Custom List, 145
Custom Plan link, 263

• D •

data, synchronization of, 288–289
Data Connection Library, 147
data security, administering, 298
Decision Meeting Workspace template, 142

Deleted Items folder, searching, 56
deployment guide, accessing, 248
digital content
  document libraries, 88–91
  Document Sets, 95–97
  slide library, 91–93
  tags and notes, 93–95
discussion board
  defined, 299
  list, 145
DNS (Domain Name System)
  considering, 247
  updating for migration, 259
Document Center template, 140–142
Document Libraries, 88–91
  content management, 89
  described, 147, 301
  Shared Documents, 96
  for site collections, 132–133
  versioning, 90–91
Document Sets
  Content Type, 96
  creating, 96
  ribbon tab, 97
  using, 95–96
Document Workspace template, 143
domain federation, 269–270
Domains link, 263

E plans, 19–20
EC2 (Elastic Compute Cloud), 12
eDiscovery, 49
editors in SharePoint Designer
  Column Editor, 158
  Content Type Editor, 158
  External Content Type Editor, 159
  Image Editor, 159
  List and Library Editor, 158
  Page Editor, 158
  Script Editor, 158–159
  Text Editor, 159
  Workflow Editor, 158
  XML Editor, 159
education plans, 21–22

e-mail. *See also* Exchange Online; Outlook
    application
  archiving, 31
  Conversation View, 55
  recovering after deletion, 56
e-mail accounts
  AOL, 56
  Comcast, 56
  Gmail, 56
  Hotmail, 56
  Yahoo Mail Plus, 56
enterprise applications, delivery of, 12
enterprise data, mobile access to, 289–290
Enterprise Search Center template, 143
enterprise software, self-service, 291
Enterprise Wiki template, 143
enterprises plan, 19–20, 244
events, adding to calendar, 76
Excel application
  described, 28
  presence indicator, 226
Excel Services, 100, 299
Excel Web App
  Alignment section, 181
  Cells section, 181
  Clipboard section, 181
  coauthoring workbooks, 186
  creating documents, 183
  Data section, 181
  Editing Mode, 183–184
  versus Excel, 180
  File menu, 182
  Font section, 181
  functions, 184–185
  Home tab, 181
  Insert tab, 182
  interface, 181–182
  manipulating data, 185
  Number section, 181
  Office section, 181
  Reading Mode, 183–184
  Ribbon tabs, 182
  spreadsheets, 183
  Tables section, 181
  workbooks, 182–183
Exchange, 299
Exchange Administrator, 243
Exchange e-mail, checking, 30

Exchange Online, 54. *See also* e-mail;
    FOPE (Forefront Online Protection for
    Exchange); Outlook application
  accessing, 43–47
  account protection, 294–295
  administration, 42–43
  archive folder, 48
  archiving and retention, 48
  availability, 42
  collaboration, 46–47
  deployment flexibility, 40–41
  deployment predictability, 41
  described, 299
  e-mail clients, 45
  inbox overload, 46
  integration with Lync, 225
  Mac access, 45
  managing, 266–269
  migrating data to Office 365, 256–257
  Outlook e-mail client, 44–45
  phone access, 44
  presence indicator, 225
  protecting information, 47–49
  provisioning, 42
  voicemail, 47
  Web access, 44
Express Team Site template, 143
External List list, 146
external sharing, enabling, 126–127
extranet
  defined, 299
  sites, 32–33

faculty and staff, plan for, 22
FAST Search, 125
files, taking offline and resyncing, 298
FOPE (Forefront Online Protection for
    Exchange), 298. *See also* Exchange
    Online
Form Library, 147
functions, adding in Excel Web App, 184–185

GAL (Global Address List), 60
Gartner Research, 283–284

Gmail accounts, accessing, 56
green workplace, creating, 281
Group Work Site template, 143
groups, managing for site collections, 137

• *H* •

home page, updating, 84–85
Hotmail accounts, accessing, 56
HR Announcement lists, creating, 81
HR page, building, 82
Human Resource page, making visible, 83
Hyper-V virtualization, use by Target, 17

• *I* •

IaaS (Infrastructure as a Service), 13–14
Image Editor, 159
implementation planning
  account provisioning and licensing, 245
  administrator responsibilities, 243
  communication, 245–246
  concept of, 241–242
  e-mail strategies, 244
  enterprises plan, 244
  Exchange Administrator, 243
  finding partners, 248–249
  hardware inventory, 245
  Internet bandwidth, 245
  issue tracking, 244
  Lync Administrator, 243
  migration needs, 246
  network administrator, 243
  Project Manager, 243
  resources, 243
  SCRUM methodology, 244
  SharePoint Administrator, 243
  software inventory, 245
  synchronization meetings, 244
  tasks, 242–243
  trainer, 243
  training, 245
Import Spreadsheet list, 146
inbox
  grouping conversations in, 30–31
  managing overload, 46
InfoPath application, 28, 299

InfoPath Forms Services, 101, 271
infrastructure
  managing, 230–231
  reducing, 286
instant messaging (IM), 54, 270. *See also*
    Lync Online
Internet. *See* cloud computing
Internet access requirements, 234–235
Internet bandwidth, 245
intranet
  Content Query Web Part, 86
  creating pages, 80–83
  default views, 83
  defined, 299
  displaying site pages, 85
  document libraries, 81
  HR Announcement lists, 81
  HR page, 82
  Human Resource pages, 80–81
  libraries, 80–81
  lists, 80–81
  lists in Team Sites, 81
  logo, 80
  Press Release subsite, 85–86
  setting as default Team Site, 79
  setting up with publishing template, 78–85
  updating home page, 84–85
invoice template, adding to site
    collection, 135
IP address, considering in migration, 259
Issue Tracking list, 146
Issues Web Database template, 143
IT department
  efficiency, 290
  interaction with business, 283
IT infrastructure, maintaining, 278–279

• *J* •

JavaScript, defined, 299

• *K* •

K plans, 20
keyboard shortcuts, using with notes,
    202–203
kiosk workers, K Plans for, 20–21

• L •

Languages and Translation list, 146
libraries. *See* SharePoint libraries
Licenses link, 263
licensing
  activating, 255–256
  software, 280
Licklider, J. C. R., 12
Links list, 146
List and Library Editor, 158
logins and licensing, preparing, 247
Lotus Symphony, 53
Lync Administrator, 243
Lync application, 28, 33–36
  activity feeds, 35–36, 222–223
  ad hoc meetings, 34
  click-to-communicate buttons, 224–225
  Contact View, 221
  Excel integration, 226
  Exchange Online integration, 225
  instant messaging, 54
  Location feature, 221
  online meetings, 34–35, 52–53
  Outlook Web App integration, 225
  photos, 35–36
  PowerPoint integration, 226
  presence, 225–226
  presence of team members, 222
  presence state, 220
  requirements, 236–237
  Soft Phone feature, 223
  switching from devices, 224
  text, voice, and video, 33–34
  user interface, 220–221
  voicemail, 223
  Word integration, 226
Lync communications system, defined, 300
Lync Online, 33. *See also* instant
    messaging (IM)
  answering calls, 216
  availability, 210
  best practices for meetings, 216–217
  collaboration, 210–211
  contact cards, 212
  contacts, 213
  conversations, 212–213
  described, 300
  domain federation, 269–270
  integration, 214
  making calls, 216
  managing, 269–270
  Notification Areas, 213
  online meetings, 214
  presence information, 88–89
  presence status, 211–212
  presenter access, 215
  presenter options, 215
  public instant messaging, 270
  sharing sessions, 215
  user information, 270
  using, 210
  video features, 216
  voice features, 216
Lync Web App
  joining Lync Online, 217–218
  versus Lync Online, 217

• M •

Mail Control page, 268
mailbox data
  managing, 269
  migrating to Office 365, 256–257
mailboxes, preparing, 247
Manage link, 263
Management group, 263
management website, 262–263
managing
  organizations, 267–268
  personal mailbox, 269
  self or others, 268–269
masterpage, defined, 300
McCarthy, John, 12
media library, creating, 93
meetings. *See* online meetings
Microsoft download center, 241
Microsoft IME Dictionary List list, 146
Microsoft .NET, defined, 300
Microsoft Office 365. *See* Office 365
migrating to Office 365
  activating licensing, 255–256
  adding users, 255–256
  configuring mobile phones, 259–260
  Exchange Online, 256–257
  IP address, 259

migrating to Office 365 *(continued)*
mailbox data, 256–257
portals, 258–259
throwing switch, 259
updating DNS, 259
mobile access, 289–290
mobile phones, configuring for migration, 259–260
Multipage Meeting Workspace template, 143
My Site. *See* SharePoint My Site

• *N* •

.NET technology, defined, 300
network administrator, 243
notebooks
closing, 201
using in OneNote Web App, 200–201
notes
proofing, 202–203
tagging, 202–203
notes and tags, adding, 93–95

• *O* •

Office 365
academic plans, 21–22
administration links, 263–264
apps, 29
benefits, 24–27
described, 171, 300
E plans, 19–20
enterprise plans, 19–20
integration of products, 89
IT control, 27
K plans, 20
kiosk workers, 20
management website, 262–263
pay-as-you-go licensing, 28–29
Plan P, 18
reliability, 26–27
security, 26–27
SharePoint Online, 25
Office 365 Marketplace, accessing, 249, 256
Office 365 plans
choosing, 239–241
E1-E4, 240

K1-K2, 240
P1, 240
Office 2010, benefit of, 26
Office 2010 integration
Backstage View, 104–106
coauthoring documents, 108–109
Outlook and Outlook alerts, 110–112
PowerPoint broadcast feature, 106–108
versioning control, 109–110
Office Professional Plus
described, 300
features, 61
Office Web Apps. *See also* web apps, described
browser and devices, 165
coauthoring in, 167
.docm files, 167
engine for user experience, 167–168
environments, 164
file types, 167
HTML (Hyper Text Markup Language), 168
JavaScript, 168
macro files, 167
versus Office Professional Plus, 166
Silverlight, 168, 302
subscription plan, 164
"On Demand" cloud computing, 279–280
OneNote application, 28
OneNote Web App
audio, 198–199
Editing View, 202
employee handbook, 198
features, 196–199
hyperlinks, 205
images, 199
interface, 200
limitations, 199
notebooks, 196–197, 200–201
versus OneNote 2010, 198–199
organization of information, 196–197
page versions, 204
pages, 203–204
pictures, 205
proofing notes, 202–203
protection, 199
Reading View, 202
Ribbon tabs, 200
search capability, 197

search functionality, 199
sections, 203–204
shapes, 199
spell checking, 203
tables, 199, 205
tagging notes, 202–203
text editing, 199
video, 198–199
online communities, 32
online documentation, consulting, 248
online meetings, 34–35
  best practices in Lync, 216–217
  connection alternatives, 217
  demoting attendees, 215
  muting audio, 216–217
  presenters, 217
  preventing audio feedback, 217
  promoting attendees, 215
  scheduling, 214
  screen display, 217
  testing audio devices, 217
  VPN connections, 216
  wired networks, 216
OOF (out of office) setup, 57–58
OpenOffice.org project, 53
organizations
  Mail Control, 268
  managing, 267–268
  Phone & Voice, 268
  Roles & Auditing, 268
  Users & Groups, 268
Outlook application. *See also* e-mail;
    Exchange Online
  archive folder, 48
  with Business Contact Manager, 300
  click-to-communicate buttons, 224–225
  Conversation View, 54–55
  described, 28
  recovering deleted items, 56
Outlook Social Connector app, 61–62
Outlook Web App
  account setup, 57
  chatting in, 295–296
  conference room setup, 58–59
  integration with Lync, 225
  OOF (out of office) setup, 57–58
  presence indicator, 225
  public groups, 60

recovering items, 56
  Scheduling Assistant, 58–59
Overview link, 264
OWA (Outlook Web Access), 30

• *P* •

Page Editor, 158
pages. *See* publishing portal template
partner, finding for implementation,
    248–249
permissions
  managing for site collections, 137
  setting in SharePoint Online, 72
Personalization Site template, 143
Pew Research Center, 14
phone, protecting confidential data in,
    294–295
Phone & Voice page, 268
Picture Library, 147
pictures, inserting, 194
plan, example of, 265
Plan P, 18
Planned Maintenance link, 264
portals, preparing, 247
PowerPoint application
  described, 28
  presence indicator, 226
PowerPoint presentations
  closing, 193
  creating, 91–93, 191–193
PowerPoint Web App
  alignments, 194
  Broadcast Slide Show, 193–194
  bullets, 194
  buttons, 189
  coauthoring in cloud, 189
  commands, 189
  content types, 192–193
  design templates, 189
  editing buttons, 190
  Home tab, 190
  Insert tab, 190–191
  macros, 189
  navigation, 189–190
  numbered lists, 194
  pictures, 194
  versus PowerPoint 2010, 188–189

PowerPoint Web App *(continued)*
  presentations, 191–193
  printing, 189
  Reading view, 192
  Smart Art, 189, 194
  thumbnails, 190
  user interface, 189–191
  View tab, 191
PowerShell interface, 301
preparing phase
  DNS (Domain Name System), 247
  logins and licensing, 247
  mailboxes, 247
  portals, 247
  support, 248
  training, 248
  web portals, 247
presence, impact on productivity, 220–224
presence indicator
  click-to-communicate buttons, 224–225
  Excel, 226
  Exchange Online, 225
  Outlook Web App, 225
  PowerPoint, 226
  SharePoint, 226
  Word, 226
presence status, indicating in Lync
      Online, 211–212
presentations. *See* PowerPoint
      presentations
presenter options, customizing in Lync, 215
Press Release subsite, managing, 85–86
private cloud
  Hyper-V virtualization, 17
  versus public cloud, 10–11
productivity. *See also* cloud productivity,
      achieving; value propositions
  administering data security, 298
  Backstage View, 297
  chatting in Outlook Web App, 295–296
  collaboration, 52–54
  on the go, 52
  increasing, 24
  instant messaging, 54
  publishing calendar, 296–297
  Service Health Dashboard, 294
  sharing workload, 295

taking files offline, 298
  three-screen strategy, 297–298
professionals plan, 18
Project Tasks list, 146
Projects Web Database template, 143
public groups, creating, 60
public versus private cloud, 10–11
Publisher application, 28
publishing portal template
  adding users, 80
  content approval, 80
  publishing pages, 83
  workflow, 80
Publishing Site templates, 144
Purchase link, 264

Record Library, 147
report, defined, 301
Report Library, 148
requirements
  bandwidth, 234–235
  browser, 235–236
  geographic, 232–233
  Internet access, 234–235
  software, 233
Ribbon, using in SharePoint Designer,
      153–154
Roles & Auditing page, 268

SaaS (Software as a Service), 13, 40–41
Salesforce.com, 10, 12
Scheduling Assistant, using, 58–59
Script Editor, 158–159
SCRUM methodology, 244
search functionality, 97–99
  business intelligence, 99
  phonetic, 99
  refiners, 98–99
security
  administering, 298
  FOPE (Forefront Online Protection for
      Exchange), 298
Security Groups link, 263

servers
  managing, 279
  role in SharePoint farms, 122
Service Health
  Dashboard, 294
  link, 264
service request
  entering, 253–254
  link, 264
Setup group, 263
Shared Documents library, 96–97
SharePoint
  development, 140
  Document Library, 301
  popularity of, 31–32
  presence indicator, 226
  technology, 301
  workflow, 302
  workspace, 302
SharePoint 2010, benefit of, 26
SharePoint Administrator, 243
SharePoint Designer
  Backstage View, 150
  breadcrumb feature, 155
  connecting to sites, 150
  described, 301
  Design section, 154
  downloading and installing, 150
  editor windows, 157–159
  features, 149, 151
  functional components, 152
  gallery windows, 156–157
  limitations, 151
  navigation features, 154–155
  Ribbon, 153–154
  settings windows, 156
  site-creation tools, 152–153
  tab order, 155
  using, 152
SharePoint farms
  administering, 123–124
  administration settings, 124
  backup, 123
  Billing Administrator, 126
  database management, 123
  delegating administration tasks, 125–126
  FAST Search, 125
  Global Administrator, 125

health monitoring, 124
multitenancy, 124–125
Password Administrator, 126
permissions, 123
recovery, 123
security, 123
servers, 122
Service Administrator, 126
service application, 123
service management, 123
Tenant Administration, 125
topology management, 124
User Management Administrator, 126
web application management, 123
SharePoint groups
  Approvers, 79
  Members, 79
  viewing, 79
SharePoint libraries
  Asset Library, 147
  Data Connection Library, 147
  Document Library, 147
  Form Library, 147
  Picture Library, 147
  Record Library, 147
  Report Library, 148
  Slide Library, 148
  Wiki Page Library, 148
SharePoint lists
  Announcements, 145
  Calendar, 145
  Circulations, 145
  Contacts, 145
  Custom List, 145
  Custom List in Data Sheet View, 145
  defined, 301
  Discussion Board, 145
  exporting tables to, 116–118
  External List, 146
  Import Spreadsheet, 146
  Issue Tracking, 146
  Languages and Translation, 146
  Links, 146
  Microsoft IME Dictionary List, 146
  Project Tasks, 146
  Status List, 146
  Survey, 146
  Tasks, 146

SharePoint My Site
  content management, 70
  described, 66, 301
  document libraries, 70–71
  editing profiles, 67–68
  managing, 273
  Note Board, 69
  notes for web pages, 69–70
  noting, 68–69
  personal content, 70
  Tag and Note tool, 69–70
  tagging, 68–69
  tags for web pages, 69–70
  viewing profiles, 67–68
SharePoint Online
  Access services, 100–101
  Administration Center, 126
  administrator responsibilities, 126–131
  blogs, 66, 71–72
  calendar list, 76
  collaboration capabilities, 52
  communication, 89
  described, 301
  design of, 68
  document libraries, 73
  Excel services, 100
  external sharing, 126–127
  extranet sites, 32–33
  fields and records, 116
  files, 25
  InfoPath Forms Services, 101, 271
  managing, 271–274
  managing external users, 295
  migrating to, 258–259
  My Site, 66, 273
  permissions, 72
  publishing portal template, 78–85
  restoring items, 74–76
  sharing links to files, 73
  Silverlight carousel, 74
  site collections, 127–128
  social features, 66
  social tagging, 66
  space conversion to %20, 73
  task list, 76
  taxonomy for Term Store, 130–131
  underscores as separators, 74
  uploading links, 133
  user profiles, 129–130, 272–273
  version control, 74–76
  viewing document history, 75
  Visio services, 101
  Wiki, 66
SharePoint sites. *See also* site collections
  Content page, 148
  described, 301
  developing, 141–144
  libraries, 147–148
  list options, 145–146
  Publishing page, 149
  Web Part page, 148
  wiki page, 148
SharePoint Team Sites. *See also* Team
    Site template
  external sharing, 77–78
  setting as default, 79
  setting up, 73–74
SharePoint templates, 140
  Assets Web Database, 142
  Basic Meeting Workspace, 142
  Basic Search Center, 142
  Blank Meeting Workspace, 142
  Blank Site, 142
  Blog, 142
  Charitable Contributions Web
    Database, 142
  Contacts Web Database, 142
  Decision Meeting Workspace, 142
  developing, 141–144
  Document Center, 142
  Document Workspace, 143
  Enterprise Search Center, 143
  Enterprise Wiki, 143
  Express Team Site, 143
  Group Work Site, 143
  Issues Web Database, 143
  Multipage Meeting Workspace, 143
  Personalization Site, 143
  Projects Web Database, 143
  Publishing Sites, 144
  Social Meeting Workspace, 144
  Team Site, 144
  templates, 141–144
  Visio Process Repository, 144

SharePoint Term Store
  features, 273–274
  importing taxonomy to, 130–131
SharePoint Workspace
  described, 28
  setting up, 112–113
  synchronization, 114
Silverlight technology, 168, 302
site collections. *See also* SharePoint sites
  activating site feature, 132
  administrator responsibilities, 132–137
  assigning owners, 129
  content and content types, 133–134
  creating, 127–128
  described, 302
  document libraries, 132–133
  document version, 133–134
  Excel template in content type, 135
  galleries, 135–136
  invoice template, 135
  look and feel, 135
  managing, 271
  permissions and groups, 137
  Resource Usage Quota, 128
  saving lists as templates, 136
  sharing sites externally, 132
  team subsite, 132–133
site-creation tools, finding, 152–153
sites. *See* SharePoint sites
Slide Library
  alerts, 93
  described, 148
  using, 91–93
slide shows, broadcasting, 193–194
small businesses plan, 18
Smart Art, adding, 194
Social Connector app, 61–62
Social Meeting Workspace template, 144
social networks, tracking, 61–62
social tagging, describe, 66
Soft Phone feature, using in Lync, 223
software
  installation, 280
  integration, 289
  licensing, 280
Software as a Service (SaaS), 13, 40–41
spreadsheets, using in Excel Web App,
    182–183

SQL Azure database component, 16
Status List list, 146
students, plan for, 22
Subscriptions group, 263–264
support
  availability, 253–254
  considering, 248
Support group, 264
Survey list, 146
synchronization of data, 288–289

• T •

tag cloud, explained, 95
tags and notes, adding, 93–95
Target, use of Hyper-V virtualization, 17
Tasks list, 146
Team Site template, 144. *See also*
    SharePoint Team Sites
templates. *See* SharePoint templates
Tenant Administration
  Billing Administrator, 126
  Global Administrator, 125
  Password Administrator, 126
  Service Administrator, 126
  User Management Administrator, 126
Term Store
  features, 273–274
  importing taxonomy to, 130–131
Text Editor, 159
three-screen strategy, 297–298
trainer, responsibilities of, 243
training
  considering, 248
  partners, 253
  tell, show, do method, 252

• U •

UC (Unified Communications), 282
user profiles
  editing, 129–130
  managing, 129–130, 272–273
users, adding, 255–256
Users & Groups page, 268
Users link, 263

• V •

vacation, cloud computing on, 281–282
value propositions. *See also* productivity
  anywhere access, 288
  enterprise software, 291
  IT efficiency, 290
  mobile access, 289–290
  offloaded responsibility, 286
  predictability of costs, 287
  reduced infrastructure, 286
  reducing complexity, 287–288
  software integration, 289
  synchronized data, 288–289
versioning
  enabling for document libraries, 90–91
  managing, 278
Visio Process Repository template, 144
Visio Services, 101, 302
Visual Studio, 302
voicemail, using with Lync, 223

• W •

web apps, described, 303. *See also* Office
  Web Apps
Web browser
  requirements, 235–236
  using as development tool, 140–141
web conferencing, 282. *See also* conference
  room setup
web pages. *See* publishing portal template
web part, 303
web portals, preparing, 247
websites. *See* SharePoint sites

Wiki
  described, 66, 303
  Page Library, 148
Windows Azure, 16
Word application
  described, 28, 303
  presence indicator, 226
word processing program. *See* OneNote
  Web App
Word Web App
  documents, 173–174
  Editing Mode, 174–175
  File menu, 173
  finding files, 171
  Home tab, 170, 172
  Insert tab, 172
  interface, 170–173
  Picture Tools tab, 173
  Reading Mode, 174–175
  styles, 175–176
  tables, 176–177
  tabs, 172–173
  View tab, 172
  versus Word, 169–170
workbooks
  coauthoring in cloud, 186
  using in Excel Web App, 182–183
Workflow Editor, 158

• X •

XML Editor, 159

• Y •

Yahoo Mail Plus accounts, accessing, 56